THE JEWISH POPE

*Ideology and Politics
in the Papal Schism of 1130*

BY

MARY STROLL

University of California, San Diego

E.J. BRILL
LEIDEN • NEW YORK • KØBENHAVN • KÖLN
1987

Library of Congress Cataloging-in-Publication Data

Stroll, Mary.
  The Jewish pope.

  Bibliography: p.
  Includes index.
  1. Papacy—History—Schism, 1130-1139. I. Title.
BX1218.S77   1987   262'.13'09021   87-21838
ISBN 90-04-08590-4

              ISSN 0920-8607
              ISBN 90 04 08590 4

PRINTED IN THE NETHERLANDS BY E. J. BRILL

To my husband, Avrum

TABLE OF CONTENTS

ACKNOWLEDGMENTS

In some ways I feel like the sports hero who, when interviewed, says modestly, "It wasn't I, who did it; it was the team." Although I could not have written this book without the "team," they bear no responsibility for its outcome.

Stanley Chodorow first excited my curiosity about the papal schism of 1130 in a seminar on church/state relations, and we have since discussed its manifold facets on numerous occasions. He and other colleagues have read earlier versions of this study, and have offered valuable suggestions. Among them are Pier Fausto Palumbo, Constance Bouchard, Gavin Langmuir, H. Stuart Hughes, Robert Lerner, and Charles Radding.

The librarians at the University of California, San Diego made herculean efforts to obtain the books I needed, and the Biblioteca Apostolica Vaticana offered me its vast resources. Its prefect, Father Leonard Boyle, was always ready to discuss my research, and he graciously permitted me to return to work in the afternoons. On several occasions I was a resident at the American Academy in Rome, and enjoyed the use of its library and the stimulating interaction with its fellows and residents. Its current director, James Melchert, made the most recent occasion especially pleasurable and productive. The Villa Massenzia run by Bryn Mawr College under the supervision of Ann and Darby Scott also provided me with a serene ambience in which to work. Part of my research was subsidized by a grant from the NEH.

For years I have been discussing the schism with my friend, Richard Popkin, and his interest was quickened enough to suggest that I submit my manuscript to the present editors. I regard it as a signal honor to publish my volume in the same series in which one of his books appears. Many people have worked tirelessly in the preparation of the manuscript. Among them are my typists, Dolores Illig and Christine Young. Kathleen Galbraith and Kathryn Wilham shepherded it through the labyrinthine process that resulted in camera ready copy with a dedication that far exceeded their professional responsibilities.

Ted, Betsy, Robin and Susan cheered me on, but most of all I am indebted to my husband, Avrum, who edited countless drafts, examined my arguments, and encouraged me to persevere. Without him, nothing.

Mary Stroll
University of California, San Diego
June 15, 1987

LIST OF ABBREVIATIONS

JL P. Jaffé, *Regesta pontificum Romanorum ab condita ecclesia ad annum post Christum natum MCXCVIII,* 2nd ed. rev. S. Loewenfeld (882-1198)

MGH *Monumenta Germaniae historica*

    Const *Constitutiones et acta publica imperatorum et regum*

    Ldl *Libelli de lite imperatorum et pontificum*

    SS *Scriptores*

PL J.P. Migne, *Patrologia Latina*

INTRODUCTION

The dual papal elections of February 1130 divided Western Christendom more deeply than any previous schism. Recent similar disputes had arisen from the competition between the pope and the emperor to work out the right order between state and church, *regnum* and *sacerdotium*. That of 1130, by contrast, was a division within the church. Each candidate was a highly respected cardinal with a distinguished record, and each was backed by eminent churchmen. Given these criteria it was not at all obvious which contender dedicated Christians should recognize.

The schism contains all of the elements of a melodrama involving intrigue, deceit, accusations of illicit sex, and moving exhibitions of unflagging loyalty. Apart from their dramatic import, the events surrounding the schism were of the utmost importance, for they concerned more than just the struggle between two papal parties. They were part, and some historians maintain, a central part of changes taking place in the church at large. In the middle of the eleventh century the papacy had led the church in an endeavor to reform itself, mainly by forcing secular powers to loosen their grip over the church. One of the most intrepid leaders of this movement, Gregory VII, even challenged secular authority in its own domain, claiming that papal authority was superior in both the spiritual and the temporal spheres. By the early twelfth century the controversy had become focused on investitures: did the secular ruler have ultimate jurisdiction over the property and administrative offices of bishoprics and abbeys, and therefore the right to invest bishops and abbots with these perquisites, or did the church? And if secular rulers had this right, did it extend to the spiritual office of the prelate? In 1122 Calixtus II and the emperor, Henry V, reached a compromise over these points of contention in the Concordat of Worms. Although the sources of imperial and papal power and the relationship between them would again become a burning issue in the mid-twelfth century in the conflict between Alexander III and Frederick Barbarossa, there was now a moment of repose in which the church could concentrate on other problems.

Having partially resolved the problem of investitures, Calixtus and his successors began to emphasize internal ecclesiastical reform and spiritual renewal under a strong papacy. These initiatives raised contentious questions such as how spiritual the church should be, how much authority the papacy should have over bishoprics and monastic orders, and what the character of the papacy itself should be. Tension arose between the Benedictine houses of Cîteaux and Cluny over how rigorously to interpret the *Rule*. There were disagreements between the popes and the abbots of Cluny and Montecassino over what authority the pope should exercise over these two venerable institutions. And in its expansive mood, the papacy collided with the ambitions of the Normans in Sicily and Southern Italy under their astute and aggressive ruler, Roger II. All of these developments were affected by the artistic and cultural renewal commonly characterized as the Twelfth Century Renaissance.

Calixtus died in 1124 while the church was just beginning to grapple with these problems and to undertake new ventures. A strong pope, he had directed events rather than merely reacting to them. The throne he had constructed in the Roman church of Santa Maria in Cosmedin symbolizes the elevated position to which he had brought the papacy. With two imposing lions functioning as arm rests, rays shoot out from a nucleus of imperial porphyry on the disk behind a pope sitting on the throne. It is small wonder that the competition to succeed such an august pope produced dissension. An armed band led by the Frangipani, one of the two most powerful Roman aristocratic families, broke up the papal election. Celestine II, elected and about to be consecrated, was summarily removed, and Cardinal Bishop Lambert of Ostia was installed in his place as Honorius II. Haimeric, appointed chancellor by Calixtus in 1123, appears to have been the orchestrator of the coup, and he played a direct role by bribing key persons to withdraw their opposition to Honorius. The most influential among these dissenters was Petrus Leonis, the head of the other leading Roman family, the Pierleoni. The Pierleoni had converted from Judaism to Christianity almost a century before, and thereafter they used their fortune acquired in banking to support the reform popes.

In 1130, with the recollection of the election of 1124 still fresh, and with the main actors still on the scene, the Romans became increasingly restive as rumors spread of Honorius' impending death. Ostensibly because of this agitation, Haimeric and a number of other cardinals brought the moribund Honorius to the monastery of St. Gregory within the area controlled by the Frangipani. During the days in which Honorius lay dying, Haimeric induced the cardinals in attendance to accept extraordinary innovations in the papal electoral procedures, arguing that the election must be accelerated because of the threat of violence. His efforts failed, however, and to assure the election of his candidate, he was ultimately forced to resort to measures which were patently illegal. As soon as Honorius died, the small number of cardinals at St. Gregory's had his body placed in a hastily dug grave. Then, without announcing the pope's death, without summoning the other cardinals, and without observing the customary three days of obsequies before proceeding to a new election, they elected Cardinal Deacon Gregory of St. Angelo as Innocent II.

Alerted to the machinations at St. Gregory's before the death of Honorius, a larger number of cardinals joined by a great many members of the Roman clergy and people had gathered at St. Mark's at the foot of the

Capitoline. There they anxiously awaited news of Honorius' condition. Only after Innocent had already been elected did word reach them that Honorius had died. Regarding the proceedings at St. Gregory's as a travesty of an election, they held their own. With the overwhelming approval of the Roman clergy and people, they elected Petrus Pierleoni, cardinal priest of St. Calixtus, as Anaclet II.[1] Thus began the schism which tore Christendom asunder for eight bitter years.

Fighting immediately broke out in Rome, and Anaclet and his followers were the victors. Innocent was forced to flee into exile, first to Pisa, and then to France. Peter the Venerable ceremoniously received him at Cluny and helped him to take the offensive against Anaclet in France. Councils were convened in France and the Empire to determine which contender was the true pope. The results of the councils and other diplomatic activity were that the church and most of the Western rulers recognized Innocent. Scotland, Aquitaine, and the Normans in Southern Italy, however, opted for Anaclet, who rewarded Roger by having him crowned king. Still in Northern Europe, Innocent asked the emperor, Lothar III, to help him secure his see in Rome. After seeing to his affairs in Germany, in 1133 Lothar marched to Rome with a small army, and installed Innocent for a short time. But with Roger's support, Anaclet remained firmly ensconced in Rome until his death in 1138.

Such in brief are the events surrounding the schism. Historians have filtered them through many prisms in order to understand why it occurred and why Innocent became the recognized pope. Some of them have viewed it as just another petty contest between Roman families—the Frangipani and the Pierleoni—vying for power. Others have also seen it as a contest for power, but as a struggle within the church among the cardinal bishops, priests and deacons. Recently the scope of the conflict has been perceived as encompassing the whole church. Innocent is thought to have embraced the

---

[1] Both popes took the names of distinguished predecessors. Anaclet I has previously been thought to have been known in the twelfth century mainly from the Pseudo-Isidorian decretals, forged in the eighth century to promote papal primacy. The three letters he allegedly wrote reveal him to be a glorifier of the Roman church. He affirms that "the roman church is the church on which all other churches depend and the head of all churches." See Paul Hinschius, ed., *Decretales Pseudo-Isidorianae et Capitula Angilramni* (Leipzig, 1863), pp. 66-75. But in the popular mind, Anaclet was especially associated with St. Peter. His biography in the *Liber Pontificalis* emphasizes that he set up St. Peter's *memoria* (sepulchre), and eventually was buried next to the apostle on whom the church was founded. The biography also stresses Anaclet's ties with the original apostles. An Athenian Greek, like Christ's immediate followers he came from the East; *Liber Pontificalis*, ed. Louis Duchesne, 2 vols. (Paris, 1886-1892, repr. 1955) vol. 1, p. 125. Anaclet was also mentioned prominently in pilgrim guides in the twelfth century. Iacobus Grimaldi mentions such a guide for St. Peter's in which he says that the *confessio et memoria Sancti Petri dicebatur primum Beatus Anacletus papa ornavit*, and that later this same Anaclet was buried next to St. Peter. *Instrumenta autentica Translationum Sanctorum corporum et Sacrarum Reliquarum E Veteri in novum Templum Sancti Petri cum multis memoriis, Epitaphiis, Inscriptionibus, Delineatione patris Basilicae demolitae, et Iconicis Historiis Sacrae Confessionis Ab eodem Summo Pontifice Magnificentissime exornata* (1619), Barb. Lat. 2733, fol. 268r.

new ideas coming from the North, while Anaclet clung tenaciously to a conception of the papacy narrowly centered on Rome. Those who hold this view believe that while Innocent fostered the new spirituality practiced by the Cistercians and canons regular, Anaclet remained enmired in an outmoded Gregorianism, continuing to see the conflict between *regnum* and *sacerdotium* as the primary focus for ecclesiastical reform. Thus, the schism is seen to transcend the scheming in Rome, and to concern basic opinions about the direction in which the church should be moving. According to this view, the conflict was ideological, not political.

Observing that Innocent and many of the members of his inner circle frequently behaved in a manner not in keeping with the principles of this new spirituality, I gradually became sceptical of this view. If they held certain values, should these values not be reflected in their actions, their style of living, and their standards of morality? Other representatives of the new spirituality saw themselves as models to emulate, and they taught by example.[2] It is true that Innocent was not expected to live like a monk, but popes also were admonished to live more simply and to devote themselves more to their pastoral duties and less to secular concerns. When at mid century in *De consideratione* St. Bernard of Clairvaux urged his protege, Eugenius III, to comport himself more in the style of the simple living Peter and less in the luxuriant ways of Peter's successors, in all probability Innocent was one of the successors he had in mind. Innocent's penchant for display was well known, and his expansion of the papal judiciary also infringed the fiery abbot of Clairvaux's conception of the papacy. Haimeric and other members of Innocent's curia deviated even more widely from the ideal of the *vita apostolica*. They commonly accepted rich gifts, and made judicial decisions according to the value of the gift received.[3]

Even though Innocent's interpretation of the papacy conflicted with the ideals of St. Bernard, the schism could still be said to have arisen over attitudes toward the new reform if Innocent promoted the more rigorous religious orders, and Anaclet did not. In fact, as cardinals both Anaclet and Innocent had supported these orders, and there is no indication that Anaclet would not have continued this policy if he had been recognized as pope. Although some of the religious leaders of the North may have known of Anaclet's warm response to the call to monks and canons to return to the *vita apostolica*, the rumors and wild accusations spread after the

---

[2] Caroline Bynum speaks of the reformers' setting an example by their own behavior; "It is itself significant that all the basic concerns of early twelfth-century spirituality—poverty and preaching, withdrawal and community, love of neighbor and love of God—were expressed in terms of models. They saw themselves as *being* models. In their own terms, they taught by example. If being a regular canon or friar meant conforming oneself to the life of Christ, one became more available as an instrument of reform for others as one became a better canon or friar." "Did the Twelfth Century Discover the Individual?" *Journal of Ecclesiastical History* 31 (1980), 13; see also by the same author, *Jesus as Mother: Studies in the Spirituality of the High Middle Ages* (Berkeley, Los Angeles, London, 1982).

[3] See John T. Noonan's recent brilliant book, *Bribes* (New York, London, 1984).

elections distorted Anaclet's actual positions. It is therefore improbable that an understanding of the true religious ideology of the two candidates prompted the reformers of the North to campaign so zealously for Innocent, and to oppose Anaclet so fiercely.

A much stronger argument can be made that the schism occurred primarily because of Haimeric's ambition to continue to exercise the very extensive powers of papal chancellor. To maintain his position he needed a pope he could influence. Gregory was such a man, but Petrus decidedly was not. He had too much prestige within the curia, and too much power in Rome. He, rather than the chancellor, would be the dominating figure. Moreover, in all likelihood he would have ousted Haimeric from his office because of Haimeric's role in the election of 1124 and his close ties with the Frangipani. Since it was probable that Petrus would be nominated, Haimeric had to take steps to forestall such an eventuality.

When he only partially succeeded in barring Petrus' election, he unleashed a propaganda campaign to mobilize support for Innocent. The most fertile ground was France, the traditional land of refuge for popes unable to maintain themselves in Rome. Since Haimeric was a Frenchman, and had spent seven years as chancellor establishing his contacts there and elsewhere, he was now in a position to capitalize on these contacts. He believed that the many influential churchmen he had befriended would now recognize his candidate. He and his supporters transmitted his version of the election and his estimation of the two candidates to such religious leaders as St. Bernard, Peter the Venerable, and Norbert of Xanten, the founder of the Praemonstratensian order of canons regular. These men then took up the cudgel and waged a forceful campaign for Innocent based on this information and their own feelings about Anaclet as a scion of a rich family of Jewish converts. Character, the legality of the election, and the positions of the two candidates on ecclesiastical issues were obfuscated in the emotionally charged atmosphere which was quickly created. Probably many ecclesiastical and secular leaders thought that they were basing their decision on Innocent's superior character and some legal points in his favor, but few of them knew what the true facts were. They simply were following what trusted men had told them.

In the following pages I attempt to demonstrate that this scenario accurately characterizes the schism. By separating their record before and after the elections from the propaganda spread about them, I attempt to determine what kind of men Innocent and Anaclet actually were, and what principles they espoused. I follow the same procedure with their advocates. Since many of them were members of religious orders, I investigate the role these orders played in the conflict. The dispute at Cluny between 1122-1126 is central for understanding the ideology and the politics of the schism, as is the debate between Cluny and Cîteaux over the interpretation of the Benedictine *Rule*. The involvement of the two popes in the affairs of the renowned and strategically located monastery of Montecassino, also illuminates their religious and political objectives.

Although some historians conclude that the question of the legality of the elections has finally been put to rest, I believe that there are still contentious issues to be examined. Beyond the question of determining which pope was legally elected, there is the further question of how much weight the church felt that legal considerations should be given in deciding which man should be pope. Even though Innocent's supporters deprecated the importance of electoral procedures for deciding which man was the true pope, nevertheless they as well as Anaclet's followers maintained that their pope had been legally elected. The sincerity of their claims and the effect of legal arguments on the outcome of the dispute must be reconsidered.

Almost no one now believes that the schism was simply an outgrowth of the competition between the Frangipani and the Pierleoni, but since both families were so deeply involved in the political and military skirmishing in Rome, it is still critical for understanding the schism to determine what their participation signified. Were their objectives narrowly parochial, for example, or were they promoting ecclesiastical programs in addition to their own fortunes? Again in the secular sphere, I analyze the alliances of the two contenders with the rulers who recognized and defended them. I consider such questions as whether Anaclet's alliance with Roger II indicates that he rejected the *modus vivendi* with the emperor reached in the Concordat of Worms, and whether the alliances reveal anything about the commitment of each pope to religious concerns as compared with worldly goals.

Finally, I evaluate the effect of the propaganda war on the outcome of the schism. The unique feature of this battle was the innuendo, and frequently the outright charge, that Anaclet remained tainted by the blood of his Jewish ancestors. Historians have differed on how widespread this sentiment was, and especially on whether it was held by the most influential people in Innocent's camp. As a result of the First Crusade and the revival of commerce, the attitude toward Jews was changing, and the changes were not uniform throughout Europe. Modern scholars are only now beginning to understand these shifts, and their findings still have not been applied to the schism. Taking cognizance of this research, I conclude that the Jewish issue was a major factor in Anaclet's defeat.

The complexity of the schism and its implications for the church have attracted many scholars. My objective is not to write another comprehensive account of the dispute; rather it is to challenge previous theories explaining why the schism occurred, and to suggest a different explanation of its ultimate outcome.

Chapter I

THE HISTORIOGRAPHICAL BACKGROUND

The schism poses special problems for the historian because so many of the sources have been lost. Innocent's zealous supporters, and especially the monks of Cluny, destroyed any bit of writing they could which might have benefited Anaclet.[1] Only a few scraps from the beginning of Anaclet's Register have escaped, preserved by the abbots of Montecassino, who supported him.[2] Innocent's partisans even tampered with Pandulphus' biographies of popes Gelasius II, Calixtus II, and Honorius II in the *Liber Pontificalis* because their author was one of Anaclet's adherents. It was not until the discovery of a Spanish manuscript of the *Liber Pontificalis* by J.M. March, edited in 1925, that Pandulphus' unaltered biographies were revealed.[3]

Before March's discovery Richard Zöpffel collected many of the sources relevant to the schism.[4] Approaching the problem from a legal perspective, he emphasized that Nicholas II's *decretum de electione papae* of 1059 did not provide specific guide lines for resolving a disputed election, and especially for determining what the function of cardinal bishops should

---

[1] A comprehensive review of the historiography of the schism can be found in Pier Fausto Palumbo, *Lo Scisma del MCXXX*, Miscellanea della R. Deputazione Romana de Storia Patria (Rome, 1942), pp. 603-638. This account is supplemented by an article in which he brings the literature until 1962 up to date. "Nuovi Studi (1942-1962) sullo scisma di Anacleto II," *Bollettino dell'Istituto storico italiano per il medio evo e Archivio Muratoriano* 75 (1963), 71-103. For different evaluations of the more recent sources, see Herbert Bloch, "The Schism of Anacletus II and the Glanfeuil Forgeries of Peter the Deacon of Monte Cassino." *Traditio* 8 (1952), 161, n. 6.

[2] Thirty eight letters or parts of letters are preserved in Codex 159, a thirteenth century parchment copy at Montecassino. None have their destination, the initial salutation is lacking, and the dates are incomplete. Two are not Anaclet's bulls, but letters dealing with his election. The Biblioteca Vallicelliana in Rome contains a sixteenth century paper copy of the fragmented register at Montecassino, codex G 99. Christiano Lupo and C. Baronius brought out early editions of these letters, and in the *Patrologia Latina* Migne integrated them with the few bulls surviving from various provenances. PL 179:690-732. For a discussion of the sources see Pier Fausto Palumbo, "La Cancelleria di Anacleto II," *Studi Salentini* 17 (1964), 3-53 at pp. 4-5. The article is reprinted from *Scritti di paleografia e diplomatica in onore di Vincenzo Federici* (Florence, 1944), pp. 81-131.

[3] José Maria March, *Liber Pontificalis prout extat in codice manuscripto Dertusensi* (Barcelona, 1925). Hereafter cited as *Lib. Pont. Dert.* Peter William, a Cistercian monk of Saint-Gilles near Rheims, altered Pandulphus' text c. 1142.

[4] Richard Zöpffel, *Die Papstwahlen and die mit ihnen im nächsten Zusammehange stehenden Ceremonien in ihrer Entwicklung vom 11. bis zum 14. Jahrhundert*, Nebst eine Beilage: *Die Doppelwahl des Jahres 1130* (Göttingen. 1872).

be.[5] He thought that there was competition among the cardinal bishops, priests and deacons, and that when the election was split, there was no legal way to determine which contender was pope. His arguments are so partial to Innocent, however, that they must be read with caution.

Emil Mühlbacher, writing only a few years later, handled the sources much more open-mindedly. While continuing to concentrate on the electoral decree of Nicholas II, he also brought out the importance of the factionalism among the Roman families, especially the competition between the Frangipani and the Pierleoni.[6] The Pierleoni had converted to Christianity under Leo IX, and not only had become the bankers for the papacy, but also its mainstay from the time of Paschal II. The Frangipani had supported the reform papacy through the reign of Paschal, but thereafter their support became erratic. When Paschal's chancellor was elected Gelasius II in 1118 the Frangipani twice attacked him, forcing him to flee to France. Calixtus II kept them under control, but they reasserted themselves again in the election of Honorius II in 1124. Haimeric used them to disrupt the consecration of Celestine II, and to impose Cardinal Bishop Lambert of Ostia as Honorius II. They supported Innocent in 1130, and since Anaclet was an offspring of the Pierleoni, the split election of 1130 came to be seen primarily as a struggle between two Roman families.

Writing in 1879 in the Jahrbücher series of German kings, Wilhelm Bernhardi viewed the schism from the perspective of the empire. He broadened the investigation to include valuable information on the relationship between both contenders and the emperor, Lothar III. He also described their interaction with Roger II, the Norman ruler of southern Italy. More than previous writers, he was impressed with the effects of Petrus Pierleoni's Jewish ancestry as a cause for his failure to be accepted as pope.[7]

A break-through in the scholarship of the schism occurred in 1939 when Hans-Walter Klewitz, a talented young German historian, who was

---

[5] The legal problems were exacerbated by the existence of two texts—the original, which emphasized the special position of cardinal bishops, and a corrupted text partial to the emperor. The latter had been incorporated into such Italian collections as those of Deusdedit, Anselm of Lucca, Bonizio of Sutri, and the Abbey of Farfa. The original text is edited in MGH Const. et Acta 1:537-541. For a discussion of the legal issues see Bernard Jacqueline, *Episcopat et Papauté chez saint Bernard de Clairvaux* (Saint-Lo, 1975), pp. 65-73; Hans-Georg Krause, *Das Papstwahldekret von 1059 und seine Rolle im Investiturstreit* (Rome, 1960); R. Holtzmann, "Zum Papstwahldecret von 1059," *Zeitschrift der Savigny-Stiftung für Rechtsgeschichte* KA 27 (1938), 135-153; Robert L. Benson, *The Bishop Elect: A Study in Medieval Ecclesiastical Office* (Princeton, 1968), p. 42, n. 81; D. Haegermann, "Untersuchungen zum Papstwahldekret von 1059," *Zeitschrift der Savigny-Stiftung für Rechtsgeschichte* KA 56 (1970), 157-193; W. Stuerner, "Der Königswahlparagraph im Papstwahldekret von 1059," *Studi Gregoriani* 9 (1972), 37-52.

[6] Emil Mühlbacher, *Die streitige Papstwahl des Jahres 1130* (Innsbruck, 1876).

[7] Wilhelm Bernhardi, *Lothar von Supplinburg* (Berlin, 1879, new ed. 1975). See also Erich Caspar, *Roger II. (1101-1154) und die Gründung der normannischsizilischen Monarchie* (Leipzig, 1907). For works concerning the effects of the Jewish origins of the Pierleoni see Palumbo, *Lo Scisma*, p. 634, n. 3.

later killed in the Second World War, approached the problem by a proso-pographical analysis of the College of Cardinals between the pontificates of Paschal II and Honorius II.[8] He concluded that the cardinals fell into two parties based upon their response to the Concordat of Worms. The party supporting Petrus, inflexible Gregorians, was hostile to the compromise of 1122. It drew its members from the older, Italian, primarily Roman cardinals. The party supporting Innocent was younger, more international in character, and more reconciled to the compromise with the emperor.

The renowned historian of the papacy, Johannes Haller, was not impressed with Klewitz' conclusions, however.[9] He did not think that Klewitz had succeeded in demonstrating that the cardinals fell into two parties, and he was not convinced by the "new spirit" theory. Haller called attention to Petrus Pierleoni's distinguished reputation, said that Petrus was the legally elected pope, and that he was so recognized by the Romans. He also emphasized the defamation of Anaclet's character because of his Jewish ancestry. Claiming that Haimeric would have lost influence if Petrus had been elected, Haller put the main responsibility for the schism on him.

The most detailed study of the schism to date is the extensive mono-graph of Pier Fausto Palumbo.[10] The student, and later the assistant of the distinguished historian of medieval Rome, Pietro Fedele, Palumbo is well qualified to speak about the conditions of Rome, and especially about the noble Roman families and the development of the roman commune. Although he is not antagonistic to Klewitz's approach, he is critical of some aspects of his work, and did not build upon it. A major cleavage between Palumbo and Klewitz and his followers is that Palumbo does not see the Concordat of Worms as a watershed after which new attitudes developed toward ecclesiastical reform. He maintains that tensions between *regnum* and *sacerdotium* continued to exist and that the leaders of the new monastic and canonistic orders had close relations with secular rulers.[11] The church, he believes, continued to decline both in spiritual power and as a moral force, and as a result the tone of much of the polemical literature was anti-Roman. He sees the campaign of hate against Anaclet, who up until that time had been esteemed, as a part of this tradi-tion. Like Bernhardi, Palumbo holds that Petrus' Jewish ancestry played a significant role in his rejection as the legitimate pope.[12] He also concludes that in the war of words the flood of propaganda flowing from Innocent's chancery compared with the relative trickle from Anaclet's had a profound effect on the outcome of the schism.[13]

---

[8] Hans Walter Klewitz, "Das Ende des Reformpapsttums," *Deutsches Archiv für Geschichte des Mittelalters* 3 (1939), 371-412. repr. *Reformpapsttum und Kardinalkolleg* (Darmstadt, 1957) pp. 267-351; this is the ed. I have used.

[9] Johannes Haller, *Das Papsttum: Idee und Wirklichkeit* 2, pt. 2 (Munich, 1965).

[10] Palumbo, *Lo Scisma*.

[11] Ibid., 82-83.

[12] Ibid., xiv-xv; 54, 95.

[13] Ibid., 10.

Franz-Josef Schmale, writing in 1961, thought that Palumbo's account was too descriptive, and stated frankly that he was writing in opposition to it and in continuance of the research of Klewitz.[14] Rather than recording events chronologically, he said that he intended to get behind them to understand the motivations of both parties.[15] In his view, the explanation that Innocent had won a quick victory because of St. Bernard's interference was too facile. He also concluded that the ambition of the Pierleoni family was not the most important cause for the schism, although he sympathized with Zöpffel's emphasis on this factor. Since in general he believes that Zöpffel, like Mühlbacher, concentrated too much on political history, he is not surprised that the schism has been seen almost exclusively as a power struggle between noble parties and wrangles over rank among the orders of cardinals.

In the decade following Mühlbacher, Schmale finds no deeper insights among historians. On the contrary, he criticizes Bernhardi for being one sided in arguing that Innocent was only a creation of the Frangipani. He also does not accept Bernhardi's reasoning explaining why the Frangipani refused to accept Petrus Pierleoni as pope, viz. that they were a proud family which had already raised Honorius II to the papacy, and did not want to bow themselves before a pope of Jewish blood.[16] Unlike Bernhardi and Palumbo, Schmale sees little connection between Anaclet's Jewish ancestry and the schism, claiming that there were no racial theories at that time.[17]

He sees Klewitz' studies of 1939 as the first creative approach to the understanding of the schism since the earliest works, and Palumbo's long description as a regression. Besides criticizing the Italian scholar for placing too much emphasis on the development of the Roman commune as a cause for the schism, he views Palumbo's work as an attempt to justify Anaclet as the legally elected pope, who was recognized as the head of the church in a broad area of Christianity.[18] He sees the main difference between himself and Palumbo, however, in their assessment of what sort of phenomenon the election was. According to Schmale, Palumbo saw it as overwhelmingly political, not connected with ideas of religion or

---

[14] Franz-Josef Schmale, *Studien zum Schisma des Jahres 1130* (Cologne, 1961), vol. 3 of *Forschungen zur kirchlichen Rechtsgeschichte und zum Kirchenrecht*, ed. H.E. Feine, J. Heckel, and H. Nottarp.

[15] Ibid., 1-2, 6.

[16] Ibid., 4; Bernhardi, *Lothar*, p. 302.

[17] Ibid., 71, n. 90. Schmale notes that no one called attention to Anaclet's Jewish origin before 1130. It was only mentioned then, he claims, because Anaclet acted in such an anti-Christian way that people were reminded of his Jewish origin. They believed that his Jewishness had been only superficially covered, and that his family's conversion to Christianity had been feigned to serve their personal goals. Here, Schmale seems to contradict himself. He recognizes that people did have a very negative stereotype of Jewish behavior. They just did not associate it with Anaclet until his election.

[18] Ibid., 7.

dogma, and dependent upon real necessities of faith or new aspirations.[19] Schmale, on the contrary, sees the uniqueness and meaning of the schism in the spiritual differences of the parties representing each pope.[20]

A critical part of Schmale's theory is the tenet that the progressive and conservative parties were not confined to Rome, but were European-wide. He correlates the new, strict monastic movements with the party of Haimeric and Innocent, and the older Benedictine orders with Anaclet, but with one refinement. Even though Cluny was an old order, he must account for Peter the Venerable's massive support for Innocent. He does this by associating Cluny under its previous abbot, Pontius, with Anaclet, and what he sees as a reformed Cluny under Peter the Venerable with Innocent. He never seems to be completely satisfied with this solution, however, for he also believes that traditional Benedictinism did not have the drive to spearhead a new reform movement.

Schmale parts company from other historians, who also see a connection between the new monastic movements and the schism at Rome, in that he believes that even more than the monks, the canons regular infused the church with the new spirit.[21] St. Bernard's influence, he thinks, was significant, but not decisive.[22] In a second departure he emphasizes that the primary impetus for the reform came from the curia rather than from the new orders. They owed more to Innocent, he claims, than he to them.[23]

Summing up his view, Schmale says that the essential meaning of the schism is that Innocent incorporated the new tendencies of the church, no matter how you evaluate them. Anaclet did not recognize these tendencies, and therefore was rejected. Schmale believes that because Anaclet concentrated his vision so exclusively on Rome, he did not see that the reform movement had created a new, broader church. He remained an almost tragic figure, committed to an outmoded Gregorianism.[24]

Palumbo replied to Schmale's attack on his monograph in an article designed to bring the scholarship since the publication of his book up to date.[25] He accuses Schmale of making dangerous insinuations rather than relying on concrete data,[26] and he charges that Schmale's scholarship is imprecise and inaccurate.[27] Moreover, Palumbo's examples show that Schmale's scholarship was not randomly inaccurate, but that the mistakes contributed to the cogency of his arguments. For instance, Schmale states

---

[19] Ibid., 10, n. 24.
[20] Ibid., 10-11.
[21] Ibid., 269.
[22] Ibid., 262-264.
[23] Ibid., 263, n. 12.
[24] Ibid., 285.
[25] Palumbo, "Nuovi Studi." See n. 1 for full citation.
[26] Ibid., 95.
[27] Ibid., 98.

that there were 20 cardinals who voted for Innocent and 5 cardinal bishops, while Palumbo demonstrates that there were only 17 and 4.[28] Palumbo also points out that Schmale claims as his own innovation what he already had said, viz. that the schism of 1130 was born within the reform church and interested all of Christianity.[29] But what strikes a particularly sensitive chord is that Palumbo thinks that Schmale is permitting his own religious convictions to intrude into his assessments, and that he sees Palumbo as the defender of Anaclet, the Anti-Christ.[30]

In matters of interpretation Palumbo stands on his conviction that the quarrels among the Roman nobility were relevant to the schism. He also maintains that Innocent's reception north of the Alps was due mainly to the zealous efforts of St. Bernard. Palumbo is not persuaded by Schmale's thesis that Innocent's party stood for peace with the emperor while Anaclet's did not, and he questions whether profound ideological differences separated the two parties or only rivalries and disputes. For instance, he sees no evidence to support the inference that Anaclet sought the support of the Romans and southern Italians because he shared their conservative views on the nature of ecclesiastical reform and the position of the papacy within the church. A more probable explanation, he suggests, is that because of his immobility, he had no alternative sources.[31] And finally he thinks that Pandulphus' account demonstrates just how political the election was, and how little it had to do with anything "spiritual."

In 1972 Stanley Chodorow entered the fray between Palumbo and Klewitz/Schmale. In a book on Gratian's contribution to Christian political theory in which he also analyzes church politics in the mid-twelfth century, Chodorow argues that Gratian was not a recluse, compiling law in a political vacuum, but was associated with the group of new reformers led by Haimeric and St. Bernard.[32] While noting the objections of Palumbo, Chodorow builds on the works of Klewitz and Schmale. In the process he had to deal with an objection to their theory from another source.

In a study analyzing the downfall of Pontius of Cluny, Gerd Tellenbach had attacked the view held by Klewitz and Schmale that in the time of Pontius, Cluny had grown old, slack through riches, and increasingly alienated from the ideals of St. Benedict.[33] Viewing Cluny from the

---

[28] Ibid., 100, n. 1.

[29] Ibid., 97-98.

[30] Ibid., 96-97.

[31] Ibid., 99.

[32] Stanley Chodorow, *Christian Political Theory and Church Politics in the Mid-Twelfth Century: The Ecclesiology of Gratian's Decretum* (Berkeley, Los Angeles, London, 1972), esp. pp. 5-6, 46-47.

[33] Gerd Tellenbach, "Der Sturz des Abtes Pontius von Cluny und seine geschichtliche Bedeutung." *Quellen und Forschungen aus italienishen Archiven und Bibliotheken* 42/43 (1963), 13-55, at p. 16.

perspective of the development of monasticism from the tenth through the thirteenth centuries, Tellenbach did not see the overthrow of Pontius as a symptom of the religious decadence of Cluny and the old Benedictinism. He conceded only that the new orders were different, not better.[34] Further, Tellenbach said that there is no evidence for the existence of European-wide parties centered in the curial party of Innocent and Haimeric on the one hand, and the party of Anaclet on the other. He argued that there is neither proof of a new spiritual direction taken by Honorius, Innocent, and Haimeric, nor of a connection between Anaclet and the dispute between Pontius and Peter the Venerable.[35]

Chodorow, however, is not convinced by Tellenbach's criticism of the views of Klewitz and Schmale. He says that Tellenbach may be essentially correct in his assessment of the situation in Cluny in the 1120's. However, he does not think that it follows from the fact that Tellenbach could find no evidence of a connection between the dispute in Cluny and the party dispute within the church, that there was no dispute between European-wide parties.[36] Chodorow admits that Tellenbach has discovered a lacuna in the interpretation of Klewitz and Schmale, that of characterizing the intellectual content of the parties, but he does not concede that the omission means that their theory was wrong. Chodorow believes that it is correct, and sets himself the task of describing the ideology of the parties to make it complete.[37]

He concentrates his investigation on the Pierleoni family, which he believes gained dominance over the papacy between April 1111 and March 1112 when Paschal II appointed Petrus Pierleoni to the cardinalate. He argues that from then until the negotiations in 1121-1122 preceding the Concordat of Worms the curia and the pope were solidly in the hands of Petrus and his supporters. Calixtus II and Henry V were able to reach a compromise on investitures only because this faction failed to control the papacy during the crucial period before 1122. Chodorow agrees with Schmale that it was the Pierleoni faction, dissatisfied with the Concordat, which raised an uproar at the Lateran Council of 1123 when Calixtus' concessions to Henry V were being read. After their failure Chodorow believes that they went into opposition against the conciliatory party of Calixtus and his newly-appointed chancellor, Haimeric. As a result, he concludes that Calixtus "became the staunch enemy of the Pierleoni representing all the elements in the Church opposed to the Roman faction's policies and outlook."[38]

In effect Chodorow is extending the Klewitz/Schmale thesis back a

---

[34] Ibid., 53.

[35] Ibid., 54.

[36] Chodorow, *Christian Political Theory*, p. 25.

[37] Ibid., 27.

[38] Ibid., 31, n. 21.

decade. Fitting Calixtus along with the Pierleoni into the two-party schema, he sees the pope, a Frenchman, as representative of the church at large, and the Pierleoni, Roman noblemen, as representative of the local powers, which, he avers, had always had a pernicious effect upon the papacy. Later Anaclet would continue to receive local support, while Innocent would attract his followers from the church at large. Chodorow notes that the sub deacons, the career servants of the papal curia, sided with Anaclet, and that he promoted many of them to the cardinalate. Innocent, by contrast, drew upon members of the church at large for his cardinals.[39]

Chodorow believes that the central point of opposition between the parties during the 1120's was the policy of enmity or friendship toward the emperor, or in other words, the continuation or resolution of the investiture contest.[40] He argues that Haimeric felt that there was no need to continue the traditional papal alliance with the Normans since the emperor was no longer a threat, while Anaclet, still holding that there was a battle to be fought on the imperial front, sought an alliance with the Normans. Thus, he concludes, while Haimeric could begin to work for general reform of ecclesiastical society, Anaclet continued to fight against the emperor to win the contest over investitures.

Chodorow believes that he has established the existence of two European-wide parties and the fundamental differences in their orientation. Since he holds that the monastic reformers represented the basic ideals and political outlook of the Innocentians,[41] all that needs to be done in determining the intellectual content of the curial party is to refer to the activities and voluminous writings of the reformers in the North. He notes their great emphasis on moral regeneration and their attempt to root out the worsening problem of heresy. He admits that the party of Anaclet may have been concerned with similar issues, but he alleges that there is no evidence that they actively sought these goals.[42]

Chodorow's study completed the Klewitz/Schmale line of research, and the thesis has been treated more as a fact than as a theory since the 1980's. In an article written on the schism in France as late as 1981 Aryeh Grabois accepts it without question.[43] He differs from Schmale only in his belief that Anaclet was regarded not simply as a less worthy rival of Innocent, but as a Jewish pope. However, more discrete studies of the cardinals have been undermining the thesis for the last two decades, and in an

---

[39] Ibid., 35, n. 28. Chodorow gets his statistics from an article by Reinhard Elze, "Die päpstliche Kapelle im 12. und 13. Jahrhundert," *Zeitschrift der Savigny-Stiftung für Rechtsgeschichte*, KA 36 (1950), 165-166.

[40] Ibid., 39.

[41] Ibid., 40.

[42] Ibid., 41. Chodorow considers Peter the Venerable's tracts against Jews and Moslems as attacks on heresy.

[43] Aryeh Grabois, "Le Schisme de 1130 et la France," *Revue d'histoire écclésiastique* 76 (1981), 593-612.

article written in the same year (1981) on the colleges of cardinals under Innocent and Anaclet, Werner Maleczek takes account of these studies.[44] He still believes that the root of the schism must be sought within the college of cardinals, but thinks that the principles the cardinals represented can better be determined from examining their records after, rather than before the elections, when there is more information. From his meticulous research he concludes that there were no parties with distinct ideologies at the time of the elections; there was only a coalescence into groups based upon immediate circumstances. Neither side tried to institute a new program after the election, he notes, and the fact that so many cardinals shifted from Anaclet to Innocent after the election indicates to him the absence of strong ideological commitments.

In only one area, Maleczek states, can Innocent's curia be said to be progressive and Anaclet's conservative—in their judicial system. By drawing more and more cases to his forum Innocent extended his authority and created dependents. Anaclet, by contrast, largely left the dispensation of justice to Roger, whose special prerogative it was under the ecclesiastical regulations of South Italy. Thus, Maleczek concludes, Innocent emancipated himself from the constraints under which he labored at the origin of his papacy and became an international papal monarch, while Anaclet quickly isolated himself.

Maleczek's study points the way to a reconsideration of the total panoply of events and relationships which are relevant, or which have been seen to be relevant, to the schism. From this new investigation Innocent and Haimeric are revealed not as leaders of a European-wide party seeking the moral regeneration of the church, but as tough minded pragmatists. Although they promoted the reform orders, and no doubt admired their religious convictions, their own records do not suggest that a commitment to the same ideals moved them to secure Innocent's election even at the expense of a schism. For a complex series of reasons Innocent and Haimeric did gain the allegiance of the leaders of these movements, however, and in so doing they had at their disposal a machine so powerful that it virtually converted most of Europe to Innocent's side.[45]

---

[44] Werner Maleczek, "Das Kardinalskollegium unter Innocenz II. und Anaklet II.," *Archivum Historiae Pontificiae* 19 (1981), 27-28.

[45] Colin Morris mentions the effectiveness of correspondence with a wide range of friends as being fundamental to an attempt to control policy, and he says further that on occasion such friendship networks could be employed ruthlessly as pressure groups. Specifically he states that "In the schism of 1130 the victory of Innocent II in the north of Europe was mainly due to a group of people who appear to have been in close touch with one another: Saint Bernard, Saint Norbert, Peter the Venerable, and the papal chancellor Haimeric." *The Discovery of the Individual 1050-1200* (London, 1972), p. 104. More recently, Timothy Reuter refers to a circle of friends from Northern France, who were in frequent contact with the papacy. After refuting the main tenets of the Klewitz/Schmale thesis, Reuter concludes that the close interaction of this circle led to Innocent's quick recognition. Reuter's arguments will be considered in greater detail below. "Zur Anerkennung Papst Innocenz II: Eine neue Quelle," *Deutsches Archiv für Erforschung des Mittelalters* 39 (1983), 395-416.

Chapter II

CALIXTUS II AND THE PIERLEONI

In order to understand the events which led to Innocent's victory, let us track back in time to the ending of the Investiture Contest. One of the most intriguing configurations in the intricate web woven by the *dramatis personae* in this pivotal period was the filament connecting Calixtus With the Pierleoni. On the surface the new Roman family appeared to support the former Burgundian archbishop, who was thought to have been elected pope in part because of his family connections extending all the way to the emperor himself. Some historians, however, believe that this seeming harmony was only a facade, which Petrus Pierleoni stripped away when he led a revolt in the Lateran Council of 1123 decrying the compromises in the Concordat of Worms.[1] The essence of their theory can be summarized in the following paragraphs.

It begins by noting that Anaclet spent his formative years during the investiture struggle, and postulates that he invariably took an inflexible stand against the emperor. Calixtus also had a record of stiff opposition to the emperor. In the Council of Vienne, for example, he criticized Paschal II for refusing to excommunicate the emperor for extracting the privilege on investitures granted when the pope and many of his cardinals were in imperial captivity.[2] But holders of this view believe that unlike Petrus, Calixtus softened his position when he became pope in 1119.

They reason that as a Frenchman, he was attracted to the views of the influential French canonist, Ivo of Chartres. Ivo was notable as the

---

[1] Chodorow, *Christian Political Theory*, pp. 30-34; see also Chodorow's article, "Ecclesiastical Politics and the Ending of the Investiture Contest: The Papal Election of 1119 and the Negotiations of Mouzon," *Speculum* 46 (1971), 638-639; Gerhoh, canon of Reichersberg, reports the outbreak, MGH Ldl 3:280; for the Lateran Council see Joannes Mansi, *Sacrorum Conciliorum Nova et Amplissima Collectio* 21 (Venise, 1776), pp. 277-286, 299-304; Charles-Joseph Hefele, *Histoire des Conciles d'àpres les documents originaux* with new trans. & notes by H. Leclercq, 5:1 (Paris, 1912), pp. 630-644; for the Concordat of Worms and all of its sources see ibid., 602-630.

[2] The papal/imperial negotiations, Paschal's captivity, and the Lateran Council of 1112 are described in the *Liber Censuum de l'Église Romaine,* ed. Paul Fabre & Louis Duchesne, Bibliothèque des Écoles Française D'Athènes et de Rome, 2e serie, 2 vols., vol. 1 (Paris, 1905), pp. 409-414; for the Council of Vienne of 1112 see Mansi, *Collectio Sacrorum Conciliorum* 21, pp. 73-78; Hefele/Leclercq, *Histoire des Conciles* 5:1, p. 531; Gerold Meyer von Knonau, *Jahrbücher des Deutschen Reiches unter Heinrich IV. und Heinrich V.* 6 (Berlin, 1907, repro. 1965), pp. 242-244; Mary Stroll, "Calixtus II: A Reinterpretation of his Election and the End of the Investiture Contest," *Studies in Medieval and Renaissance History* 3 (1980), 3-53 at pp. 9-14.

theoretician of the agreements over investitures worked out between the English and French kings and their churches. Calixtus tried to negotiate a similar compromise with Henry V at Mouzon in 1119, they argue, but the conservative Italian cardinals he had inherited thwarted his efforts. Their leader was the young cardinal deacon, Petrus Pierieoni. They believe that by 1122 Calixtus had consolidated his power, and was less reliant upon the support of Petrus and his powerful family. He chose three cardinals not under their influence to negotiate with the emperor, and this time he was successful.

According to the theory Petrus and his faction were unhappy with this truce, and led the revolt in the Lateran Council of 1123 when the provisions of the Concordat were read. Calixtus would not tolerate this act of insubordination, and immediately took steps to take control of the curia. Within a month of the council he appointed Haimeric, a fellow Frenchman, as chancellor, and he made Leo Frangipani commandant of the forces of the city of Rome.[3] Since Haimeric supported the Concordat of Worms, he would guide the church away from its concentration on the problems of church and state, and lead it toward an emphasis on internal ecclesiastical reform. Advocates of this view see the Frangipani as a counterweight to the power of the Pierleoni. Less hostile to the emperor, they would be more effective in providing the military support needed in the new climate of detente. The appointment of Leo is seen as even more significant than Calixtus' promotion of Petrus from cardinal deacon to cardinal priest on December 17, 1120.[4]

Calixtus died in 1124, and adherents of the theory hold that his loyal chancellor assumed the responsibility of insuring that the next pope would continue his policies. The conservative cardinals, still in the majority, saw the election as an opportunity to regain their ascendancy. There was bound to be a clash, and there was. When the conservatives elected Celestine II, Haimeric and the Frangipani broke up his consecration by force, and imposed cardinal Bishop Lambert of Ostia as Honorius II.[5] The new pope's main virtue was his dedication to a policy of peace with the emperor, a commitment he had demonstrated as a negotiator of the Concordat of Worms.

In the hope of legally electing the next pope, the theory concludes, Honorius and Haimeric created a large number of like-minded cardinals. Not having had time to achieve a majority within the College of Cardinals

---

[3] JL 7069; Schmale, *Studien zum Schisma*, p. 105.

[4] Schmale, op. cit., p. 23. For Petrus' promotion see Luigi Pellegrini (Mario da Bergamo), "Cardinali e Curia sotto Callisto II (1119-1124)," pp. 507-556 of *Raccolta de studi in memoria de S. Mochi Onory* (Milan, 1972), p. 526 & n. 100; Rudolf Hüls, *Kardinäle, Klerus und Kirchen Roms 1049-1130*, vol. 48 of *Bibliothek des deutschen historischen Instituts in Rom* (Tübingen, 1977), p. 225; Helene Tillmann, "Ricerche sul collegio Cardinalizio nel sec. XII," *Rivista di Storia della Chiesa in Italia* 26 (1972), 323-325; Klewitz, "Das Ende," p. 227.

[5] *Lib. Pont.* 2, p. 327.

by Honorius' death in 1130, however, Haimeric was forced to manipulate the electoral process to prevent Petrus' election. The chancellor's faction elected Gregory of St. Angelo as Innocent II, but not accepting a *fait accompli*, the Pierleoni party elected Petrus as Anaclet II. Formulators of this theory believe that the French monastic reformers and canons regular supported Innocent because they thought that he would pursue the policies initiated by Calixtus and Haimeric, and continued by Honorius. It was to be anticipated that the Normans in Southern Italy, the cardinals from Rome and Southern Italy, and the older Benedictine houses—the mainstay of the Gregorian papacy—would support Anaclet.

As appealing as this argument is, it does not accurately characterize curial politics from the time Petrus became a cardinal until the election of 1130. Petrus and Calixtus were not ideological foes, and there never was any break between them. Moreover, Petrus was not the predominant figure in the curia from the Lateran Council of March 1112 until the negotiations preceding the Concordat of Worms. It is even improbable that he was a cardinal in 1112, since the first time he is known to have been a signatory as a cardinal is in 1113.[6] Fresh from his studies in France, and a brief sojourn as a monk at Cluny, Petrus could not possibly have shunted aside the veterans of the wars over investitures and become the most powerful member of the curia. He was too young and inexperienced, and he was out of Rome most of the time. Until 1125 he spent much of his time abroad, either in France in the entourage of Gelasius and Calixtus, or as a legate to England and to France.[7]

Rather than substantiating that the curia under Calixtus was solidly in the hands of Petrus, his family and supporters, a careful analysis of the cardinals indicates that other cardinals had more authority.[8] Petrus' future opponent, Cardinal Priest John of Crema, a man regarded by some as a person of dubious character, appended his signature to more papal bulls than any other cardinal.[9] These signatures show that of all of the

---

[6] Chodorow (*Christian Political Theory*, p. 30) says that Petrus was raised to the cardinalate between April 1111 and March 1112. Hüls says that it was c. 1112 (*Kardinäle*, pp. 86, 225), but Tillmann claims that it was not until 1113 ("Ricerche," p. 323). The first act, which Petrus signed is dated in that year.

[7] Palumbo, *Lo Scisma*, pp. 141-145; Pellegrini, "Cardinali," p. 525.

[8] In addition to the studies on the cardinals cited in this chapter, see also Barbara Zenker, *Die Mitglieder des Kardinalkollegiums von 1130 bis 1159*, (Diss. Würzburg, 1964). Dr. Zenker was Schmale's student, and appears to be influenced by his views.

[9] Pellegrini, "Cardinali," p. 520; Pandulphus reports that Honorius II suspended him from office, but then inexplicably restored him. "Hic Johannem Cremensem, hominem litteratum et providum, sed turpis fame magis quam opus sit, suspendit a cardinalatus officio; sed ipse scit et Deus qualiter eum postea restituerit." *Lib. Pont. Dert.*, p. 208. For further sources on John's alleged depravity see March's n. 24, pp. 214-215 and Palumbo, *Lo Scisma*, pp. 265-266. Many of the charges against John rose out of his legateship to England and come from English rather than curial sources. Schmale, however, minimizes these charges, and refers to him as "ein durchaus reformtreuer Mann," *Studien zum Scisma*, pp. 34-38. It is suggestive that the two cardinals who appear to have been Calixtus' closest advisors, John and Lambert, were both career curialists and both Italian. There is no sign here of any new reform party inspired by the French monastic reformers. John will be discussed below.

cardinals, he was the most frequently in the pope's entourage. Calixtus also used John for important diplomatic assignments, and gave him command of the military expedition to Sutri to capture the antipope, Gregory VIII. But Pellegrini, who has made a careful study of the curia under Calixtus, concludes that Lambert of Ostia was the dean of the cardinals. Whenever particularly sensitive or important decisions were to be made, he was on hand.[10]

As we shall see when we discuss Petrus' record as a cardinal, he cannot be shown to have been the leader of a conservative contingent among the cardinals,[11] but apart from the question of whether there was such a faction within the curia which opposed Calixtus' progressive policies, no one had the power to control the curia in opposition to the pope's wishes. Calixtus had shown his mettle as archbishop of Vienne, when he was even willing to threaten Urban II to achieve his ends. He masterfully controlled the council of Rheims of 1119, and from the moment he entered Rome riding a white horse, and wearing a jewel encrusted garment, there was no question of who was in command.[12] Showing that he had the support of all of the major factions there, he was always able to leave Rome for long periods of time without incident. Moreover, the Pierleoni were not all-powerful. Both Paschal and Gelasius had been forced to flee Rome in spite of their support. Calixtus, therefore, did not have to compromise his principles in order to keep their loyalty.

If Calixtus had wished to favor Petrus only enough to keep his good will, but not enough to allow him to hinder his own policies, he would have asked him to accept a minimum number of assignments of as little importance as possible. Instead of treating him honorably, but giving him little power, Calixtus showed his confidence in Petrus by asking him to carry out important diplomatic duties throughout his whole reign. He not only appointed Petrus to repeated legateships, but he granted him exceptionally broad powers. When he asked Petrus to be his representative in England, he appointed him as both legate *a latere* and as vicar. Petrus simultaneously held the legation for France, Scotland, Ireland, and the surrounding islands. Calixtus also brought Petrus back to Italy from time to time to participate in particularly important business. The negotiations between Pisa and Genoa for the control of the church of Corsica are an example.[13]

---

[10] Ibid., 543.

[11] Ibid., 548.

[12] Uodalscalcus de Eginone et Herimanno, MGH SS 12:446; the clothes were not merely decorative, but had imperial overtones. See the description of imperial attire in the *Graphia Aurea Urbis*, a twelfth-century compilation of legendary descriptions of the founding of Rome, selections from the *Mirabilia*, and the *Libellus de caerimoniis aulae imperatoris*. The descriptions are taken from the Donation of Constantine, and therefore have political implications as well. Roberto Valentini and Giuseppe Zucchetti, eds., *Codice Topografico della Città di Roma* 3 (Rome, 1946), pp. 101-102, and editors' notes, pp. 67-76; for the Council of Rheims see Mansi, *Collectio Sacrorum Conciliorum* 21, pp. 233-256; Hefele/Leclercq, *Histoire des Conciles* 5:1, pp. 569-591.

[13] Petrus' legateships will be discussed below; for the negotiations over the church of

If Calixtus had initiated a campaign to curtail Petrus' power after the Lateran Council of 1123, then there should have been a sharp drop off in Petrus' participation in curial business. The opposite was the case. Petrus took part in more acts after the Council than before.[14] On May 16, 1122 he appeared as *judex datus* in a papal document for the monastery of St. Remigius at Rheims.[15] The following year on April 26th he signed Calixtus' celebrated bull for Genoa,[16] and on April 15th he signed a privilege for Pavia.[17] Two other documents also indicate Calixtus' esteem for Petrus. On June 7, 1123 he confirmed the possessions of Petrus' cardinalate church of Santa Maria in Trastevere,[18] and in the fall after the Lateran Council he sent Petrus back to France with a warm recommendation to Louis VI.[19]

Santa Maria was the title church of St. Calixtus, and by assigning Petrus the church of his eponymous predecessor, Calixtus was deliberately identifying himself with Petrus. Moreover, the dependencies which Calixtus confirmed were vast—many properties, some far flung, and nine churches.[20] The first mentioned was St. Calixtus. In the same bull Calixtus also confirmed a new Station on the Octave of the Nativity, i.e. the Feast of the Circumcision. Calixtus transferred the station from S. Maria ad Martyres, where it had been celebrated from the seventh century. By the time the bull was issued, the first celebration of the station had already occurred:

> In the year of the Lord's incarnation 1123 . . . a Station was given in the church of S. Maria in Trastevere on the Octave of the Nativity of the Lord by the Lord of the Roman Church, Pope Callixtus. And this was with the assent, pleasure, and prayers of all of the bishops, cardinals, deacons, and the entire Roman clergy. Which Station he himself celebrated for the first time with the aforesaid lords and all of the Lateran

---

Corsica see MGH SS 18:356; Palumbo, *Lo Scisma*, pp. 69, n. 3, 144. The document is of particular significance because of the huge payments made by the Genoese negotiators in return for a favorable settlement. Petrus personally received no money, but his father and brothers received 155 marks of silver, and his mother gifts of jewelry. Leo Frangipani received a much smaller payment, 40 marks, but Schmale has nevertheless seen this gift as indicative that Calixtus was beginning to use the Frangipani as a counterweight to the Pierleoni (*Studien zum Schisma*, pp. 22-23). That the Frangipani were again reconciled with the papacy is indisputable, but that they were used as a counterweight to the Pierleoni is by no means demonstrated by this evidence. If anything, the text shows the continuing influence of the Pierleoni by the much larger size of their gifts.

[14] Palumbo, *Lo Scisma*, p. 145.

[15] PL 163:1246-1247.

[16] PL 163:1287-1290.

[17] PL 163:1292-1293.

[18] Ulysse Robert, *Bullaire du Pape Calixte II* (Paris, 1891), nr. 408, p. 210.

[19] PL 163:1297. September 30, 1123: "Sane charissimum filium nostrum P. sedis nostrae presbyterum cardinalem nobilitati tuae attentius commendamus."

[20] For Calixtus' confirmation of the churches and possessions of Santa Maria in Trastevere, and the transfer of the Station of the Circumcision, see Dale Kinney, *S. Maria in Trastevere from its founding to 1215* (diss. New York University, 1975), pp. 198-204.

scholae, solemnly and surrounded by a great throng of Roman people. And he especially ordered that in the future it be solemnly celebrated annually by the Roman popes.[21]

The description of the celebration testifies to Petrus' high stature among the cardinals and every level of clergy, and Calixtus' wish to associate himself publicly and ostentatiously with Petrus. The transfer of a station from one church to another was a rare phenomenon in the Roman church, because the church impelled to relinquish it lost prestige and the revenues from pilgrims and votive gifts. The donor church not only gained these benefits, but also the honor of being selected as a church where the sacrosanct liturgy, attributed to the Holy Spirit, could be enacted. The stational liturgy was regarded as being absolutely perfect, and anyone who did not perform it flawlessly invited criticism, not only from Rome, but from all of Europe. By bestowing this great honor on Santa Maria, Calixtus showed unequivocal confidence in Petrus as a religious leader. The fact that all of the clergy, and especially the cardinals, were pleased with the transference of the Station to Santa Maria is independent evidence of the respect Petrus commanded within the church in 1123. It is a strong refutation of the charges hurled at Petrus at the time of the papal elections.

From their perspective, Petrus and his supporters affirm that there was no friction between Petrus and Calixtus.[22] Pandulphus is a case in point. In his biographies of Calixtus and Honorius, he is uniformly commendatory toward the former, and disdainful of the latter. There is even a hint that he wanted to contrast the two popes by characterizing Calixtus as "holy" and Honorius as corrupt.[23] When Peter William altered the biography of Calixtus to make it fit with the picture which the Innocentians wanted transmitted, he probably realized the impact that this contrast would have on the reputation of Honorius, and by extension on Innocent. To avoid an invidious comparison he changed "holy" to "royal." By describing Calixtus as holy rather than royal, Pandulphus not only showed great respect for Calixtus, but also approval of his religious attitudes.

Supporting this written evidence is the recently much discussed mural painted in the apse of the chapel of St. Nicholas in the Lateran palace. Built by Calixtus, the chapel was destroyed in the eighteenth century. We are therefore dependent upon descriptions and reproductions of it made between the sixteenth and the eighteenth centuries. In an article on the schism of Anaclet and the Glanfeuil forgeries Herbert Bloch analyzed this mural. He agrees with Gerhard Ladner's felicitous description of it as "the

21 *Necrologium ecclesiae S. Mariae trans Tiberim*, ed. Pietro Egidi, *Necrologi e libri affini della provincia di Roma* I: *Necrologi della città di Roma* (Rome, 1908), pp. 88-89; Kinney's trans., *S. Maria in Trastevere*, p. 200.

22 Palumbo, *Lo Scisma*, p. 137.

23 *Lib. Pont. Dert.*, p. 203. March offers the explanation in his notes (p. 209) of why Peter William deleted "holy" and replaced it with "royal."

apotheosis of the victorious papacy."[24] The painting is divided into two zones. In the upper zone a pope stands on either side of the Virgin, Queen of Heaven. According to the drawing made by Gaetani in the seventeenth century the popes are Sylvester I and Anastasius I. Kneeling at the Virgin's feet are popes identified as Calixtus II and Anastasius IIII. In the lower zone St. Nicholas is flanked by popes of the reform to which were added Leo I and Gregory I, models for the reform popes.

Between the two zones is a dedicatory verse. At the end of the nineteenth century Louis Duchesne was able to demonstrate that the verse had been changed. Whereas it once had read that Calixtus had built the chapel, and that Anaclet had painted it, someone altered it to read that Calixtus had both constructed and decorated the chapel. Duchesne also showed that Anaclet II, not Anastasius IIII was the figure kneeling at the left of the Virgin across from Calixtus II.[25] Someone, quite possibly Innocent himself, who had politically significant paintings executed in rooms close to the chapel, expunged the name, "Anacletus II."

The painting has signified different things to different historians. Bloch says that it is graphic testimony in support of Klewitz' view that Anaclet was the last representative of the Gregorian reform, which thereafter was superseded by the new reform of St. Bernard.[26] Chodorow echoes Bloch's conclusion that the mural expresses Anaclet's consciousness of being the end of an era, and he also notes that it is striking that Honorius II has been left out. To him the omission reinforces Pandulphus' ascription of the origins of the schism to the elevation of Honorius II.[27] This observation is partially correct, for Pandulphus does show his revulsion for Honorius, and he emphasizes the dissension within the curia over the mode of Honorius' election. Elements of continuity persisted during Honorius' pontificate, however,[28] and the argument that by this painting Anaclet symbolized that he was at the end of an era is not convincing. If he had wanted to make this point, he should have stood out alone rather than juxtaposing himself with Calixtus. In his eyes he and Calixtus were the last two reform popes, but he in no way implies that he would not have a successor in the same tradition.

---

[24] Bloch, "The Schism of Anacletus II," pp. 178-180; by the same author, *Montecassino in the Middle Ages* (Rome & Cambridge, Mass., 1987?) 2, pp. 964-966. Professor Bloch very kindly showed me the proofs. Gerhard Ladner, "I mosaici e gli affreschi ecclesiastico-politici nell'antico palazzo Lateranense," *Rivista di archeologia Christiana* 12 (1935), 270. By the same author, *I Ritratti dei Papi nell'Antichità e nel Medioevo* vol. 1 *Dalle origini fino alla fine della Lotta per le Investiture*. Monumenti di Antichità Christiana Pubblicati dal Pontificio Istituto di Archeologia Christiana, II Serie, IV (Vatican City, 1941), pp. 202-218; Ursula Nilgen, "Maria Regina—Ein politischer Kultbildtypus," *Römisches Jahrbuch für Kunstgeschichte* 19 (1981), pp. 3-5, 24 & passim.

[25] Louis Duchesne, "Le nom d'Anaclet II au palais de Lateran," *Mémoires de la Société de Antiquaires di France*, 5th ser., 9 (1888), 197-206; Bloch, "The Schism of Anacletus II," p. 179, n. 83; Richard Krautheimer, *Rome: Profile of a City, 312-1308* (Princeton, 1980), p. 190.

[26] Bloch, "The Schism of Anacletus," p. 180.

[27] Chodorow, *Christian Political Theory*, pp. 38-39, n. 33.

[28] These will be discussed below.

The painting's most revealing clue for understanding the ecclesiastical politics of this period, however, is Anaclet's specific association of himself with Calixtus. The symmetry of the painting unmistakably pairs the two popes, both clasping the feet of Mary, and set off from the other popes by wearing the square halo. There is no evidence here of a power struggle between the two men, or of conflicts over religious ideology. Rather, Anaclet is dramatically emphasizing that he and Calixtus were part of a long tradition of reforming popes, and that Honorius was an aberration in that noble tradition.

The painting is iconographically very rich, and there may be still more to be gleened from it. Scholars who have analyzed this painting have concentrated on the identification of the figure of Anastasius IIII with Anaclet II, but as far back as the beginning of the nineteenth century, Philippe Lauer argued that "Anacletus I" had been changed to "Anastasius I." He noted that the figure is not wearing a tiara, a sign that he had to have preceded Sylvester I, since according to Christian iconography, the tiara is attributed to popes only after Sylvester. In his recent book on Rome, Richard Krautheimer also identifies the pope named Anastasius I as Anaclet I.[29] In addition to the other evidence, it makes sense that Anaclet would have put the pope after whom he had named himself above himself in the fresco rather than Anastasius I. The implication is far more suggestive, especially since Anaclet I is paired with Sylvester I. The forged Donation of Constantine specifies Sylvester as the pope to whom Constantine granted the ruling powers in the West, when he departed for the East. Sylvester thus symbolizes the pope's temporal authority—his *plenitudo potestatis*. By contrast, Anaclet I signifies St. Peter. Thought to have been ordained by Peter himself, his biography in the *Liber Pontificalis* also states that he set up Peter's *memoria* (sepulchre), and that he was buried next to him.[30] Accordingly, by identifying himself with Anaclet I, Anaclet II identifies himself with St. Peter, and therefore with papal leadership of the church. He does not reject the pope's temporal authority, since he juxtaposes himself with Calixtus, who is placed in the same relationship with Sylvester I as he is with Anaclet I, but his closest attachment is with the papacy before it possessed any temporal authority.

There is yet another level on which to interpret the connection between Anaclet I, representing St. Peter, and Anaclet II. St. Bernard frequently referred to St. Peter with his simple-living ways as the model for the popes of the second quarter of the twelfth century to emulate. Contrasting their involvement in worldly affairs, their ostentation, and their preoccupation with judicial concerns, he admonishes them to copy the unaffected style of St. Peter.[31] Portraying himself as a smaller figure,

29 Krautheimer, *Rome*, p. 190; Philippe Lauer, *Le Palais de Latran* (Paris, 1911), p. 170.

30 *Lib. Pont.* 1, p. 125.

31 Bernard of Clairvaux, *Five Books on Consideration: Advice to a Pope*, vol. 13 of Cister-

realistically depicted as a young man rather than as embodying the abstract qualities of a saint, Anaclet accentuated his humble position within the church, and his empathy with the *vita apostolica*.

The painting is also evidence that Calixtus did not shift his reliance on the Pierleoni to the Frangipani after the Concordat of Worms. As one time supporters of Henry V, they, more than the Pierleoni, have been seen to be sympathetic to the emperor, and accordingly as better allies for charting a new course after the reconciliation of 1122. Although Pandulphus notes that Calixtus had some of the Frangipani towers destroyed with the added priviso that they never be rebuilt, proponents of this view do not regard these severe measures as evidence to the contrary.[32] They argue that the Frangipani gradually made their own accommodation with Calixtus, and that this can be seen from their participation in the negotiations over the church of Corsica, and then "not much later" from Calixtus' grant of the command of the militia of Rome to Leo Frangipani.[33] Chodorow more specifically states that Calixtus granted Leo this command as one of the two steps he took after the Concordat of Worms to counter the power of the Pierleoni.[34]

For understanding the relationship of Calixtus with the Frangipani and the Pierleoni it is not of great moment that he granted the command to Cencius rather than to Leo, although it could be important for understanding the Frangipani.[35] Leo was more of a statesman, and Cencius more bellicose (it was he, who had captured Gelasius), and some scholars think they see a split in the family along those lines. The nature of the force is of the utmost importance for assessing how Calixtus was utilizing the two families, however. The body of troops was not the militia of Rome, but the *masnada*, a much smaller band of militia.[36] The size is

---

cian Fathers series, ed. & trans., John D. Anderson & Elizabeth T. Kennan (Kalamazoo, Mich., 1976), p. 117: "You will not deny it unless you deny you are the heir of him whose throne you hold. This is Peter, who is known never to have gone in procession adorned with either jewels or silks, covered with gold, carried on a white horse, attended by a knight or surrounded by clamoring servants. But without these trappings, he believed it was enough to be able to fulfill the Lord's command, 'If you love me, feed my sheep.' In this finery, you are the successor not of Peter, but of Constantine." Bernard goes on to say that for the time being these things may be allowed, but he admonishes Eugenius to concentrate on his pastoral responsibilities.

[32] *Lib. Pont. Dert.*, pp. 194-195: "Hic pro pace seruanda turres Cencii, domne Bone et Iniquitatis dirui et reparari non ibidem precepit. Iniquitas quidam homo fuit uicinus Cencii domui." See n. 16 of March, p. 200 for the explanation of members of the Frangipani family.

[33] Schmale, *Studien zum Schisma*, pp. 22-23.

[34] Chodorow, *Christian Political Theory*, p. 32.

[35] The evidence that Calixtus granted Cencius command of the *masnada* is found in the biography of Honorius II. Pandulphus states that Cencius used the armed band to force Petrus Leonis and other nobles to acclaim Honorius: "Inde Petrus Leo, etsi nollet, inuitus et quidam alii nobiles de sola fraude clamati, coacti a masnada Cencii Fraiapane, que ei a papa Calixto commendata remanserat, adoraverunt omnes, etsi saperet malum." *Lib. Pont. Dert.*, pp. 204-205.

[36] Palumbo, *Lo Scisma*, p. 137, n. 3.

significant. Calixtus was not handing over the security of Rome to the Frangipani, but was only giving Cencius command of a relatively small band of militia. Certainly Calixtus was using the Frangipani, just as he used Leo in the negotiations with Genoa over the church of Corsica, but he was using them in a very carefully controlled way. In no way could he be considered to be favoring them to the detriment of the Pierleoni by granting them this command.

In ordering that three towers of the Frangipani be destroyed in the interests of preserving peace, and yet granting them military power, Calixtus appears to have been inconsistent. But the astute pope no doubt knew what he was doing, for there is a vast difference between the threat posed by a tower, and that posed by a possibly insubordinate leader of a small band of militia. Calixtus' rationale may have been that he wanted the family to maintain the loyalty that they had exhibited when they were on hand to meet him upon his arrival in Rome, and which Leo had solemnized by an oath.[37] But given their record, he did not want them to have any substantial military strength. Thus, in order not to alienate the family, and yet not to give them too much power, he commanded that the towers be destroyed, but put Cencius in charge of the *masnada*. If this were his strategy, it worked brilliantly. At the end of his reign it was said that Rome was so peaceful that it almost seemed as though the Age of Augustus had returned.

For Schmale and Chodorow, who see Cencius' appointment as indicative of Calixtus' change of policy, the timing is also critical. Chodorow believes that it roughly coincided with Haimeric's appointment and peace with the empire, accordingly with the onset of Calixtus' new orientation. Since Pandulphus does not specify when Calixtus appointed Cencius, however, the pope could have done it at any time, even at the beginning of his reign. The commission, therefore, can be seen neither as evidence of a shift away from the Pierleoni and toward the Frangipani, nor as a signal that Calixtus was embarking upon a new policy of ecclesiastical reform.

From every perspective, then, Calixtus demonstrated that he had the highest respect for Petrus, after, as well as before the Concordat of Worms. He granted him the most sacred honors, and he asked him to represent the papacy in the most important diplomatic assignments. Neither the appointments of Cencius Frangipani and Haimeric nor the uproar at the Lateran Council of 1123 indicate that Calixtus had lost confidence in his long time ally. Ironically, the person who voiced his opposition to the Concordat of Worms most emphatically was Gerhoh of Reichersberg, who had reported the uproar, and who supported Innocent.[38] The fact that

---

[37] PL 163:1180-1181; In a jubilant letter to Stephen, his *camerarius*, Calixtus noted that Leo Frangipani was among the noblemen on hand to welcome him to Rome, and that Leo later swore an oath to him.

[38] Gerhoh of Reichersberg, *Libellus de ordine donorum sancti spiritus*, MGH Ldl 3:279-280. Gerhoh reports the disruption of the Lateran Council of 1123, and adds his own thoughts: "In proximo futurum speramus, ut et illud malum de medio fiat, ne pro regalibus, immo

Gerhoh would object to the Concordat and yet recognize Innocent suggests that the parties to the schism did not originate in their response to the compromise over investitures. We will also find that their ideological underpinnings cannot be found in the dispute at Cluny of 1122-1126, or in Cluny's squabbles with Cîteaux, its rival for the allegiance of idealistic young Benedictines.

---

iam non regalibus, sed ecclesiasticis dicendis facultatibus ab episcopis hominium fiat vel sacramentum, sed sit episcopis liberum res ecclesiarum possidere de iure concessionis antiquae, sicut mater aecclesiarum Romana ecclesia possidet quae de iure oblationis vel traditionis antiquae tenet." Chodorow (*Christian Political Theory*, p. 62, n. 64) says that Gerhoh looked upon the Concordat of Worms as a hopeful beginning of the process of depriving the secular powers of all their authority in ecclesiastical elections, but in fact, Gerhoh seems to be saying just the opposite. For an analysis of the incident at the Lateran Council and the relationship between Calixtus and the Pierleoni see my article, "Calixtus II," esp. pp. 49-50.

Chapter III

PONTIUS AND ANACLET

Shortly before the upheaval of the papal schism a dispute erupted at Cluny, which rocked the relatively peaceful world of Western monasticism, and deeply involved the papacy. The conflict centered around the abbot, Pontius, and ended in a violent clash between him and his successor, Peter the Venerable. Some scholars see the dispute as part of the first rumblings of the papal schism. They interpret it as the northern counterpart of the division within the curia, and believe that it delineates the ideological guidelines of each of the papal contenders in the schism. To them the evidence is very strong that Anaclet was ideologically associated with Pontius, and Innocent with Peter. Anaclet had taken orders at Cluny under Pontius, and even though the abbot had died by 1130, these scholars believe that his followers must have supported Anaclet because they shared a common monastic philosophy. This probability appears to be strengthened by Peter the Venerable's vehement rejection of Anaclet, and his unstinting support of Innocent.

According to this perspective, one has only to observe the values upheld by each abbot to know the religious philosophy of the two cardinals vying for the papacy.[1] Here the differences appear to be clear cut. While the advocates of this view believe that Pontius permitted the standards of Cluny to degenerate, they hold that Peter the Venerable restored, and further tightened discipline under pressure from the Cistercians.[2] Accordingly, when St. Bernard harshly criticized the excesses of Cluny, he was referring to the reign of Pontius rather than the rule of Peter the Venerable.[3] Therefore, even though he was a member of an older Benedictine house, Peter is seen to have represented the monastery's most enlightened tendencies, and his support of Innocent is viewed as a compelling argument that Innocent also extolled these same principles. Churchmen recognized him as pope for this reason, and conversely, they rejected Anaclet because they saw him as spiritually aligned with the

[1] Chodorow, *Christian Political Theory*, p. 42, n. 37.

[2] Ibid., 22-26. John Van Engen questions whether there was a crisis in the older Benedictine houses during this period. "The 'Crisis of Cenobitism' Reconsidered: Benedictine Monasticism in the Years 1050-1150," *Speculum* (1986), 269-804.

[3] For a discussion of this issue see Adriaan Bredero, "Cluny et Cîteaux au XIIᵉ siècle: les origines de la controverse," *Studi Medievali* 12, nr. 1 (1971).

outmoded traditions of the old Cluny. Today this view is being challenged
by a number of scholars, who are reinvestigating the reign of Pontius and
the dispute at Cluny.

The salient events of the controversy are not clear because its two main
sources—*De Miraculis* of Peter the Venerable, and the *Historia Ecclesiastica*
of Ordericus Vitalis—conflict.[4] Ordericus, a Norman monk, is considered
to be a reliable reporter to the degree that he had access to accurate information, and his account is generally substantiated by others. Peter, however, was directly involved in the dispute, and understandably could not
entirely detach himself from it. Also, his memory may have been somewhat vague, since he did not write his version until 20 years after the
events. Nevertheless, until recently scholars accepted it with little scepticism. Now they are detecting discrepancies, which make them take Ordericus' account, written only 10 years after the conflict, more seriously.[5]

The dispute evolved roughly as follows. Peter the Venerable contended
that there had been grumbling against Pontius within Cluny since 1112
because of his poor administration, and many other sources attest that
bishops in overlapping territories resented Cluniac exemptions. However,
to the outside world Pontius appeared as one of the pillars of the reform
papacy from his consecration by Archbishop Guy of Vienne (later Calixtus
II) in 1109 until 1122.[6] In that year he suddenly arrived in Rome, where

---

[4] *De Miraculis*, PL 189:922-926. The account of Pontius is found in cc. 12 and 13 of book
2 of Peter's biography of Matthew, cardinal bishop of Albano, formerly of the Cluniac
monastery of St. Martin-des-Champs, and grand prior of Cluny. See Pietro Zerbi, "Intorno
allo scisma de Ponzio, Abate di Cluny," in *Studi storici in onore di Ottorino Bertolini* 2, ed. Pacini (Pisa, 1971), 835-891 at p. 836, n. 1 for a discussion of *De Miraculis*. The best edition of
the *Historia Ecclesiastica* is edited by Marjorie Chibnall, *The Ecclesiastic History of Orderic Vitalis* (Oxford, New York, 1969, 1972-1978). The events concerning the dispute at Cluny are
in Book XII, vol. 6 (1978), pp. 311-316. See also by Chibnall *The World of Orderic Vitalis*
(Oxford, 1984).

[5] Tellenbach, "Der Sturz," p. 16. Tellenbach noticed that Peter did not mention Pontius'
painful imprisonment in the Septizonium. Instead, Peter affirmed that Pontius died from an
epidemic not mentioned in any other source. These discrepancies suggested to him that at
least Peter did not present an accurate account of details, and that perhaps his distortions
went beyond details. Geoffrey of Vigeois mentions Pontius' imprisonment in the Septizonium. *Ex Chronico Gaufredi Vosiensis*, ed. M. Bouquet, *Recueil des Historiens des Gaules et de la
France* 12 (Paris, 1806, new ed. 1968) p. 432:. "Et ut breviter multa perstringam, jussu Apostolici Pontius frater Comites *de Melgoire* sine audientia captus, in turre quae dicitur ad
Septem-Salas usque ad obitum, videlicet v. Kal. Januarii, in custodia tentus est. Sepultus est
quasi pauper, imo captivus, apud S. Andream." Ordericus also reports that Pontius was imprisoned. Chibnall, *Ecclesiastic History* 6, p. 314.

[6] *Ex Chronico Cluniacensi*, ed. Bouquet, *Recueil* 12, p. 313: "Successit ei in Abbatiae regimine venerabilis vitae vir nomine Pontius, tam carnis quam mentis nobilitaie clarissimus,
communique totius sanctae Fraternitatis electione promotus, VII. Idus Maii a domino
Widone Viennensis Ecclesiae reverendo Archiepiscopo consecratus, et in sede sua cum magna totius populi exultatione locatus est." Both Abbots Hugh I and Peter the Venerable were
consecrated by archbishops of Besançon (Hugh and Anseric). Hugh II, the follower of Pontius, seems not to have been consecrated at all. Since Guy was acting in the place of the
archbishop of Besançon about the time of Pontius' election, it may have been in this capacity
that he consecrated Pontius. Guy continued to have contact with Pontius and Cluny
throughout Pontius' abbacy; e.g. Dedicatio Capellae—1118: "Anno incarnationis Domini
1118. xvij. Kal. Septemb. consecratum est Oratorium hoc cum Altari a reuerendissimo Arch-

Calixtus informed him that some of his brothers had raised complaints against him. Upset by these charges, Pontius is said to have convinced a reluctant Calixtus to accept his resignation. Then, with or without papal permission (disputed), he set out for the Holy Land after a brief stop at Montecassino. Allegedly angered by Pontius' abrupt, unauthorized departure, Calixtus ordered an immediate election in Cluny, and the choice fell on the aged Hugh of Marcigny. As Hugh II he lived only a few months, and was in turn succeeded by Peter, later surnamed the Venerable. After defending the Holy Land, Pontius returned to Italy in 1124. Rather than travelling on to Cluny he went to a small priory near Tarvisio in Northern Italy, where he remained as abbot until the spring of 1126.[7]

He then journeyed to Cluny, where his arrival occasioned an uprising in which the abbey was ravaged. Acting for Honorius II, Archbishop Humbald of Lyons excommunicated him in April, and Cardinal Peter of St. Anastasia arrived as legate *a latere* in time to hold a council in Lyons on May 26, 1126. After Pontius had refused his threefold summons to submit to judgment, Peter confirmed Humbald's excommunication and placed Cluny under an interdict until Pontius would leave.

During the summer of 1126 Honorius summoned both parties to the dispute to Rome, and both responded, giving hostages as a sign of their intent to appear. Pontius, however, refused to retract the position which had led to his excommunication, and according to Peter the Venerable, claimed that only St. Peter in heaven could judge him. Accordingly, Pontius was condemned as a schismatic and died in prison in December 1126. He was buried as a pauper in the church of St. Andrea. Shortly thereafter Honorius wrote to the monks of Cluny telling them that even though Pontius had died impenitent, he had nevertheless granted him an honorable burial out of respect for Cluny.

In 1958 Hayden White wrote a seminal paper interpreting these events in a novel way. He observed that it was a strange concourse of events which transformed Pontius, a mainstay of Gregorian orthodoxy, into a nemesis both of the papacy and the monastic movement as a whole. He did not see the cause of the abbot's downfall in the previously held views of his decadence, however, but found it in the changes in Cluny and Rome when Honorius was elected. He concluded that Pontius was the first victim to fall in a revolution that heralded the end of the Gregorian papacy in Rome and the end of the old style monasticism in the West.[8] In

---

iepiscopo Viennensi domno Widone." Martin Marrier, *Bibliotheca Cluniacensis* (Paris, 1614), p. 564; Calixti II, Papae diploma, de confirmatione Bouis Curtil. Anno 1122 v. Kal. Ianuar. ". . . Propterea fili in Christo beatissimi PONTI quem nos in Viennesis Ecclesiae regimine positi nostris per Dei gratiam manibus in Abbatem consecrauimus, & personam tuam & locum, cui Deo auctore praesides, totis dilectionis visceribus amplectentes . . ." ibid., 581-582.

[7] In a recent monograph on Hugh I and Pontius H. E. J. Cowdrey has argued that Pontius returned to Cluny in 1126 rather than the usually accepted date of 1125. *Two Studies in Cluniac History 1049-1126.* II. *Abbot Pontius of Cluny (1109-22/26)*. Studi Gregoriani XI (Rome, 1978), p. 241.

[8] Hayden White, "Pontius of Cluny, the *Curia Romana* and the end of Gregorianism in Rome," *Church History* 27 (1958). p. 197.

White's view, Pontius was allied with the party of Petrus Pierleoni, while Haimeric and Honorius were associated with the abbot's enemies.[9]

Unlike Chodorow, White does not associate Calixtus with the new reform movement, but places him squarely within the old Gregorian tradition along with Pontius. As compared with Pontius, however, he sees Calixtus as decadent. He asserts that before Calixtus became pope he was mainly noted for his attempt to defraud the saintly bishop Hugh of Grenoble of the archdeaconry of Salmorenc, and that after his election he was characterized by a curia which rivaled the opulence of a Byzantine court. White is therefore not surprised that there is no record that St. Bernard ever corresponded with this degenerate pope. He believes that St. Bernard saw Cluny, Pontius, Calixtus and the curia as all of the same ilk. To the ascetic abbot curial and Cluniac decadence were two aspects of the same problem.[10]

This theory shook the whole edifice constructed to explain the background of the schism, and ignited scholars to reconsider their basic assumptions. Placed under the harsh lights of their scrutiny, its flaws emerge. The first is its basic premise—the linkage between Pontius and Calixtus. Rather than a bond, what one observes is a history of tension between the two powerful religious leaders going back to Calixtus' election. Pontius seems to have coveted the highest office for himself, and rather than leading the groundswell for the Burgundian archbishop, he appears to have done everything he could to thwart it. As the loser, he earned the enmity of the victor.[11] The abbot and the pope were later formally reconciled, but they never became close.

---

[9] See Chodorow's analysis of White, *Christian Political Theory*, p. 22, n. 9.

[10] White, "Pontius of Cluny," pp. 203-206. For the characterization of the dispute between Archbishop Guy of Vienne and Bishop Hugh of Grenoble see Jules Marion, *Cartulaires de l'église cathédrale de Grenoble, dits Cartulaires de Saint-Hughes* (Paris, 1869), pp. 49-57. Marion summarizes the affair on pp. XXXIII-XL. For proof of St. Bernard's hostility toward Pontius, White relies heavily on a letter written by Bernard to his cousin, Robert of Chatillon. Robert had been an oblate at Cluny, but moved by the example of his cousin, as an adult he had transferred to Clairvaux. There, however, he complained about the harsh life, and while Bernard was away, the grand prior of Cluny rescued the unhappy young man. Bernard bitterly castigated the prior in a letter to Robert, and took advantage of the occasion to criticize Cluny for its slack standards. The letter has previously been dated 1119, and thus during the abbacy of Pontius, but now most scholars are convinced that it was not written until 1124-1125 during the abbacy of Peter the Venerable. The dating will be discussed below. *Sancti Bernardi Opera*, ed. Jean Leclercq and H. Rochais, vol. 7, I. *Corpus Epistolarum 1-180* (Rome, 1974), Ep. 1, pp., 1-11. The conventional analysis of this letter is found in Watkin Williams, *Studies of St. Bernard of Clairvaux* (Manchester, 1935), pp. 135-149.

[11] *Historia Compostelana*, ed. Henrique Florez, vol. 20 of *España Sagrada* (Madrid, 1765), p. 282 (misnumbered, p. 284): Geoffrey of Vigeois. ed. Bouquet, *Recueil* 12, p. 432: "Contigit praeterea Romanum Antistitem [Gelasium] Cluniaco venire, mori ac sepelire: qui ab Abbate [Pontio] visitatus, aciem oculorum prolixius in illum deflexit. Dixitque ei Abbas; 'Quid me aspicis?' Aeger respondit: 'Quia video in Papatu moriturum.' Ex tunc animus Pontii gliscere coepit, sperans se Papam futurum iri; sed fefellit eum dubia spes. . . Tumulato Pontifice Cluniaco, [Guidonem] Archiepiscopum de Vienna, qui erat frater Comitis illius ejusdem urbis, summum Pontificem statim Cardinales elegerunt. Pontius his contradicere voluit, sed non valuit." White, "Pontius of Cluny," p. 202; for an analysis of Pontius' part in the election see Stroll, "Calixtus II," pp. 20-23.

It could even be speculated that Calixtus helped to engineer Pontius' downfall, and that part of his motivation was the settlement of an old score. The two quick letters he wrote shortly after Pontius' departure for the Holy Land raise doubts that the abbot had clearly abdicated. The first congratulates Peter the Venerable on his election, while the other warns the monks of Cluny not to raise a protest on account of Pontius, who, he assures them, had resigned his office without any hope of recovery.[12] The necessity to reassure the monks even after the rule of Hugh of Marcigny shows that those monks loyal to Pontius still did not trust the veracity of Calixtus' first announcement that he had abdicated. The phrase, "without any hope of recovery," is a clue that they suspected that Pontius had done something short of abdicating. If he really had permanently stepped down, why did he himself not inform the monks at Cluny in order to avoid any misunderstanding?

But even though Calixtus and Pontius may not have been politically or ideologically aligned, might the events at Cluny still not reveal allegiances adumbrating the future parties of the papal schism? Ordericus Vitalis insists that Pontius had no intention of seizing power in the spring of 1126, but was merely traveling in Gaul. Finding Peter the Venerable absent, he decided to visit his old friends. When they wanted to greet him in the style befitting his once exalted rank, the grand prior, Bernard, prohibited them from doing so, and they exploded in a rage. Even though Pontius protested against it, the surrounding burgers and knights, who idolized him, took up arms, and a general fight ensued. In contrast to Ordericus' description, Peter the Venerable asserts that Pontius had intended to seize Cluny, and he accuses his predecessor of multiple atrocities.[13]

Neither account was first hand. Ordericus probably got his information from the general chapter meeting of 1132, while Peter's came from Pontius' enemy, his former prior, Bernard. Peter the Venerable had dismissed Bernard, and instated Matthew of St. Martin-des-Champs with the mandate to rectify the laxity in monastic discipline. Then, amazingly, given his sharp criticism of Cluny under Bernard's management, Peter two years later reappointed the former prior to his old post. Since Bernard's strength lay in his ability as an administrator, Peter's charges have a somewhat hollow ring.[14]

The return of Bernard to his old post also casts doubt on the existence of two parties at Cluny, the one composed of morally flaccid followers of Pontius, and the other of those who emulated the rigorous Cistercian interpretation of the *Rule*.[15] The hypothesis that the curia divided along

---

[12] JL 6991, PL 163:1256; JL 6992, PL 163:1256.

[13] *De Miraculis* PL 189:923-924.

[14] Chibnall, *Ecclesiastic History* 6, pp. 312-314; PL, 189:924; Cowdrey, *Abbot Pontius of Cluny*, pp. 244-245.

[15] White argues that when Matthew of St. Martin-des-Champs instituted reforms based

parallel lines, and that Pontius could have counted on the support of the conservative faction if he agreed to have his case heard before the pope, becomes accordingly even more tenuous.[16]

Although he obeyed Honorius' summons to come to Rome, Pontius declined to be tried. Ordericus does not mention any trial after his refusal to appear, and Geoffrey, prior of Vigeois, says that a tradition survived which held that there never was one. Peter the Venerable, however, does describe a trial of Pontius' followers.[17] The following recapitulation of its high points purports to demonstrate that the dispute at Cluny mirrored the ideological divisions within the curia. Pontius' adherents mounted a very simple defense. Denying that Pontius had ever abdicated, they insisted that he had only asked Calixtus for permission to make a pilgrimage to the Holy Land, and that the pope had granted his request. Haimeric then

---

upon the Cistercian interpretation of the *Rule* that the older members of the order—the bulk of Pontius' support—found these regulations to be too strict. Some priors began to argue that Pontius, not Peter, was the rightful abbot, and they organized a coup when Pontius appeared in 1125. He believes that even though Pontius may have had no intention of seizing power, that nevertheless the men of the old order and the surrounding laymen rose to his defense. "Pontius of Cluny," pp. 207- 208. From this scenario White believes that Cluny was already divided over the interpretation of the *Rule* before Pontius arrived, but Zerbi finds no basis for this view. "Intorno allo Scisma," p. 882, n. 50.

[16] White thinks that Pontius thought that he could win his case in Rome even though his protector, Calixtus, was dead. What Pontius did not realize, according to White, was that his old-guard friends had been ousted from power in the coup which brought Honorius to the papacy in 1124, and that Haimeric, a devotee of Cistercian asceticism, and St. Bernard's friend, was the real ruler there. From his reading of Pandulphus' account of the stormy proceedings surrounding Honorius' election, White concludes that there was still a conservative faction among the cardinals, and that the cleavage between them and those loyal to Haimeric emerged into the open in the schism of 1130. White, "Pontius of Cluny," p. 211; *Lib. Pont. Dert.*, p. 205. White's interpretation of Pandulphus is disputed by Zerbi, who thinks that he is anticipating the schism. "Intorno allo Scisma," p. 886.

[17] Chibnall, *Ecclesiastic History* 6 p. 314; Geoffrey of Vigeois, *Chronicon*, PL 188:840; Peter the Venerable, PL 189:925. White believes that after Pontius discovered that he was not to be tried by his old friends, he retreated to his cardinalate rights and Gregorian principles to defend himself, and refused to be judged by the illegally-elected Honorius. "Pontius of Cluny," p. 211; Tellenbach, "Der Sturz," p. 29, n. 49 claims that White's assertion that Pontius did not accept Honorius as the legally-elected pope does not make sense since Pontius treated Honorius as pope by obeying his summons to Rome, and by putting up hostages. In defense of White, he did say that Pontius did not really understand what was going on in Rome until he arrived there, and may only then have learned the details of the Pope's election. I, however, do not believe that Pontius was either so incredulous or so uninformed.

By cardinalate rights White is probably referring to the report in *Pontii Cluniacensis Abbatis Gesta Quaedam* where it is reported that during Calixtus' visit to Cluny in 1120: "Eadem die, communi suorum assensu assidentium, largitus est felix Papa Calixtus Cluniacensi ecclesiae, speciali et propriae suae, ut abbas Cluniacensis semper et ubique Romani fungatur officio cardinalis, manuque propria ipse te Papa annulo vestivit. . . ." Bouquet, *Recueil*, 14 p. 197. See also *Histora Compostelana*, ed. cit., pp. 284-286. Klaus Ganzer points out that although the Chronicle of Hirsau also mentions Calixtus' grant of the cardinalate dignity to Pontius, no papal documents directed to Cluny ever designate him as a cardinal, and he did not sign any papal bulls. Ganzer speculates that Pontius was given certain privileges of a cardinal, but did not receive a regular appointment. Klaus Ganzer, *Die Entwicklung des Auswärtigen Kardinalats im Hohen Mittelalter: Ein Beitrag zur Geschichte des kardinalkollegiums vom 11. bis 13. Jahrhundert* (Tübingen, 1963), pp. 80-81.

refuted their claims by producing Calixtus' Register, and reading a letter from the pope to Pontius warning him never to molest Cluny. Calixtus reminded him that he had surrendered the abbey into papal hands without hope of recovery, and threatened him with anathema if he ever attempted to regain his rule there. Thereupon Matthew of St. Martin-des-Champs, representing Peter, arose and demanded that Honorius restore Peter to his rightful place as abbot. Honorius so ruled, and then deprived Pontius of his remaining ecclesiastical honors.

Although this description is allegedly based on Peter the Venerable's account, Peter does not mention that Haimeric produced the Register of Calixtus. The Register is mentioned, but in an entirely different context—in a letter describing the trial written by Honorius to Peter the Venerable on October 20, 1126. The pope says that when Pontius' defenders claimed that the abbot had never relinquished his office, but had been defrauded of it, he had Calixtus' Register produced. He directed that three letters be read from it refuting the monks' claim: one to Pontius, another to the monks of Cluny, and the last to Peter himself.[18] Given the existence of these letters, which so easily refuted the charges of Pontius' followers, it seems incredible that they had the temerity to deny that Pontius had abdicated. Either they must have been deceived, or they were lying if Calixtus wrote the letters, and was telling the truth. Later I shall challenge these assumptions, but their relevance in the present context is that if Calixtus made the incriminating statements, then the letters would undermine the conclusion that he protected Pontius as a fellow Gregorian.[19]

Peter the Venerable's contention that the entire curia condemned Pontius brings out an even more fundamental weakness in the theory. Since one of its most basic tenets is that from the time of Honorius' election the curia was split into conservative and progressive factions, then part, even the majority, of the cardinals should have defended Pontius.[20] The

---

[18] The letter of Honorius is JL 7268:; those of Calixtus are JL 7137 and JL 7138; PL 166:1265-1268; the fragments are on p. 1267. See Tellenbach, "Der Sturz," pp. 21-25 for a discussion of when Calixtus could have written these letters. Zerbi thinks that Tellenbach was correct to date them at the end of Calixtus' papacy. "Intorno allo scisma," p. 874.

[19] White, "Pontius of Cluny," p. 212. Further evidence that there was no major difference in the attitude of Calixtus toward the problems of Cluny from that of Honorius is that Peter the Venerable described the pontificate of Honorius as following in perfect continuity with that of Calixtus. PL 189:924: "Decesserat jam e vita suprascriptus venerandus papa Calixtus, nec se inferiorem papam Honorium accepert successorem." Zerbi calls attention to Peter's emphasis on the continuity of the two popes, "Intorno allo scisma," p. 840.

[20] White suggests that the anomaly can be explained by Haimeric's curious concept of unanimity. If Haimeric could claim that his candidates in the papal elections of 1124 and 1130 had been unanimously elected, why could he not claim that the curia unanimously condemned Pontius in 1126? White believes that Haimeric had a penchant for hyperbole, and should not be taken literally. "Pontius of Cluny," p. 213. A difficulty with this argument is that Peter the Venerable, not Haimeric reported the proceedings of the trial. White deals with this difficulty by arguing that although Peter wrote the account, he based it upon information transmitted by Haimeric. In n. 106, p. 219 he cites as his sources Orderious Vitalis, PL 188:895; letter 48 of Honorius, PL 166;1267; letter 55, ibid., 1272. As support of his posi-

unanimity of the curia's condemnation of Pontius must stand as counter evidence to the view that there was such a division within the curia, and that Pontius represented the conservative wing.

Likewise, Pandulphus' biography of Honorius reveals that nothing more than preconditions for a split within the curia existed during Honorius' reign.[21] The fluidity of cardinalate groupings can perspicuously be seen from Pandulphus' revelation that two of the later staunch supporters of Anaclet did not reject Honorius. Peter of Pisa, the foremost authority on canon law within the curia, remained friendly with Honorius even after most of the cardinals had objected to the way in which he had been forced upon them in flagrant violation of electoral procedures.[22] Peter of Porto participated regularly in curial business, and strikingly, it was he to whom Honorius delegated the task of reading Pontius' condemnation.[23] If Peter, Petrus Pierleoni, and Pontius all had belonged to a party defending Gregorian principles, then Peter would have shown himself to be a poor ally by reading the sentence.

In conclusion the background to the papal schism of 1130 cannot be found in an analogy between the divisions at Cluny and a split within the

---

tion that Haimeric was an eyewitness, he says that Peter the Venerable stated that at Honorius' request Haimeric produced Calixtus' Register. In fact Peter does not reveal the person to whom Honorius made his request; moreover, White fails to support his contention that Peter's absence from Rome during the trial necessitated Haimeric's report. He cites Ordericus, who does not mention a trial, but who does say that after the riot at Cluny "instead of returning to Cluny, he [Peter] proceeded to Rome without loss of time, and laid before the pope what had occurred, to which the monks who had suffered in the affair bore witness." (In the Chibnall edition the statement is on p. 314; her translation on p. 315 differs slightly, but the meaning is the same.) Ordericus continues, stating that Peter remained in Rome while Pontius was summoned and refused to plead to the charges. Only then did Honorius dismiss Peter to Cluny with apostolic letters and the emblems of dignity.

Likewise, Honorius' two letters, which White cites say nothing either about Peter's presence in Rome or absence from it during the trial. One cannot even assume that since Honorius was describing the trial of Pontius' defenders in the letter of October 20, 1126, that Peter was not there to gain first hand knowledge, for in the letter Honorius is describing not just the trial, but the whole history of the dispute, including events in which Peter himself participated. Moreover, Honorius reports that Peter did come to Rome after the depredations of Cluny, and he does not say when he left. PL 166:1266: "Statuto itaque termino, nostro te conspectui praesentasi." There is accordingly no proof that Peter was not in Rome at the trial, and no reason to believe that the account of the trial in De Miraculis was Haimeric's.

[21] Lib. Pont. Dert., p. 205; In contrast to White's belief that Pandulphus reveals that a schism already existed within the curia during Honorius' reign, Zerbi concludes that Pandulphus only discloses that some of the preconditions for the schism of 1130 existed. "Intorno allo scisma," p. 883, n. 51.

[22] Klewitz, "Das Ende," p. 213.

[23] Peter the Venerable, PL 189:925: ". . . Portuensi episcopo jubet. Fert ille jussus sententiam, et ut ipsa ejus verba referam: 'Pontium,' inquit, 'invasorem, sacrilegum, schismaticum, excommunicatum, ab omni ecclesiastico honore vel officio sancta Romana et apostolica Ecclesia in perpetuum deponit, et Cluniacum, monachos vel cuncta ad idem monasterium pertinentia, abbati qui impraesentiarum est, cui injuste subtracta fuerant, restituit.' " Schmale (Studien zum Schisma, p. 57) minimizes Peter of Porto's participation in the administration of Honorius, emphasizing that he was one of those who opposed the irregularities of Honorius' election.

curia. The dispute within Cluny was not one of the reverberations of a revolution, which had taken place within the curia.[24] The further argument—that Anaclet represented Pontius' outmoded conception of monasticism and ecclesiastical reform, and that his adherence to these views was one of the basic reasons why the progressive elements of the church opposed him in 1130—has led historians astray in their quest for understanding the meaning of the papal schism. Indeed, as we shall see, Pontius may have been the monastic radical, and Peter the Venerable the conservative.

---

[24] Tellenbach, "Der Sturz," pp. 39-40.

Chapter IV

TENSIONS WITHIN CLUNY AND THE PAPAL SCHISM

Peter the Venerable's harsh criticisms of Pontius continue to reverberate in spite of reservations about his objectivity. Some scholars still see the standards at Cluny as having become lax through brilliance and riches under Pontius' stewardship. Even more egregious as they see it, the house, which had been the prototype of ecclesiastical reform had become arrogant, and no longer willing to submit unconditionally to papal authority.[1] Now, however, revisionists of various hues are beginning to see Pontius as a worthy abbot, whose reputation has suffered unfairly from the repeated blows of historiography.[2] They argue that he fell either because Calixtus shifted curial policy in favor of bishops at the expense of monasteries, or because he intrepidly defended Cluny's independence against papal incursions. In either case, the old attribution of his fall to an adherence to an increasingly decadent form of Benedictinism has suffered its own blows. Its corollary—that the church rejected Anaclet in part because of his commitment to a Pontian style of Benedictinism inculcated during his novitiate at Cluny—is tottering. No longer can Anaclet be seen as the standard bearer for a conservative party within the curia, who tilted with the new reformers in the papal schism, and eventually was unhorsed. The schism is not a story of religious progress versus flabby complacency.

Papal sources, as well as Peter the Venerable's account, are suspect. In fact, some of them are so puzzling that one might even speculate that a case was being fabricated against Pontius. When, for example could Calixtus have written the three sharp letters which Honorius contends were read at the trial of Pontius' supporters? There would have been no occasion for the pope to have written them while Pontius was in the Holy Land. Since Pontius did not return until July or August of 1124, and Calixtus died in December of that year, the only time they could have been written was during the short interval in between.[3] But it is

---

[1] Schmale, *Studien zum Schisma*, pp. 134-135, 255, n. 6.

[2] In a series of articles Adriaan Bredero has shown the origin and progress of the historiography, which he contends has distorted Pontius' image. His most recent article is "Une Controverse sur Cluny au XIIe siècle," *Revue d'histoire écclésiastique* 76 (1981), 48-72.

[3] Tellenbach ("Der Sturz," p. 22 & n. 29) says that the usually reliable Meyer von Knonau mistakenly reports that Pontius returned at the end of 1123. Cowdrey (*Abbot Pontius of Cluny*, p. 234) points out that the earliest evidence of his presence in Europe is in the charters of Henry V of July 25, 1124 at Worms, and of August 5, 1124 at Bövingen, Luxemburg.

improbable that they were written during this period, because as late as April 1125 Honorius still permitted Cluniac monks to visit Pontius if they had permission from Peter.[4] Thus, there still was no open conflict, and presumably no reason for Calixtus to have written his letters.[5] Although other authors have not suggested that Honorius might simply have forged the letters as evidence to be used against Pontius' supporters at the papal tribunal, this possibility would make sense of the otherwise perplexing set of circumstances.

Since both the papal sources and Peter the Venerable's account are at least questionable, Ordericus' suggestion that Pontius fell because of the tension between Cluny and disgruntled bishops appears to be more trustworthy.[6] His account seems to be reinforced by canons 4 and 16 of the Lateran Council of 1123, which emphasize the authority of the *ordinarius*. Even though the special monastic privileges created in the past remained unaffected, the two canons nevertheless could be interpreted as revealing a disposition in favor of bishops over abbots in cases of exemptions. They could have given a signal to the local bishops that the pope would favor them in their confrontation with Cluny. In this scenario the embattled Pontius' would have succumbed to superior force while defending the rights of Cluny in the face of demands of the local bishops.[7]

The question then might be raised whether the new papal policy toward bishops was part of a broader policy of ecclesiastical reform. Since the Cistercians conspicuously consented to live under the jurisdiction of the *ordinarius* and Cluny and Montecassino jealously guarded their independence, perhaps the canons in the Lateran Council of 1123 signified a tilt in favor of the new houses against the old. This conjecture is especially attractive because Honorius moved against the chief defenders of the liberties of Cluny and Montecassino—Pontius and Oderisius. Innocent also attempted to undermine the liberties of Montecassino, but continued to grant privileges to the newer houses. This favoritism could manifest an

---

[4] JL 7194; PL 166:1227.

[5] Tellenbach, "Der Sturz," pp. 22-24.

[6] Ibid., 27-35. Tellenbach forcefully argues this hypothesis.

[7] For the Lateran Council, Mansi, *Collectio Sacrorum Conciliorum* 21, pp. 277-286; Hefele/Leclercq, *Histoire des Conciles* 5.1 pp. 630-644. Canon 4 states: "Nullus omnino archidiaconus aut archipresbyter sive praepositus vel decanus animarum curam vel praebendas aecclesiae sine judicio vel consensu alicui tribuat; immo, sicut sanctis canonibus constitutum est, animarum cura et rerum aecclesiasticarum dispensatio in aepiscopi judicio et potestate permaneat. Si quis contra hoc facere aut potestatem quae ad aepiscopum pertinet sibi vindicare praesumpserit, ab aecclesiae liminibus arceatur." As Archbishop Guy of Vienne, Calixtus had already shown a disposition against an increase of monastic power within diocesan churches. In a letter written to his nephew, Amedeus, Count of Maurienne, in 1115 he asked Amedeus not to allow monks to occupy churches in the diocese of Maurienne, which laymen possess: "De justitia et defensione, Maurianense ecclesiae, multas tibi gratias habemus et reddimus, insuper rogamus, et pro Dei amore ex officio nostro injuncto praecipimus ut ecclesias, de quibus nuper investivisti Maurianensem ecclesiam, illi auferri non sinas et alias quas laici possident a monachis occupari non permittas." Ulysse Chevalier, *Cartulaire de l'abbaye de Saint-André-le-Bas de Vienne* (Lyons, 1869), App. 72, p. 281.

identification with the reforming ideology of the newer houses, and a rejection of the allegedly threadbare Benedictinism of the older. But as I shall argue, the two popes attacked the venerable old monasteries for different reasons, and in neither case did the reasons have anything to do with ideology.[8]

Further, Pontius' association with Anaclet, along with any ideological implications it might have, is tenuous. Pontius' close Cluniac confederate, Aegidius of Tusculum, did support Anaclet in the elections of 1130, but he was an exemplary monk and cardinal. Even Peter the Venerable had the highest respect for him. His approbation, therefore, would have to be construed as a signal honor.[9] No one knows how Pontius would have responded to the schism, and likewise, there is no indication of how Petrus Pierleoni reacted to the dispute at Cluny. Indeed, no evidence ties him to Pontius after he left Cluny to become a cardinal. Moreover, even if he had been associated with Pontius, that connection would still not demonstrate that he tolerated lower standards of conduct for churchmen, or a less aggressive disposition toward pursuing ecclesiastical reform. Until 1122 all of the contemporary sources show Pontius to be a worthy abbot, and even Calixtus is supposed to have been reluctant to accept his resignation. On the other side, although Peter the Venerable had problems with St. Bernard, nothing indicates that Pontius did. On the contrary, he is known to have granted the tithes of the parish of Arconville to Clairvaux, an act suggesting that he and Bernard were on good terms, and that he was not hostile to the Cistercians.[10] Thus, the old equation of Innocent with Peter the Venerable, St. Bernard, and other new reformers on the one side, and Anaclet with such alleged upholders of an outmoded Benedictinism as Pontius and Aegidius of Tusculum on the other, cannot be held to elucidate the schism.

Even though Peter singles out Pontius for administrative inadequacies, he does not charge him with initiating a moral decline at Cluny. Peter defended the Cluniac interpretation of the *Rule* and believed that the Cistercians had deviated from *charitas*. Nevertheless, he was greatly influenced by their moral force, and tightened the regulations at Cluny in response to their criticisms.[11] He first brought in Matthew of St. Martindes-Champs to deal with such problems as *noxia vel superflua in cibis, in potibus, in moribus*, and many years later, in 1132 and 1146, he directed his

---

[8] Tellenbach, "Der Sturz," p. 42.

[9] Aegidius was one of Anaclet's strongest supporters. He was born near Auxerre, and became a monk at Cluny in 1119. In 1121 Calixtus raised him to the cardinalate. After Anaclet's death he went over to Innocent, but like all of the other former supporters of Anaclet, Innocent deprived him of his office in the Lateran Council of 1139. See Zenker, *Die Mitglieder*, pp. 43-44; Hüls, *Kardinäle*, pp. 142-143.

[10] *Recueil des chartes de l'abbaye de Clairvaux*, ed. J. Waquet, fasc. 1 (Troyes, 1950) no. 5, pp. 7-8.

[11] In a long letter to Bernard. Ep. 111, *The Letters of Peter the Venerable*, ed., intro., & notes by Giles Constable, 2 vols., vol. 1 (Cambridge, Mass., 1967), pp. 274-299.

reforms towards what he considered to be excesses.[12] But Peter conceded that the relaxation had begun in the reign of St. Odo, and he does not accuse Pontius of hastening any decline.[13]

It thus seems to be improbable that a leveling off of religious and moral zeal in Cluny highlighted by the asceticism of the new orders caused the downfall of Pontius. Likewise, the dispute at Cluny does not point to an alliance between the new orders and the papacy in pursuit of a more spiritual direction of the church. What united them, rather, was their zeal to curtail the privileges of Cluny.[14]

The one area in which Pontius may have exaggerated Benedictine norms was in Cluny's liturgical service, and especially in the liturgy for the dead. This striving after a flight from the world, and the emulation of Christ and the apostles had been increasing among Cluniac monks since the eleventh century.[15] Paolo Lamma, the distinguished Italian scholar, has suggested that Pontius was a product of this trend rather than the instigator of a shift toward secularism.[16] His observations, so contrary to the picture of Pontius painted by Peter the Venerable, are compelling. If he is right, Anaclet would have been nurtured in an ambiance as divorced from the world as that of the Cistercians, but where liturgy rather than self-abnegation was the expression of otherworldliness.

After he left Cluny, Pontius evinced a penchant for the emulation of Christ. Upon his return from the Holy Land he seems to have been caught up in the popular religious movements, which found their expression in itinerant preachers and hermits. In his *Panegyricus* of Peter the Venerable, Peter of Poitiers wrote that Pontius himself became a kind of prophet to the local populace after he settled in Italy.[17] This passage

---

[12] "Nam noxia vel superflua quaeque in cibis, in potibus, in moribus quam maximo persequens, licet ea de causa multa nunc reticenda passus fuerit, ea tamen ad congruum finem, etsi non statim, Deo praecipue, meque cum quibusdam aliis pro viribus juvante, perduxit." *De Miraculis*, Lib. II, PL 189:922; for the reform decrees *Petri Venerabilis abbatis Cluniacensis noni Statuta Congregationis Cluniacensis*, ibid., 1023-1024; Tellenbach, "Der Sturz," pp. 46-47.

[13] PL 189:1025: "Hos si nominare sigillatim necessitas imperaret, ostendarem a primo sancto Odone usque ad ultinum sanctitatis titulo insignitum Hugonem sanctum Patrem, universos de institutis consuetudinibus plurima suis temporibus, urgente tamen necessitate, utili semper causa mutasse."

[14] Tellenbach, "Der Sturz," pp. 50-64.

[15] Ibid., 53.

[16] His views are found in two works. Paolo Lamma, "Su alcuni temi di storiografia cluniacense," *Spiritualia cluniacense* (Todi, 1960); Paolo Lamma, *Momenti di storiografia cluniacense* (Rome, 1961).

[17] Petri Pictavensis monaci, *Panegyricus Petro venerabili dictus in primo adventu ejus ad Aquitaniam secundam*, PL 189:47-58 at p. 54. Speaking of Pontius, Peter of Poitiers writes:

Unum de magnis subito advenisse prophetis,
Rumor in occiduis partibus ortus erat.
Jamque novam sectam vulgaris fecerat error,
Dum putat hunc aliquem rustica turba Deum.
Iste novum Moysen, hic Daniel, ille Joannem: Alter
Eliseum, vel Salomona vocat.

suggests that rather than being a strict Gregorian and a representative of the old order, the man whom Honorius and the curia condemned in 1126 was a dangerous innovator.[18] According to this reading Peter the Venerable, not Pontius, was the conservative. It was Peter, who rejected both the new monasticism and the pauperistic tendencies of the Cistercians.[19]

This interpretation of the *Panegyricus* may stretch the evidence too far, but there is no doubt that the complaints of Peter the Venerable over Pontius' inadequacies as an administrator are exaggerated. In fact, Pontius coped surprisingly well with the financial problems plaguing Cluny in the twelfth century. Some of them at least were attributable to the costs of constructing the huge basilica begun by Hugh I. Hugh had been able to count on funds from Spain, but after the destructive warfare following the death of King Alphonso VI of Castile, they were cut off, from 1111 at the latest. By engaging in delicate diplomacy with Alphonso's daughter and successor, Uracca, and with leading Spanish magnates, Pontius succeeded in getting the flow of donations started again by 1114. These revenues assured the continued construction of the basilica as well as that of other Cluniac houses.[20]

But the economic difficulties did not disappear, and although they mainly arose out of situations over which Pontius had no control, he received the blame.[21] It was his bad fortune that the crisis came around 1125, the time of the great troubles at Cluny. Not only Peter the Venerable, but also Ordericus accused him of waste. It is improbable that either of them understood the complicated causes of Cluny's economic malaise,

---

Lamma, "Su alcuni temi," p. 272, n. 19; Cowdrey (*Abbot Pontius of Cluny*, p. 237, n. 38) thinks that Lamma reads too much into the *Panegyricus*.

[18] Lamma, *Momenti di storiografia*, p. 74, n. 1.

[19] Ibid., 176; Pietro Zerbi criticized Lamma for basing his conclusion that Pontius exemplified the new *vita religiosa* on only one source. "Intorno allo scisma," p. 875; Zerbi also failed to understand why Lamma judged the account of Peter the Venerable so harshly, accusing Peter of using words of "unusual violence." ibid., 885, n. 53; Lamma, "Su alcuni temi," p. 271. Zerbi admired Tellenbach's reconstruction of the schism, but felt that like other German historians Tellenbach was excessively sceptical of *De Miraculis* and of papal sources; op cit., p. 865.

[20] Cowdrey, *Abbot Pontius of Cluny*, pp. 1-8, 200-202.

[21] Georges Duby, "Économie domaniale et économie monétaire: le budget de l'abbaye de Cluny entre 1080 et 1155," *Annales Économies, Sociétés, Civilizations* 7 (Nendeln/Liechtenstein, 1952, repr. 1977), 155-171, esp. pp. 164-171. On p. 165 Duby speaks of some of these difficulties: "Au premier examen, c'est bien une diminution des ressources en argent qui parait à l'origine du déséquilibre budgétaire. Avec le XIIe siècle, pour des motifs a la fois économiques et politiques, beaucoup d'anciens revenus tarrissent. L'ordre commence à perdre de sa cohésion et certaines filiales acquittent mal leurs redevances. Le trouble croissant qui agite l'Occident, les competitions entre les principautés rivales rendent plus difficiles le mouvement des fond. Les aumònes enfin se font plus rares. Les grands princes, engagés dans des entreprises de plus grande envergure, ont maintenant de pressants besoins de'argent et. . . e'ils montrent à Cluny autant d'amitie que leures ancèstres, ils sont beaucoup moins généreux." See also Duby, *La Société aux XIe et XIIe siècle dans la région màconnaise* (Paris, 1955, repr. 1971), pp. 275-280; Bredero, "Une controverse sur Cluny," pp. 66-68.

but the juxtaposition of the financial problems and the upheaval in Cluny must have made Pontius seem responsible for these difficulties. The best information we have today, however, indicates that Pontius' financial organization was sound. Charges that he wasted the goods of his monks, or that he tolerated abuses of food, drink, and excesses in the manner of life at Cluny are unsubstantiated.[22]

Even though Peter the Venerable enlisted Matthew of St. Martin-des-Champs to deal with these alleged excesses, he made no pretense of transforming the life of Cluny into the Cistercian model. He defended Cluniac traditions and he actively solicited the funds, which allowed him to complete Hugh's great edifice in time for Innocent to consecrate it on his first journey into exile. But not all of his efforts were so successful, and economic problems continued to afflict Cluny. Peter lamented the loss of the tithes subtracted from Cluny, and he bitterly inveighed against the Jews, who, he thought, took advantage of Christians in financial dealings.[23] The administrative troubles in Cluny, therefore, did not stop with Pontius' deposition, and probably were only tangential to it.

Since Peter's complaints about Pontius' administrative deficiencies fail to explain the troubles at Cluny and their possible relation to the papal schism, scholars have sought clues from the interview between Calixtus and Pontius. A variant of the view that Pontius fell because of Calixtus' new stance in favor of bishops begins with the assumption that Pontius indubitably did resign his abbacy in response to the charges brought against him by certain monks. In expressing reluctance to accept his abdication, Calixtus was not implying confidence in Pontius, but was only observing a ceremonial courtesy. In fact, according to this view, Calixtus actively desired Pontius' abdication because the princely abbot opposed his new orientation toward bishops. The complaints were a blessing from heaven. Obviating the necessity of facing the issue head on, they provided the pope with the perfect opportunity to disencumber himself of an incubus hindering the pursuit of his policy.[24] Pontius cooperated by resigning in a moment of passion, but as his anger dissipated, so did his will to abdicate. But it was too late. Calixtus had moved with alacrity to order an election at Cluny to choose a new abbot.[25]

---

[22] Cowdrey, *Abbot Pontius of Cluny*, p. 204. Adriaan Bredero concludes that both Pontius and Peter the Venerable desired to impose a more strict authority over Cluniac abbeys, and that Pontius was more sensitive to the difficulties than Peter. "Pons de Melgueil et Pierre le Vénérable," *Mélanges E.-R. Labande: Études de Civilisation médiévale*, ed. under the direction of the University of Poitiers by C.É.S.C.M. (Poitiers, 1974), pp. 63-75.

[23] Peter complains about the Jews in a letter to King Louis of France. *The Letters of Peter the Venerable*, ed. cit., 1, nr. 130, pp. 327-330; on p. 329 he says: "Insuper ut tam nefarium furum Iudaeorumque commercium tutius esset lex iam uestusta sed uere diabolica, ab ipsis Christianis principibus processit, ut si res aecclesiastica uel quod deterius, aliquod sacrum uas apud Iudaeum repertum fuerit, nec rem sacrilego furto possessam reddere, nec nequam furem Iudaeus prodere compellatur." See also Lamma, *Momenti di storiografia*, p. 182.

[24] Zerbi, "Intorno allo scisma," pp. 862-865.

[25] Ibid. 866. Chibnall, *Historia Ecclesiastica* 6, p. 312: "Papa Poncio sine licentia et

According to Ordericus, however, Calixtus did not act immediately, but only later out of anger because Pontius had neglected to request his permission before departing for the Holy Land. If his report is accurate, Pontius would twice have acted rashly, presenting the pope with two compelling reasons for ordering a new election. Pontius' fortuitous gift of exactly the justification Calixtus needed in order to rid himself of the thorn in his side seems to be almost too opportune, especially since Pontius did not have the reputation of being impetuous.[26] Moreover, according to both Peter and Ordericus, Pontius was not on bad terms with the pope, and there was therefore no need for him to defy papal authority by neglecting to request license to depart. And most basically, if Pontius had in fact resigned, why would Calixtus have needed an added excuse to order a new election?

An abundance of other evidence raises one's sceptical antennae about the accuracy of either Ordericus' or Peter's characterization of the interview between Pontius and Calixtus. Reason to doubt his abdication, for example, is revealed in the account of Peter the Deacon, the chronicler of Montecassino during this period. Peter relates that after his meeting with Calixtus in 1122, Pontius visited Montecassino with twelve attendants, an entourage befitting an abbot. There he referred to himself as abbot ("I would rather be a *decanus* in Montecassino than abbot of Cluny"), and added that after returning from the Holy Land he would resign his pastoral charge at Cluny and enter Montecassino as a simple monk.[27] Other sources indicate that after he returned he did not carry out his desire, but continued to refer to himself as abbot of Cluny. He witnessed two imperial charters as "abbas Cluniacensis," and in 1125 he wrote a letter from Tarvisio to the monks at Cluny in which he referred to himself as

---

benedictione sua imprudenter abeunte ira incaluit, et Cluniacensibus ut idoneum sibi rectorem eligerent precepit." It is significant that Peter the Venerable not only does not say that Pontius failed to ask for permission to depart, but specifically mentions that he did, and that he received it; PL 189:923. One is suspicious that both Calixtus and Pontius are said to have acted out of anger rather than out of cool consideration in pursuit of such critical goals.

[26] Cowdrey (*Abbot Pontius of Cluny*, pp. 204-213) argues that there are two lines of evidence suggesting weakness in Pontius' character: the first concerns Pontius' unprecedented request after he became abbot that Paschal confirm Cluny's privileges without his personally coming *ad limina*; the second is his insensitive handling of Cluniac abbeys (as opposed to priories). Cowdrey concludes, however, that these weaknesses were of minor and peripheral importance when compared with the generally satisfactory character of his rule of Cluny, and with his relationships with external authorities. I think that it is stretching the point to see in Pontius' background any evidence of rashness, which could make this explanation for his actions in 1122 plausible.

[27] *Die Chronik von Montecassino*, ed. Hartmut Hoffmann, MGH SS 34:541: "'Mallem prius esse decanus Casinenesis quam abbas Cluniacensis.' Demum vero fratrum vestigiis provolutus illorumque se orationibus commendans Ierosoliman petit beato Benedicto spondens post suum regressum pastoralem curam relinquere, et Deo attentius in hoc sancto Casinensi cenobio deservire." Tellenbach, "Der Sturz," p. 25 and n. 37; Cowdrey, *Abbot Pontius of Cluny*, pp. 230-231.

"abbas indignus."[28] The tone of the letter is very humble. He accepts his repudiation by the monks with good grace, and states that he has handed over the reigns of government to another abbot. He closes with a plea for unity, and admonishes his brothers that on no account should they create a schism because of him. The letter implies that Pontius renounced the rule of Cluny out of affection for the abbey, and as an effort to keep the situation there from deteriorating even further. Nevertheless, even then his followers refused to accept it, and many of them remained faithful to him until the very end. Peter the Venerable's report that almost all of them had already deserted him in 1122 is a gross exaggeration.[29]

These monks continued to recognize Pontius as abbot even after the election and death of Hugh II. In a letter written to the monks of Cluny on October 21, 1122, one week after signing the Concordat of Worms, Calixtus chastised them for their insubordination. Not only did he admonish them not to cause any trouble over Pontius, who, he assured them, had resigned, but he also stated expressly that the pope himself was the source of abbatial power.[30] The claim was without precedent, for even though Cluny had always been directly under the authority of the bishop of Rome, heretofore it had exercised full autonomy. It was a claim of momentous proportions, and Calixtus was acutely aware of its impact.

---

[28] The two Imperial charters are the ones referred to in n.3 establishing the dates of Pontius' return. The one for July 25, 1124 from Worms is a charter for the monastery of Camaldoli, and is found in *Memorie e documenti per servire all'istoria del ducato di Lucca* 5, pt. 1 (Lucca, 1844), p. 429, n. 2; St. 3199. The other for August 5 is a charter for the monastery of Vallombrosa, and is found in *Deliciae eruditorum seu ueterum Anekdoton opusculorum collectanea*, ed. J. Lamius, 3 (Florence, 1737}, pp. 176-177; St. 3200.

The letter written to the monks at Cluny in 1125 was discovered in the archives of Vercelli by A. Wilmart, and published as "Deux pièces relatives à l'abdication de Pons, abbé de Cluny, en 1122," *Revue Bénédictine* 44 (1932), 351-353. The text is in bad shape, and not all of it can be read. Using more advanced technology Zerbi improved upon Wilmart's transcription; "Intorno allo scisma," pp. 877-882. He reconstructs the opening sentences as follows: "Quoniam placuit uos propter indignitatem et inutilitatem nostram repudium nobis mittere, gratum habemus. Nos quoque per manus apostolici alterius uobis abbatis regimen concessimus." Zerbi compliments Tellenbach for seeing the importance of this letter, but thinks that Tellenbach excessively accentuates its legal aspects (p. 881). He also rates Pontius' reference to himself as "abbot" less importantly, and suggests that the title might refer to Pontius' position at Tarvisio. Tellenbach, "Der Sturz," p. 24 & n. 34. White does not mention the letter, but Cowdrey discusses it, *Abbot Pontius of Cluny*, pp. 231-232. He emphasizes that Pontius did not admit the finality of his abdication, and says that given the ambiguity of the situation, the struggles, which were to follow, were not surprising. He also calls attention to intriguing evidence, in which, if it is not a forgery, Calixtus contradicts himself by referring to Pontius as the abbot of Cluny after 1122. Calixtus states that on April 3, 1123 he confirmed the possessions and rights of the priory of Payerne "ob petitionem cari nostri Poncii abbatis Cluniacensis." Robert, *Bullaire du pape Calixte II*, p. 169.

[29] *De Miraculis* Lib. II, PL 189:922: "Dissentientes illi ab eo, et quod multa mobilitate vel levitate animi, nullis bonorum consiliis acquiescendo, ut dicebant, res monasterii pessundaret, inter se nunc pauci, nunc plurimi, tandem pene universi murmurabant." Tellenbach, "Der Sturz," pp. 27-28.

[30] JL 6992; PL 163:1256-1257: "sicut ei nos monasterium ipsum ex parte beati Petri et Romane commiseramus Ecclesie . . ." Zerbi, "Intorno allo scisma," p. 870.

Popes were sensitive about interfering in the liberties of any monastery, and Cluny was not just any monastery.[31] This extension of papal rights heightened Pontius' significance. Whereas in the past he had only symbolized the preservation of the liberties of Cluny in the face of episcopal power, now in addition he became the symbol of the defense of Cluny against the incursions of Roman authority.

A strong case can be made that this was the underlying cause for the need to get rid of Pontius, and that all of the subsequent events were simply the playing out of the drama. The tormented abbot realized upon his arrival in Rome that his doom had already been sealed. The denouement was foregone, for Honorius had already indicated his sentiments by appointing Pontius' long-standing enemy, Archbishop Humbald of Lyons, and Humbald's confederate, Cardinal Deacon Peter, as papal legates to review his case.[32] But even though Pontius' conviction was inevitable, it did not imply that a de facto schism existed, or that Pontius' "old" conception of monasticism lost out to the "new" of Peter the Venerable.[33]

Adriaan Bredero also rejects the old/new equation, and concentrates more on Pontius' image as a practitioner of the new *vita religiosa*. In addition to Peter of Poitier's *Panegyricus* other sources also lend themselves to this portrayal. Robert of Torigny, the author of the chronicle of Mont-

---

[31] Honorius II showed this consciousness when he sent two cardinals to deal with the problems of Farfa in 1125. In creating a new abbot, Adenulf, they were fastidious not to infringe the ancient privileges of the abbey. Gregory di Catino, *Chronicon Farfense*, ed. Ugo Balzani, 2 vols. (Rome, 1903), vol. 2, p. 314.

[32] For Peter see Zenker, *Die Mitglieder*, pp. 70-71; Hüls. *Kardinäle*, p. 149; L. Spätling, "Kardinallegat Petrus im Pontifikat Honorius II," *Antonianum* 38 (1963), 162-192. Spätling demonstrated that Cardinal Peter of Santa Maria in Via Lata was identical with Cardinal Priest Peter of St. Anastasia. Honorius promoted him in 1127/1128. Pandulphus called him "Boccaruncione" (*Lib. Pont. Dert.*, p. 207), and Anaclet accused him of raiding the treasures of Cluny (JL 8376). Presumably this act would have occurred during the violence at Cluny in 1126. Spätling's views of the discord in Cluny and the significance of Pontius and Peter the Venerable are similar to Klewitz' and Schmale's.

[33] Zerbi argues that Tellenbach was right to emphasize that Peter the Venerable tenaciously defended the traditions of Cluny, and that White and Schmale were wrong in concluding that the same forces operated in Cluny as operated in the papal schism. He believes that Pontius fell because he could not accept the new status of Cluny under the pope, and the curtailment of its liberties to the advantage of bishops. "Intorno allo scisma," p. 888. In an article on the monastic policy of Peter the Venerable, Giles Constable accepts the views of White, Klewitz and Schmale. He notes that White and Tellenbach associated the Pontian schism with the shift in papal policy in the 1120's, and with the opposition of the new monasticism to the old. "In this conflict, Pontius and the 'old' Cluniac Cardinal Peter *Leonis* (the future anti-pope Anacletus II) and Cardinal Gilo of Tusculum were on one side, and Peter the Venerable and Prior Matthew of Saint-Martin-des-Champs, who in 1127 became cardinal-bishop of Albano, on the other." The unsuccessful effort to restore Pontius marked the end of the old Cluniac spirit and the victory of the new, more strict tendencies. Constable holds that when Anaclet and Innocent were elected, each represented the opposite side in the struggle of the 1120's. Naturally, he says, Peter the Venerable supported Innocent. Giles Constable, "The monastic policy of Peter the Venerable," *Pierre Abélard: Pierre le Vénérable*, no. 546 of Colloques Internationaux du centre National de la Recherche Scientifique (Paris, 1975), pp. 119-142 at pp. 122-123.

Saint-Michel, did not write until 1140, and confused Calixtus with Paschal, but nevertheless Bredero concludes that his text merits as much credence as those of Ordericus and Peter the Venerable. Robert contends that Pontius attempted to limit the excesses of the monks in food and clothes, and that those who were dissatisfied made false accusations against him in Rome. Not deigning to justify himself in the face of these accusations, Pontius resigned his office and departed for Jerusalem.[34]

Support for Robert of Torigny's characterization of Pontius comes from an unexpected source—St. Bernard's famous letter to his cousin, Robert of Chatillon.[35] In his letter Bernard moves from castigating Cluny for surrepticiously removing Robert from Clairvaux while he was absent, to criticizing the customs of Cluny in general. Damien Van den Eynde's new dating of this letter between the end of 1124 and the summer of 1125 throws this critical period open to a fundamental reevaluation.[36] Previously the letter had been thought to have been written in 1119, when Pontius was abbot, but the new dating makes it fall within the reign of Peter the Venerable while Matthew of St. Martin-des-Champs was prior. One interpretation of this letter is that it was part of St. Bernard's campaign of attacking the customary Cluniac interpretation of the *Rule*, defended most vigorously by Matthew. While Matthew opposed Cistercian conceptions of Benedictinism, Pontius responded more receptively to their perspective.[37]

St. Bernard's strategy may have been as follows. Seizing upon the pretext of the internal disputes in Cluny to attack its interpretation of the *Rule* he wrote the letter to Robert, not as a personal communication, but as open propaganda. He followed the letter with the *Apology*, which also harshly criticized the customs of Cluny. Rather than opposing Pontius, St. Bernard saw him as more inclined toward his own spiritual outlook. He may even have been defending him against the archpromotors of Cluniac traditions—Peter the Venerable and Matthew of St. Martin-des-Champs. Indeed, Matthew may have been the prior, who fetched Robert from Clairvaux, and returned the young monk to Cluny. It is even possible that in his letter Bernard was implicitly encouraging Pontius to return to Cluny.[38]

---

[34] *Roberti de Monte Cronica*, anno 1117 MGH SS 6:486: "Pontius abbas Cluniacensis cum vellet ad unguem corrigere excessus et in cibo et in vestitu quorundam monachorum, qui exteriora eiusdem monasterii negotia tractabant; Insurrexerunt in eum, et crescente simultate, accusaverunt eum in presentia Paschalis pape, de quibusdam gravissimis capitulis, licet falsis." Adriaan Bredero, "Cluny et Cîteaux au XIIᵉ siècle: les origines de la controverse," *Studi Medievali* ser. 3 vol. 12, nr. 1 (1971), 135-175, at pp. 165-167.

[35] *Sancti Bernardi Opera*, ed. cit. 7, pp. 1-11.

[36] Damien Van den Eynde, "Les premiers écrits de saint Bernard, " in Jean Leclercq, *Recueil d'études sur saint Bernard et ses écrits* 3 (Rome, 1969), pp. 395-396.

[37] Bredero, "Cluny et Citeaux," p. 141 & n. 26; 168-169.

[38] Ibid., 147, 171-175.

In essence, this theory reverses the conventional alignments. Rather than Peter the Venerable and St. Bernard being advocates of the new monasticism and Pontius of the old, St. Bernard and Pontius would represent the new, and Peter the Venerable and Matthew of St. Martin-des-Champs the old. This view would totally confuse the previously accepted interpretation of the parallels of 1130. The alleged association between Anaclet and Pontius could mean that Anaclet embraced the new spiritual tendencies, while Innocent would be unidentifiable, supported both by St. Bernard (the new) and Peter the Venerable (the old). This consequence shows that something is basically wrong with the whole model characterizing Innocent and Anaclet by their adherence to old Cluniac or to Cistercian interpretations of Benedictinism. Its flaws have catapulted scholars back to the drawing board.[39]

Since Bredero does not adopt this model, he has no difficulty in maintaining his view that the life of Cluny during Pontius' abbacy, and especially at the moment of abdication, was severe. Pontius had been forced to intensify the austerity of living, to emphasize manual labor, and to reduce the liturgical service, he believes, because Hugh I had been too old to enforce discipline and to oversee his priories properly. Financial problems increased because the ancient benefactors of Cluny became increasingly reluctant to pay their tithes. Bredero remains convinced that Peter the Venerable simply extended the reform begun by Pontius.[40]

Why then, he asks, is the life of Cluny thought to have deteriorated under Pontius, but to have improved under Peter? He attributes this confusion mainly to the ambiguity of Pontius' character. On the one hand he perpetuated "the new vogue" of Cîteaux, and on the other he continued to behave like a grand lord, defending the independence of Cluny from episcopal power. This behavior made him vulnerable to attack by those who chafed under his strict policies, and who demanded a return to the ancient traditions of Cluny. The same ambivalence characterized his behavior in his interview with Calixtus, Bredero conjectures. The pope believed that he had abdicated, while he thought that his gesture was only a temporary expedient, and he still considered himself to be abbot. When Calixtus did not accept the equivocation and demanded total obedience, Pontius responded by refusing to accept papal authority.[41]

Zerbi still defends his position that the new papal orientation toward bishops was crucial. He also continues to hold that the composition of the

---

[39] Zerbi was astonished by Bredero's radical interpretation of the relationship of St. Bernard to Pontius and Peter the Venerable, and the two men agreed to meet to debate their differences. With Dom Jean Leclercq acting as moderator, they did so in 1973. For the transcript of the debate see Jean Leclercq, Adriaan Bredero, Pietro Zerbi, "Encore sur Pons de Cluny et Pierre le Vénérable," *Aevum* 48 (1974), 134-149.

[40] One reason for drawing this conclusion is that Peter never said that he was reforming customs introduced by Pontius. Ibid., 139-141.

[41] Ibid., 142.

party supporting Pontius was fundamentally conservative, consisting not only of those monks loyal to the tradition of independence of Cluny, but also of the *milites, burgenses*, and *rustici*. He strongly disagrees with the hypothesis that Bernard's letter to Robert and the *Apology* were intended to support Pontius. Would it make sense, he asks, for the champion of episcopal rights to ally himself with the champion of the monastic rights of Cluny? Moreover, given Pontius' strained relations with the Holy See in 1124-1125, would Bernard have jeopardized his already great prestige to intervene on his behalf?[42] Zerbi admits that Pontius imposed a rigid regimen on the monks to finance Hugh I's great basilica, but he is sceptical that the controversial abbot instituted reforms and a rigorous economy at Cluny.[43]

Zerbi, however, does take seriously Peter of Poitiers' claim in the *Panegyricus* that Pontius became a religious hermit.[44] He sees Pontius as a relic of the Cluny, whose abbots had functioned as third parties in relations between emperors and popes. Now Pontius had to adjust to a new situation in which the pope was striving to establish a papal primacy, which could function through bishops alone. In this new scheme of things there was no longer room for the Cluny of Pontius with its distinct personality and autonomous functioning. Upon returning from the Holy Land, he recognized that Cluny had embarked upon a new course under Peter the Venerable, and he then turned to the hermitic life. Zerbi continues to maintain that the Cistercian model influenced Pontius as well as Peter the Venerable, and he urges caution in attaching the labels of "old" and "new" to either of them. Such a complicated situation, he says, cannot be reduced to such broad generalities.[45]

The latest, and most comprehensive reassessment of Pontius reaches the same conclusion. It notes that almost until 1122 contemporary sources show that Pontius held the loyalty of many, if not most of his monks, and that the internal life of Cluny was not deeply disturbed either spiritually or materially.[46] Under Pontius, as also before and after his time, popes

---

[42] Ibid., 144-147.

[43] Zerbi believes that Bredero was misled into concluding that Pontius was an austere reformer by relying too heavily on Robert of Torigny. Ibid., 145.

[44] In a new study since his debate with Bredero. Pietro Zerbi, "Cluny e Cîteaux. Riflessioni e ipotesi sui rapporti fra i due, 'ordines' durante lo scisma di Ponzio (1122-26)," *I Cistercensi e il Lazio. Atti delle giornate di studio dell'Istituto di storia dell'Arte dell'Università di Roma* (Rome, 1978), p. 240. I am indebted to Philip Smith, reference librarian at UCSD for finding this reference for me.

[45] Ibid., 243. For an excellent analysis of the debate between Zerbi and Bredero see J. B. Van Damme, "Bernard de Clairvaux et Pons de Cluny, controverse au suject d'un controverse," *Cîteaux* 25 (1974). Van Damme agrees with the 1125 dating of St. Bernard's letter to Robert, but he concludes that the letter of Pontius to Cluny edited by Wilmart was written in 1122. He adds a few nuances to the work of Bredero and Zerbi, especially in his careful reading of the *Apologia*.

[46] Cowdrey, *Abbot Pontius of Cluny*, p. 187.

upheld the distinctive features of Cluniac monasticism with no hint that
Pontius had taken a wrong direction. When Bernard attacked Cluny, it was
Cluniac monasticism that he criticized, not any abuse of Pontius' rule.[47]
Further, there was no partisan duality in Cluny corresponding with two
groups within the papal curial "that of Abbot Pontius which, like the Ana-
cletans at Rome, represented the by now obsolescent traditionalism of the
eleventh-century reformers, and that associated with Peter the Venerable
which, like the Innocentians, championed the vigorous spiritual and
ascetic tendencies of more recent decades."[48] One obvious discrepancy in
pairing parties within the curia with those at Cluny is that Aegidius of
Tusculum, Pontius' protégé, both quickly recognized Peter the Venerable
as abbot, and also supported Anaclet. Another is that Matthew of St.
Martin-des-Champs was a diehard Cluniac, who had no profound spiritual
or monastic differences with Pontius.[49]

Ordericus' view that troubles with bishops contributed to Pontius'
downfall continues to be taken seriously, but the hypothesis that a
younger group of reformers favoring bishops over monks accounts for the
abbot's eclipse, is viewed with scepticism. It is noted that both the
appointment of Haimeric as chancellor and the insertion of canons re-
stricting the concession of exemptions to monasteries in the Lateran
Council of 1123 occurred a year after Pontius' departure. Moreover, since
these canons left the provisions of earlier papal privileges such as those of
Cluny unaffected, Calixtus' initiatives in the Lateran Council cannot be
construed as a lessening of papal support for Cluny. On the contrary, a
continuity in papal policy surrounding the crisis years of 1122-1126 can be
seen from papal confirmations of Cluny's privileges without major changes
during and after those years.[50]

The reasoning is overwhelmingly persuasive, therefore, that there was
no immediate or close connection between the troubles at Cluny, which
led to Pontius' departure in 1122, and the emergence of two groups of
cardinals in the later stages of Calixtus' reign. The older view, which sees
Pontius as the perpetrator of a superannuated form of monasticism is not
convincing. Its corollary that Anaclet was philosophically tied to Pontius'
outmoded attitudes toward ecclesiastical reform is accordingly without
foundation. Pontius' fall is symptomatic of changes occurring in the
papacy during the reigns of Calixtus and Honorius, but those changes had
more to do with the consolidation of papal power than with ecclesiastical

---

[47] Ibid., 261.

[48] Ibid., 261-263.

[49] Ibid., 263.

[50] Ibid., 264. Giving his own assessment of the crisis of 1122 Cowdrey states: "The troubles in 1122 were not the result of papal support for the bishops against the monks. Rather,
their background was Calixtus' anxiety to support to the full the claims of both parties, even
when they were not easily compatible."

reform. Let us now take a fresh look at what happened in the dramatic meeting between Pontius and Calixtus in 1122 to see how it illuminates the political and ideological ambiance preceding the papal schism.

Chapter V

THE DISPUTE AT CLUNY REINTERPRETED

Two figures stand out as keys to the unraveling of the dispute at Cluny and its intermeshing with the papal schism—Calixtus II and Matthew of St. Martin-des-Champs, later cardinal bishop of Albano. Both actively participated in Pontius' deposition, and to comprehend why is to see how ideology and politics intersected. For understanding the compost out of which the schism grew it is critical to determine whether Calixtus removed Pontius as abbot because he saw him as an impediment to a more religious form of Benedictinism, or whether he found him to be a hindrance to the expansion of papal authority. By examining the past behavior of this complex pope, we will gain a deeper insight into which of these alternatives motivated him. Matthew's response to the new reform will further illuminate Calixtus' objectives, and will add to the evidence that ideological differences did not produce the papal schism.

Calixtus is an enigma. Moving from a position of total intransigence on investitures, it was he who made the concessions to the emperor, which achieved the *modus vivendi* between *regnum* and *sacerdotium*. Several explanations could account for this dramatic shift, but they also could be sirens leading the unwary mariner astray. Among them is the French connection—that Calixtus was French, and that he appointed a French chancellor. From this Gallic influence it might seem to follow that Calixtus would hold the conciliatory view on investitures of the great canonist Ivo of Chartres, and the ascetic attitudes of St. Bernard. In fact, this reputed French connection is only a siren, luring the bewitched sailor into dangerous shoals rather than safe waters, for neither the premises nor the conclusions are wholly accurate.

Even though Calixtus is generally thought of as French, he was born in Besançon in the Kingdom of Burgundy, the third kingdom of the empire. As the sole surviving son of Count William of Burgundy, he became the chief power in the area as the archbishop of Vienne. Only the emperor seriously contested his authority, and in that context his tough position on investitures makes eminent sense. But when he became pope, he was operating in a different world. He had to think in less parochial terms, and to do what was right for the church at large. He could not consolidate his authority over the church and undertake new enterprises as long as he was bogged down in a dispute with the emperor centered on investitures. Even if it meant compromising tenaciously held positions, the goals were worth the sacrifice. Calixtus swallowed hard, and signed the Concordat of Worms.

This new found flexibility on the relationship between *regnum* and *sacerdotium* had nothing to do with the spirituality fostered by the Cistercians and other new orders. Although like all popes in this period Calixtus promoted the new orders, he himself in no way was ascetic, and he was a reformer only the the broad sense of the term. As archbishop of Vienne he lied, forged documents, and threatened Urban II with force in order to obtain the archdeaconry of Salmorenc. He interfered in the liberties of the monks of St. Barnard of Romans in his province of Vienne, and then allowed his men to ravage their property when they tried to defend their rights. When he was too weak to deal with the emperor in the negotiations of Mouzon in 1119, he added new conditions at the last minute, which scuttled the tentative agreement. He then assigned John of Crema the task of reporting to the delegates of the Council of Rheims that the emperor had been responsible for the failure. In the negotiations between Pisa and Genoa over the church of Corsica he was so venal that even the worldly Cardinal Bishop Lambert of Ostia would have nothing to do with them.[1] Calixtus did not oppose the ideals of the new monastic movements—indeed, he fostered them—but his priority was the strengthening of his office, whether as archbishop or as pope. His relationship with Pontius must be seen in these terms.

As archbishop of Vienne Calixtus had consecrated Pontius in 1109, and thereafter the two powerful prelates had frequent contacts. However, as I have pointed out, Pontius was unhappy with Guy's election as pope, which was held in Cluny. He urged that the election not be recognized until the cardinals in Rome had agreed to it. Pontius may have felt that Guy would not bring peace to a troubled church, since he had always been so inflexible on issues of *regnum* and *sacerdotium*. It was Pontius who had been involved in efforts to bring about a *modus vivendi* with the empire while Guy was still on the barricades. It also was he rather than Guy who was a careful student of the works of Ivo of Chartres.[2]

In spite of the rupture between the two men at the time of Guy's election, Pontius played a shadowy role in the unsuccessful negotiations with Henry V at Strassburg and Mouzon in 1119. Whether Pontius'

---

[1] For the threat to Urban and the archdeaconry of Salmorenc see Marion, *Cartulaires de l'église de Grenoble*, pp. 49-57 & n. 10, ch. III above. For the interference in the liberties of the monks of St. Barnard of Romans see Paul Giraud, *Essai historique sur l'abbaye de St. Barnard et sur la Ville de Romans* (Lyons, 1856), 2 *Cartulaire de Romans et autres pièces justificatives inédits servant de preuves a la Première Partie*, nr. 5 bis, pp. 12-13. For the negotiations of Mouzon see Mansi, *Collectio Sacrorum Conciliorum* 21, pp. 233-256; Hefele/Leclercq, *Histoire des Conciles* 5:1, pp. 569-591, and Stroll, "Calixtus II," pp. 30-41, & passim for a discussion of these incidents. The charter of the Genoese is recorded in *Iacobi Aurie Annales Ianuenses*, MGH SS 18:356.

[2] Pontius asked Ivo for his canonical collections, and Ivo sent them. Ivo of Chartres, ep. 231, 262, PL 162:233-235, 266-267; Cowdrey, *Abbot Pontius of Cluny*, p. 191.

participation came from his own initiative or Calixtus' is not clear, since their reconciliation took place only after the negotiations in 1120 while Calixtus was in Cluny on his way to Rome. Likewise, Calixtus' defense of Pontius from accusations made against Cluny by Archbishop Humbald of Lyons representing a consortium of bishops at the Council of Rheims in 1119 occurred before their reconciliation. For this reason Calixtus' defense cannot be interpreted as a personal endorsement of Pontius, but rather as an attempt to gain the good will of Cluny. Calixtus had not yet occupied his see in Rome, and the anti-pope, Gregory VIII, still functioned. He needed Cluny's resources and backing to establish himself in Rome and to unseat Gregory.

Once he was securely ensconsed in Rome and had begun to consolidate his authority over the church at large, Calixtus was then in a position to make the compromises with the emperor, which he had been too weak to concede in 1119. He was willing to recognize the emperor's right to invest bishops with their *regalia* in return for peace so that he could continue to strengthen papal authority over the church, and to expand it into Spain and the Near East. The bishops would serve as the best conduits for the dissemination of a more centralized authority, and they would also have a second function. They would help to curtail the independence of the great monastic systems which Calixtus wanted to bring more directly under his control. He did not wish to favor the bishops at the expense of the abbots, but he did wish to use their complaints to increase papal power, especially over Cluny.

Calixtus' coolness, if not hostility, toward Pontius after the abbot's reservations about his election gave the bishops their opportunity to gain some leverage in their confrontation with Cluny. In 1119, the same year in which Calixtus became pope, Humbald was elected archbishop of Lyons. There is no direct evidence that Calixtus had anything to do with Humbald's election, but since Lyons was in the Kingdom of Burgundy, and since Guy was the most powerful figure there, it is well within the realm of possibility. It is at least suggestive that while Pontius refused to recognize Calixtus' election until it had been confirmed in Rome, Humbald welcomed him ceremoniously into Lyons as pope before that confirmation had been received.[3] There had been no serious trouble between Lyons and Cluny since Gregory VII's vindication of Cluny in 1079-80, but Humbald immediately ended that halcyon interlude.[4] Even though Calixtus did not respond to his complaints against Cluny in the Council of Rheims in 1119, the archbishop may rightly have detected some ambivalence on the pope's part.

Calixtus continued to defend Cluny in the face of repeated attacks from Humbald, Bishop Berard of Mâcon and other bishops, but his support was

---

[3] Cowdrey, op. cit., p. 222; Stroll, "Calixtus II," p. 22.

[4] Ibid., 221.

ambiguous. At the same time that he confirmed the privileges of Cluny, he also confirmed Humbald as primate of France (January 5, 1121), and created a very narrowly defined *banleuca*—boundaries within which no one might attack Cluny's temporal subjects or lands. This restricted territory may have served as an incentive for bishops to attack outside of it. Probably the vagary of the *banleuca* among others finally made it impossible for Pontius to deal with the repeated assaults upon his monks, churches and lands.[5] He, had attempted to persuade his subjects to obey the pope's directives rather than Humbald's, but his efforts only earned him the accusation of having acted with excessive violence. Peter the Venerable made the charge twenty years later to contrast his own good relations with Lyons with Pontius' thorny ones.[6]

Whether Calixtus was earnestly trying to help Cluny in the face of the bishops' onslaught, or whether the bishops detected a softness in his efforts, which encouraged them to persevere, Calixtus did not succeed in checking the attacks against Cluny. Ordericus reports that they built up into an increasing crescendo by 1122. They led to the loss of many domains and to great dislocations within the mother abbey when many of the oppressed monks fled there. These upheavals exacerbated Cluny's economic difficulties, and the serenity of life at Cluny deteriorated. Those who blamed Pontius for not dealing with these multiple problems more effectively complained to Calixtus.[7]

During the meeting between Pontius and Calixtus in Rome, the pope informed the abbot of their complaints. Presumably upset by their accusations, Pontius departed for the Holy Land. But had he resigned his office? How can one explain the contradiction between Calixtus' assertion that he had abdicated, and the stubborn insistence of his defenders that he had not? The resolution of the contradiction depends upon the veracity of Calixtus' report, and upon each participant's perception of what had taken place in the interview. A possible solution is that Pontius and Calixtus each had a different understanding of the seriousness or the finality of Pontius' resignation.[8] While Pontius considered his move to be tentative,

---

[5] Ibid., 224, 227-228, 256.

[6] Constable, *The Letters of Peter the Venerable* 1, p. 260: "Seruaui igitur et semper ut dictum est seruare proposui inter nostros et uestros pacis et concordiae bonum, nec quosdam etiam antecessorum in sepe commouendo animos uestros secutus sum . . ." Cowdrey (*Abbot Pontius of Cluny*, p. 225) appears to accept Peter's judgment, but one must always be sceptical of what Peter says about Pontius.

[7] Chibnall, *Ecclesiastic History* 6, p. 310: "Quidam contra Poncium archimandritam zelo commoti sunt, ipsumque apud Calixtum papam Romae accusauerunt quod in actibus suis uehemens esset ac prodigus, et monasticos sumptus immoderate distraheret in causis inutilibus."

[8] In one of Bredero's most recent articles he says that Pontius had decided not to return to Cluny temporarily, but to undertake a pilgrimage to Jerusalem. Calixtus then informed Pontius of the complaints coming from Cluny. Bredero says that apparently the pope thought that it was not opportune for Pontius to withdraw himself *pour un temps* from the controversy at Cluny. Thus, Bredero argues, cause and pretex for the abdication are closely related, and the cause is equivalent to the reason for which Pontius was denounced at Rome.

Calixtus understood it to be final. This reconstruction of what happened is not convincing, however, for the abdication of the abbot of Cluny was far too serious a matter to be left shrouded in ambiguity.

More probably Pontius did not step down, and Calixtus simply misrepresented what had taken place during the interview. He had both the motivation and the capacity for doing so. He is known to have been dishonest in the dispute over the deaconry of Salmorenc with Bishop Hugh of Grenoble, and in his attempt to prove the primacy of the archbishopric of Vienne over that of Arles. Also, in not reporting to the delegates at the Council of Rheims of 1119 that he and his advisors had presented Henry V with new demands at their meeting in Mouzon, and thus in omitting a crucial reason for the breakdown of the negotiations, Calixtus was at least less than candid.[9] To shade the truth in order to win what were very high stakes—more direct control over Cluny—was not beyond Calixtus' ethical sensibilities.

No one can ever be sure what happened at the meeting, or what Calixtus and Pontius were thinking, but the following account makes sense of the evidence we have. Pontius readily responded to Calixtus' summons. Their relationship had at least outwardly remained good since their reconciliation, and the pope's letter to Bishop Berard of Mâcon in January 1121 demanding that he desist from molesting Cluny showed that it was in order at the time.[10] A year later Calixtus was still expressing his good disposition toward Pontius.[11] When Pontius arrived in Rome, he and Calixtus discussed the problems at Cluny, and the pope told him that the monks were discontented with the way he was handling the many difficulties there. They agreed that Pontius would temporarily relinquish the administration to someone else, who did not have his history of antagonism with the bishops. He would then go on a pilgrimage to the Holy Land. With that understanding, Pontius departed. On the way he paid a visit to Montecassino. There, reflecting upon his growing weariness with ruling his huge order, and probably with ecclesiastical politics in general, he uttered his pregnant remark that he would rather be a *decanus* in

Adriaan Bredero, "Pierre le Vénérable: les commencements de son abbatiat à Cluny (1122-1132)," pp. 99-118 of *Pierre Abélard; Pierre le Vénérable: Les courants philosophiques, littéraires et artistiques en occident au milieu du XIIe siècle*, Colloques internationaux du centre national de la recherche scientifique # 546—Abbaye de Cluny 2 au 9 juillet 1972 (Paris, 1975), p. 107.

[9] For the dispute between Hugh of Grenoble and Guy of Vienne see n. 10, ch. III; for the dispute over the primacy between Vienne and Arles, and Guy's forged letter see Wilhelm Gundlach, "Der Streit der Bisthümer Arles und Vienne um den Primatus Galliarum," 2 "Die Epistolae Viennenses," *Neues Archiv der Gesellschaft für ältere deutsche Geschichtskunde* 15 (1890); for the account of the negotiations of Mouzon and the report to the Council of Rheims see *Hessonis scholastici de concilio Remensi relatio* MGH SS 12:422-428; Chibnall, *Ecclesiastic History* 6, pp. 264-276; see also Stroll, "Calixtus II," pp. 6-9.

[10] JL 7112; Tellenbach, "Der Sturz," p. 33 & n. 58.

[11] January 9, 1122; A. Bernard & A. Bruel, *Recueil des chartes de l'abbaye de Cluny* 5 (Paris, 1894), p. 312; for further references to their good relationship see n. 6, ch. III.

Montecassino than abbot of Cluny. He even speculated that he might resign his office after he returned.[12]

After his sojourn at Montecassino Pontius proceeded onward to the Holy Land to let the tense situation in Cluny abate. Calixtus, however, moved immediately to assert his authority over the abbey. As soon as Pontius was safely out of the country, he declared that Pontius had resigned his office. Then, in order to justify his unprecedented intervention in the affairs of Cluny, he contended that Pontius had departed without his permission and blessing. In his alleged indignation, he commanded that the monks elect a proper abbot to preside over them.[13] The man they chose, the elderly Hugh of Marcigny, has always been seen as a compromise candidate, and it is regarded as puzzling that so elderly an abbot would be elected under such trying circumstances. It may be significant, however, that Hugh came from Besançon, the city in which Calixtus was born, and where the power of his family was centered. This confluence might indicate that there was a connection between Hugh and the pope such as to make Hugh amenable to accepting the abbacy under these ambiguous conditions.[14] Pontius' followers, who were not convinced that he had resigned, did not strenuously object to Hugh, because he was old, and they hoped that after he died, Pontius could return. When Hugh died and Pontius did not return, and instead Peter the Venerable was elected, they became much more vocal in their discontent. This restiveness provoked Calixtus' letter of October 21, 1122, declaring that he was the source of abbatial power, and cautioning the monks against raising a scandal on Pontius' account.[15]

In the Holy Land Pontius must have been informed about what was happening in Cluny, but he chose not to return to defend his rights in order not to exacerbate the situation. He helped to defend the Holy Land for the Christians, and only returned to the West two years later when the situation in Cluny should have stabilized.[16] Determined not to reopen old wounds, he buried himself in a tiny monastery in northern Italy where he became a kind of saint to the local population. Gradually, however, his

---

[12] *Die Chronik von Montecassino*, MGH SS 34:541: " 'Mallem prius esse decanus Casinenesis quam abbas Cluniacensis.' "

[13] *De Miraculis* PL 189:922.

[14] Chibnall, *Ecclesiastic History* 6, pp. 310-312. It may also be significant that archbishops of Besançon consecrated Hugh I and Peter the Venerable. See also PL 189:923. Since both Ordericus and Peter the Venerable based their reports of this meeting on papal accounts, the motivation of anger on Calixtus' part and anger and rashness on Pontius' cannot be trusted. We do not have Pontius' side of the story.

[15] JL 6992; PL 163:1256-1257; Zerbi, "Intorno allo scisma," p. 870. As archbishop of Vienne, Calixtus had intervened in the affairs of an abbey in his province in similar ways. For a description of his illegal intervention in the election of the abbot of St. Barnard in Romans, and the allowance of his vassals to devastate the property of those who objected, see ns. 1, 3 above.

[16] Anselmi Gemblacensis cont. ad anno 1123, MGH SS 6:379.

loyal followers sought him out, occasioning the letter from Honorius in April 1125 commanding the Cluniac monks to obtain permission from Peter before visiting him.[17] Realizing that he was becoming a rallying point for the discontent in Cluny, Pontius wrote the letter to the monks at Cluny found in the Vercelli archives.[18] He told them that he had handed over the rule of the abbey to another abbot, and admonished them to be obedient to the new administration. In no wise, he said. should they foment a schism on his account.

Not until 1126 did he venture a trip back to his homeland. Since he had been out of the political maelstrom for many years, and had tried to dampen any of his followers' efforts to reinstate him in his former office, it is improbable that he had any ambitions to regain his abbacy. Ordericus' report that the prior, Bernard, rather than Pontius, fomented the plot which led to the uprising, has the ring of truth.[19] The motives of Bernard, Pontius' former prior, and the man whom Peter the Venerable reinstated after the tenure of Matthew of St. Martin-des-Champs, are already suspect. In an almost Iago-like role he appears to have convinced the surrounding knights and burghers, who still remembered the open-handed Pontius with great affection, to intrude Pontius and his entourage into the monastic compound. Pontius knew that his supporters among the monks would not act without his bidding, but he had not anticipated the intervention of the laymen. They forced him into a situation, which he could not control, and unwillingly he became the object of the open split, which he had sought so long to avoid.

Rather than setting up an independent inquiry to examine the revolt at Cluny, Honorius appointed two prelates hostile to Pontius—his ancient enemy, Archbishop Humbald of Lyons, and Cardinal Deacon Peter, whom the Anacletians would regard with the deepest scorn. As was to be expected, Humbald found Pontius to be responsible for the afflictions at Cluny and excommunicated him. Peter confirmed the sentence after Pontius refused to respond to his summons. In spite of the pope's prejudicial treatment, Pontius acceded to his bid to come to Rome, perhaps out of necessity in order to have the interdict lifted from Cluny. He may also have thought that he could no longer refrain from telling his version of the events at Cluny, and what had happened in his interview with Calixtus. He concluded that a hearing in the presence of the pope and the curia would offer him a suitable forum. But once in Rome it became clear that there was no chance for an honest trial. Rather than recanting sins which he had not committed, and thereby jeopardizing his followers in Cluny, he relinquished his right to a hearing. His followers, however,

---

[17] JL 7194; PL 166:1227.

[18] See n. 28, ch. IV.

[19] Chibnall, *Ecclesiastic History* 6, p. 312; PL 189:924; Peter the Venerable lauds Bernard for his defense of Cluny.

could no longer remain silent, and went through the formality of confession and absolution so that they could participate in a tribunal.

They had their opportunity to proclaim that Pontius had been defrauded of his office, but Honorius was prepared for their charge. He simply produced the three letters from Calixtus' Register.[20] In the first Calixtus sharply reprimands Pontius for his inconstancy, and reminds him that he has resigned his office without hope of recuperation. In the second he informs the monks at Cluny that he is very much aware of Pontius' attempt to sew discord there, and he admonishes them to remain loyal to Peter the Venerable. In the third he reassures Peter that he has no intention of changing the situation created when Pontius abdicated his office without hope of recovery.

There are reasons to be suspicious of the letters to Pontius and the monks at Cluny. They no longer exist, and the only evidence we have that Calixtus wrote them is Honorius' report. Yet, a letter, which Calixtus wrote to the monks at Cluny in October 1122 informing them of Pontius' resignation does exist.[21] Why did Honorius not produce that letter instead of the ones not only stating the Pontius had resigned his office without hope of recuperation, but also accusing him of going back on his word, and of abetting a schism in Cluny? Since Pontius could only have been involved in such nefarious activities during the four or five months between his return from the Holy Land and Calixtus' death in December, 1124, and since he was then secreted in the little monastery in Tarvisio, where he was reported to have become a Holy Man detached from the world, when could have have incited the conspiracy? Honorius would never have allowed Cluniac monks to gain permission to visit him in April 1125 if he had been involved in such subversive activities so recently. If Pontius had really wanted to regain power, he could have gone directly from the Holy Land to Cluny, where he not only had the support of a large faction of monks, but also of the surrounding knights and burghers.

Accordingly, it is improbable that Pontius could have prompted these letters, but there were good reasons for Honorius to forge them. He not only wanted proof that Pontius had resigned—proof which he already had from Calixtus' letter of October 1122—but also he wanted proof demonstrating that Pontius instigated the violence at Cluny. These letters

---

[20] PL 166:1265-1268 at 1267. To Pontius: "Tibi praecipimus ut ab hujusmodi levitate desistas, et quam in manu nostra sine recuperationis spe refutasti Cluniacensem abbatiam nullatenus molestare praesumas. Si vero nostri praecepti transgressor exstiteris, gratiam beati Petri, et nostram amittes; et si quando ad nos clamaveris, non exaudieris." To the monks at Cluny: "Zelum inter vos et contentiones agitari multorum relatione comperimus, et vehementius aggravamur. Pontius enim qui olim vestro monasterio praefuit, concordem unitatem vestram dividere, et simplicitatem mentium vestrarum sollicitare non desinit; . . ." To Peter: "Quod autem de Pontio illo qui olim abbatiae Cluniacensi praefuit, quam omnino sine recuperationis spe in manibus nostris refutavit constituimus, nulla volumus ratione mutare." See n. 18, ch. III.

[21] JL 6992; PL 163:1256-1257; see n. 15 above.

provided that proof, which was what the trial was all about. They became the incriminating evidence, which convicted Pontius.

It could be objected to this hypothesis that Pontius and some of the Cluniac monks were in Rome, and that they would have protested that they had never received these letters. But since Pontius had not absolved himself, and was not able to participate in the trial, his cries would have gone unheard. Moreover, he probably would not even have made the attempt to exonerate himself, since it was clear from Honorius' appointment of his enemy, Archbishop Humbald of Lyons, to look into the uprising at Cluny, and from the political situation in Rome, that the pope was not going to give him an impartial hearing. As for the monks, any small group of them might not have remembered such a letter, or they might have confused it with the one written in 1122. Besides, since we do not have their account of the trial, but only that of the pope, who was writing to their opponent, Peter the Venerable, we cannot be sure what their reaction was. They could have complained, and Honorius, or his chancellor, Haimeric, simply omitted to record their protests.

It could also be objected that Honorius would never have forged letters, but I suggest that he could have, just as Calixtus did when he was archbishop. To do so would not have been out of character. One has only to remember that he allowed the Frangipani to disrupt the proceedings of a papal election, and Haimeric to bribe the opposition so that he might become pope. Pandulphus, partisan, but not necessarily inaccurate, presents a highly unfavorable portrait of him, and the greatly respected Archbishop Hildebert of Tours includes his papacy among those characterized by deception and corruption.[22] To forge a few letters, therefore, in all likelihood would not have disturbed his conscience. But in any case, the trial ended predictably. Pontius' arrest and death soon thereafter from natural or unnatural causes insured that there would he no martyr around whom the dissidents could unite. Peter became the undisputed abbot of a Cluny now more closely bound to the papacy.

Beyond papal intervention in the quarrels of Cluny, other evidence suggests that Calixtus and Honorius envisaged a broad restructuring of papal policy toward Cluny. Their objective was to make the papacy less dependent upon Cluny, and to bring the abbey more directly under papal

---

[22] Hildebert, Bishop of Tours, *Curiae Romanae Discriptio*, ed. Ortuin Gratius, *Fasciculus rerum expetendarum et fugiendarum, Opera et Studi Edwardi Brown* (London, 1690), vol. 2 App., p. 7: "Romanae sunt quos timent et qui tementur. Hi sunt quos haec peculiariter Provincia monet inferre calumnias, deferre personas, afferre minas, auferre substantias. Hi sunt quorum laudati audis in otio occupationes, in pace praedas, inter arma fugas, inter vina victorias. Hi sunt qui causas morantus adhibiti, impediunt praetermissi, fastidiunt admoniti, obliviscuntur locupleti. Hi sunt qui emunt lites, vendunt intercessiones, deputant arbitros, judicanda dictant, dictata convellunt, attrahunt ligaturos, protrahunt audiendos, trahunt addictos, retrahunt transigentes. Hi sunt quos si petas, et nullo adulante beneficium promittant, pudet negare, poenitet praestitisse. Hi sunt qui negant reverentiam Clericis, originem nobilibus, concessum prioribus, congresum sequalibus, cunctis jura . . ."

control. From the time of Urban II Cluny had been the seat of the papal *camera*, and Calixtus, who spent most of his first year as pope in France, particularly exploited Cluny's good offices.[23] His *camerarius*, Stephen, remained there after he had departed for Rome, and both Pontius and the monks of Cluny acted as middlemen in transferring the hoards of treasure from Bishop Diego of St. James of Compostella to the papacy. Diego granted these "benedictions" as support for his petition to be elevated to an archbishop.[24] In 1123, however, the *camera* was transferred to Rome, and the benedictions were brought there directly instead of passing through Cluny.[25] By assuming the administration of the *camera* Calixtus took a further step in emancipating the papacy from Cluny, and in shifting the balance of power between the two institutions in favor of the papacy.

The other key to the understanding of the relationship between the dispute at Cluny and the papal schism is the role of Matthew of St. Martin-des-Champs. As Peter the Venerable's prior, Matthew prosecuted Pontius. Indeed, arguably on the basis of the spurs he earned in his performance, he was promoted to cardinal bishop of Albano. Matthew's opposition to Pontius did not originate from differences over how Cluny should respond to the challenge posed by the Cistercians and other new Benedictine houses over the interpretation of the *Rule*, however, but from other causes. Matthew was one of the most outspoken defenders of Cluniac traditions, and he specifically argued against adopting a more stringent interpretation of the *Rule*. He feared that if the ancient statutes of Cluny were upset, Cluny would lose its prestige and influence. In a letter written between 1131-1132 to the Benedictine abbots of the chapter of Rheims, he spells out his position. The abbots had recently (probably October 18, 1131) passed some strict statutes which went well beyond the customs of Cluny. They demanded perpetual silence in the cloister, a diminution in the reading of the familiar psalms, and the suppression of certain solemnities in the celebration of offices. Matthew criticized all of these regulations, and even presented an argument in favor of ornamentation, which, he claimed, pertained to the monks as well as to the church.[26]

---

[23] *Historia Compostelana*, ed. cit., p. 284: "Ea propter Calixto Papae operae pretium erat Cluniacense Monasterium esse sibi praecordialissimum, utpote cameram & assedam suam, nempe ad confundendum matris Romanae Ecclesiae incestatorem." For an excellent description of the papal camera at Cluny see Karl Jordan, "Zur päpstlichen Finanzgeschichte im 11. und 12. Jahrhundert," *Quellen und Forschungen aus Italienischen Archiven und Bibliotheken* 25 (1933/34), 61-104. Jordan discusses the reference above on p. 98. See also Jürgen von Sydow, "Cluny und die Anfänge der Apostolischen Kammer: Studien zur Geschichte der päpstlichen Finanzverwaltung im 11. und 12. Jahrhundert," *Studien und Mitteilungen zur Geschichte des Benedictinerordens* 63 (1951), 55, 59.

[24] Jordan, "Zur päpstlichen Finanzgeschichte," pp. 83-85, 99.

[25] Ibid., 86, 99.

[26] Ursmer Berlière, *Documents inédits pour servir à l'histoire ecclésiastique de la Belgique* 1 (Mardesous, Abbaye de Saint-Benoit, 1894), pp. 91-93; Bredero, "Une controverse sur Cluny," pp. 56-60.

About this time (1132) Matthew wrote another letter to the prior and monks of the Grand Chartreuse, commiserating with them over the losses they had suffered in a gigantic avalanche.[27] The letter shows respect and admiration for the Carthusians, and reveals that monastic leaders of different ideologies could coexist amicably without the need to prove that their principles were superior to the others. Competition occurred only when there was a threat or a challenge, and Chartreuse did not present a challenge to any of the other orders. Matthew was far more concerned with the innovations in the interpretation of the Benedictine *Rule* by the abbots in the province of Rheims because they did pose a threat to the customs of Cluny. Moreover, Matthew had a personal association, because he was born in the area of Rheims, and had been a canon there. Even more importantly, St. Bernard's approval of the abbots' alternatives to the interpretation of the *Rule* greatly enhanced their significance. Bernard was very close to one of the abbots of Rheims, William of St. Thierry, who later wrote a biography of the saint. It was to William that Bernard addressed his Apologia criticizing not only what he regarded as the abuses of Cluny, but also its customs.[28] Bernard's approval of the monastic vision of these abbots, therefore, gave an entirely different dimension to what otherwise was a local movement, and elicited Matthew's strong response.

What Matthew's two letters show is that Innocent's supporters could be both advocates of the older monastic customs, and yet be receptive to the new. To see a bifurcation of the sort which has been posed to explain the papal schism is to see something which did not exist. This is why there is nothing anomalous about the fact that Matthew, a spokesman for the old customs, and Bernard, an advocate of the new, both supported Innocent. What this juxtaposition shows is that a common religious outlook was not the cement which bound Innocent to his supporters. The dispute at Cluny does not point to the existence of European-wide parties in 1130 composed of traditionalists—the old Benedictine houses and cardinals of southern Italian provenance—and spiritually-minded progressives— members of the new orders and northern cardinals. We must look to other criteria to determine why church leaders backed one candidate or the other.

---

[27] Matthew's letter is edited by H. Rüthing, "Ein Brief des Kardinals Matthaus von Albano an di Grande Chartreuse," *Revue Bénédictine* 78 (1968), 145-151.

[28] *Apologia ad Guillelmum Abbatem, Sancti Bernardi Opera*, ed. cit. 3, pp. 81-108.

Chapter VI

MONTECASSINO

The parallels between events at Cluny and Montecassino following the Concordat of Worms are striking, and it is therefore understandable that some historians do not regard it as accidental that crises developed in both monasteries about the same time.[1] They see the common cause as a shift in papal favor away from Cluny and Montecassino and toward the new, more vigorous orders and the episcopate.[2] Others urge caution in emphasizing the points of similarity between the two older monasteries and the fall of their abbots, Pontius and Oderisius.[3] Still others reject any attempt to associate them at all.[4] In a general way, this view is correct. What Cluny and Montecassino shared was an intense desire to maintain their independence, especially from papal encroachment. Their difficulties with the papacy arose from a contest over power rather than from differences over a progressive or regressive monastic ideology.

Montecassino's time of tribulations stemmed from a multiplicity of causes—some personal, some strategic, and still others resulting from a dispute over imperial and papal rights. Located on a mountain between Rome and Naples, the abbey overlooked land which local powers, the Normans, the emperor, and the pope all wanted to control. Thus, military considerations were of the utmost importance. So also was the abbey's wealth, which both Honorius and Innocent wanted to tap for their needs. What aroused little interest, however, were the living habits of the monks. The partisanship of Montecassino's abbot for Anaclet did not spring from a desire they both shared to shield the church from the breezes of reform blowing in from the North.

The main source for the history of Montecassino during this period is the Chronicle of Peter the Deacon.[5] Although Peter transmits much valuable information, historians weigh his judgments carefully because of his partiality for Oderisius. His admiration for the abbot is revealed by a series

---

[1] Hartmut Hoffmann, "Petrus Diaconus, die Herren von Tusculum und der Sturz Oderisius' II. von Montecassino," *Deutsches Archiv für Erforschung des Mittelalers* 27 (1971), 1-109 at p. 75.

[2] Chodorow, *Christian Political Theory*, p. 25.

[3] Cowdrey, *Abbot Pontius of Cluny*, p. 268.

[4] Tellenbach, "Der Sturz," pp. 37, 42.

[5] *Die Chronik von Montecassino*, MGH SS 34; for salient facts about Peter see intro., pp. X-XI.

of saints' lives which he wrote and dedicated to Oderisius when he became abbot in 1123. Oderisius came from a noble family, the counts of Sangro. Paschal II promoted him to cardinal deacon of St. Agatha no later than 1113, and as a cardinal he helped to elect Gelasius II.[6] Calixtus II confirmed his election as abbot about the time of the Lateran Council of 1123. At the same council bishops lodged complaints against the monks of Montecassino, but Calixtus rose to their defense.[7] The, scene was almost a replay of an incident during the Council of Rheims of 1119. When some French bishops stated their grievances against Cluny, Calixtus defended the abbey.

In the summer of 1123 Calixtus again exhibited his good will toward Montecassino. He stopped there on a trip to Benevento and excommunicated Count Geoffrey of Ceccano, who had seized some of the abbey's possessions. About the same time Cardinal Bishop Lambert of Ostia, the future Honorius II, arrived at Montecassino to ask for the use of the abbey of Santa Maria in Pallara in Rome. Santa Maria had been at the disposal of Lambert's predecessor, Cardinal Bishop Leo of Ostia, but Leo had also been a monk at Montecaassino. Oderisius feared that if he acceded to Lambert's request, the abbey might slip from Montecassino's control. He therefore denied the petition. Peter the Deacon says that Lambert was so angered that he vowed revenge.[8]

In 1124 Calixtus gave Oderisius a commission to use military force against Richard Pygnardus, Lord of Pico, ostensibly because Richard had imprisoned a consul. The abbot subdued the castle of Pico with his troops, and Calixtus then conceded the city to Montecassino.[9] The Lord of Pico's imprisonment of the consul was probably only a pretext for the pope's much more ambitious designs. Calixtus appears to have thought that the time was propitious for realizing his claims to territory south of the papal states, and the capture of Pico presented him with the opportunity to take the first step. In retrospect the campaign was a mistake because the price for Pico was the alienation of the Normans.[10]

---

[6] Oderisius later was also cardinal by right of being abbot of Montecassino. For the main features of Oderisius' career see Hoffmann, "Petrus Diaconus," passim; Ganzer, *Die Entwicklung des Auswärtigen Kardinalats*, pp. 75-79; Hüls, *Kardinäle*, p. 252; Zenker, *Die Mitglieder*, pp. 181-182. Following Schmale, Zenker notes that Oderisius belonged to the older generation in the college of cardinals, and that his difficulties with Honorius not only were personal, but also that they arose because of differing attitudes towards the reform and monastic life.

[7] MGH SS 34:542-543.

[8] Ibid., 545. The abbey was located on the Palatine under the influence of the Frangipani. Matthew of Albano resided there, and the Frangipani spirited Innocent to that refuge after his election. See Pietro Fedele, "Una Chiesa del Palatino: S. Maria 'in Pallara'," *Archivio della R. Società Romana di Storia Patria* 26 (1903), 343-380.

[9] Ibid.

[10] Hoffmann, "Petrus Diaconus," p. 90. One of Calixtus' first priorities after he finally occupied his see in Rome was to establish papal suzerainty over southern Italy. He himself went there in 1120 after he had been in Rome only a short time. He received homage from his vassals, and became the administrator for the Duchy of Apulia during the absence of

Oderisius did not participate in Lambert's turbulent election as pope, and indeed, Pandulphus reveals in his biography of Honorius II that the abbot cooperated with the cardinals who opposed Lambert.[11] Moreover, although Oderisius respected Honorius' learning, he did not exhibit the obedience that Honorius thought was proper to a pope, and Honorius accused him of being guilty of the sin of pride.[12] When the pope turned to him for financial support after his election, Oderisius rejected his appeal. The contrast between the abbot's willingness to expend great sums for the acquisition of Pico, and his unwillingness to grant Honorius a subsidy could not have escaped the pope's attention. It was another sign of the abbot's dissatisfaction with his election, and relations between the two men subsequently were colored by the personal animosity that these events engendered.[13]

In June 1125 Honorius visited Montecassino. Peter the Deacon records no problems, but the pope took the precaution of transferring the antipope, Burdinus (Gregory VIII), from the prison at Janula, which was under the influence of Montecassino, to Fumo, which was not. The Count of Aquino and a few monks had recently informed Honorius that Oderisius was the pope's enemy. In addition they charged that the abbot was squandering the goods of his abbey.[14] Now Honorius had ammunition to

---

Duke William of Constantinople. He wanted to prevent the incursion of Roger, the count of Sicily, on the mainland, but he failed both in diplomacy and in a personal appearance in September 1121 at the fortress of Rocca Niceforo near Catanzaro. After 15 days an epidemic broke out. Several cardinals died and Calixtus himself became seriously ill: "et demum quicquid uoluit ipse comes Rogerium cum papa semiuiuo peregit." *Lib. Pont. Dert.*, p. 194; see also ibid., 193 and March's notes 14 & 15, p. 200. For other sources on Calixtus' activities see e.g. *Annales Ceccanenses* MGH SS 19:282;

Chronica Pontificum et Imperatorum Tibertina MGH SS 31:261: "Civitates, castella, portus, lacus et alia multa beati Petri patrimonia longis retro distracta temporibus recuperavit." See Josef Deér, *Papsttum und Normannen: Untersuchungen zu ihren lehnsrechtlichen und kirchenpolitischen Beziehungen* (Cologne, Vienna, 1972), pp. 171-172. In general see the older, but still useful study of Ferdinand Chalandon, *Histoire de la Domination Normande en Italie et en Sicile* 2 (New York, 1907, repr. 1960).

[11] *Lib. Pont. Dert.*, p. 207: "Hic Oderisio uiro curiali multum ac nobili, Casinensis abbati et cardinali, non tamen absque dampno irrecuperabili monasterii, et abbatiam abstulit et tempora de eo cantari permisit, quia contra se aliquando fauerat cardinalibus."

[12] Peter the Deacon says that if Honorius could find no other fault with Oderisius, his sin of pride would be enough to damn him. MGH SS 34:549: "Et si in nullo alio culpandus est, eius tamen superbia crimen est dampnationi sufficiens, quia omnia peccata remittuntur hominibus, superbis autem Deus resistit."

[13] MGH SS 34:546. Honorius makes it clear that the good will of the papacy depended upon Oderisius' response to his request. Oderisius responded that those who had participated in Honorius' election ought to be responsible. He respected the pope's intelligence, but he obviously had other reservations about him. "Mandat dehinc idem papa nostro abbati navem Petri periclitari in fluctibus, monet uti subveniat, ut pecunie subsidium mittat, protestans illos, qui se in tanto articulo adiuvarent, habituros ut filios, qui non, ut privignos. Commotus ad talia abbas fatetur, quod ipse, qui tunc de adiutorii ope ferenda pulsabatur, interesse debuisset electioni, ut, qui particeps erat tribulationum, consors esse deberet et consiliorum. Interrogantibus fratribus de predicto pontifice, cuius filius esset, unum tamen pro certo scire, quia plenus esset litteris a capite usque ad pedes. Hec ergo causa inter eundem pontificem et abbatem perpetuum discordie malum et perenne odium suscitavit."

[14] MGH SS 34:547: "Interea cum Aquinenses comites ferali adversus Landulfum de

use against him. In a gathering of laymen at the Castle of Fumo Honorius declared that Oderisius was a fighter rather than an abbot, and he accused him of dissipating the property of Montecassino.[15] The following winter Oderisius' enemies insinuated to Honorius that the abbot even coveted papal authority, and this time (March 1126) Honorius deposed him after he had refused to respond to the customary three summons. Since Oderisius did not observe the deposition, Honorius excommunicated him and all of his followers.[16]

Such, in brief, are the events leading up to the disorders in Montecassino. Their similarities to the events at Cluny before the dispute of 1122-1126 are palpable. Charges of wasting the abbey's goods were leveled at both abbots, and both were suspected of having designs on the papacy. Violence erupted in each case. Bishops complained about the monastic exemptions of Montecassino as well as those of Cluny, and Calixtus publicly defended both abbeys against the attacks. Oderisius supported Anaclet, and although Pontius died before the papal election of 1130, his close associate, Aegidius of Tusculum, also supported Anaclet.[17] From these comparisons it is understandable that some historians see Cluny and Montecassino as embodying the same tendencies. Given these resemblances, the extrapolation that the two venerable houses stood in a corresponding relationship to the papal schism also makes sense. In both cases Anaclet is seen to represent the older style of Benedictinism with its princely abbots and its jealously guarded privileges.

Yet, these similarities are misleading if they are not balanced against major differences.[18] Economic problems, for example, greatly contributed to the crisis at Cluny, but were less important at Montecassino.

Sancto Iohanne odio deseuirent, contra eundem abbatem conqueri ceperunt, quod Landulfum illis preferret, illi pecuniam, terras et domos tribueret, se vero contempni et pro nichilo haberi. Sed cum ad ista abbas non preberet auditum, iuncti quibusdam ex nostris eum pape Honorio accusare ceperunt illum apostolice sedis inimicum, prodigum et dilapidatorem rerum monasterii astruentes." Cf. Palumbo, *Lo Scisma*, pp. 263-264 & n. 2, p. 263. Hoffmann ("Petrus Diaconus," pp. 82-84) says that it is possible that individual monks were unhappy with Oderisius and sided with the counts of Aquino in their complaints to Honorius, but he also says that dissatisfaction in Benedictine abbeys was the norm, and that he does not think that the grumblings from these monks were a significant criticism of Oderisius. Hoffmann believes that the mutiny came mainly from the outside—from the rebellious burgers of San Germano next to the monastery and from the Count of Aquino. When the count accused Oderisius of extravagance, it was merely a tactic and a pretext. He says that poverty and distress occurred only after Oderisius had been deposed, and he notes that in the Middle Ages nothing was easier than to complain about the decline in morality in Benedictine monasteries.

[15] Ibid., 547-548: "Ibi itaque in plenario laicorum conventu eundem abbatem papa Honorius evocans et enormi adversus eum odio deseviens ingenti eum increpatione redarguit militem illum, non abbatem, lapidatorem et prodigum substantie monasterii esse inclamitans . . ."

[16] Ibid., 548-549.

[17] Cowdrey, *Abbot Pontius of Cluny*, p. 267.

[18] Ibid., 268. Cowdrey insists that the factors, which brought about the fall of Pontius, must be sought within the history of Cluny and in Pontius' character deficiencies.

Conversely, Montecassino enjoyed a strategic importance not shared by Cluny. There was, nevertheless, one important resemblance—a change in the position of both Cluny and Montecassino following the conclusion of the Investiture Contest. Before the reconciliation of Calixtus and Henry V, the support of the powerful monasteries was indispensable to the papacy, but thereafter it became less critical. Popes could be more sympathetic to the complaints of the bishops and less protective of Cluny and Montecassino.[19]

In the case of Montecassino issues of *regnum* and *sacerdotium* receded into the far distance as those of territorial expansion became more dominant.[20] At first Rome and Montecassino cooperated, as they had, for instance, when Oderisius captured Pico at Calixtus' behest. But Honorius turned a blind eye when hostilities broke out between Oderisius and Richard of Gaeta, Pygnardus of Pico's overlord. Again, Honorius imposed no ecclesiastical censures when Richard of Gaeta entered the *Terra Sancti Benedicti* in 1125 and laid waste a number of fortresses. For his part, Oderisius openly began aiding the counts of Ceccano against Roman forces.[21] Clearly the interests of Rome and Montecassino no longer coincided, and Oderisius had become a liability. In great part, Oderisius fell because he hindered more than he promoted papal undertakings in the South Campagna.[22]

Even though the military confrontations are beyond dispute, not every historian believes that they were the basic reason for Oderisius' downfall. Schmale still sees religious ideology as the main point of contention between Honorius and Oderisius, and concentrates on the complaints uttered about monastic discipline at Montecassino. He admits that Honorius made strenuous efforts to bring Montecassino more directly under curial control, but he does not believe that the pope's motivation was the attainment of greater military and political benefits for the papacy. Rather, he thinks that as a reformer, the pope wanted to exert greater authority over the abbey in order to tighten monastic discipline. "Innere Ordnung und Hoheitsanspruch gingen hier Hand in Hand."[23]

---

19 Hoffmann, "Petrus Diaconus," pp. 79-82.

20 Bloch, "The Schism of Anacletus II," pp. 174-175. Bloch notes Honorius' ambition to expand the Patrimonium to the south. See *Lib. Pont. Dert.*, pp. 207-208.

21 Honorius' military activities were extensive. Giorgio Falco notes that he took over Segni, Trevi, and Maienza, that he burned Posterzo, Roccasecca, Giuliano, and Santo Stefano Prossei, and that he assaulted Ceccano. "I comuni della Campagna e della Marittima," *Archivio della R. Società Romana di Storia Patria* 42 (1919), 571-572. Falco notes (p. 573) that by the mid-twelfth century there was an important change in the administration of papal lands. In the tenth and eleventh centuries a "count," who was a local power and independent of papal authority, administered the lands. By the mid-twelfth century the popes had consolidated their power and were then able to appoint an official of the church.

22 Hoffmann, "Petrus Diaconus," p. 95. Ganzer also speculates that differences in policies over the Normans contributed to the hostility between Oderisius and Honorius. *Die Entwicklung des Auswärtigen Kardinalats*, p. 78.

23 Schmale, *Studien zum Schisma*, p. 135 & ns. 61, 62.

It is not, however, obvious that there were serious problems of excesses in the behavior of the monks during Oderisius' reign. Peter the Deacon mentions complaints over monastic discipline, but he lends them no credence. Schmale nevertheless puts more trust in the complaints than in Peter, whom he regards as Oderisius' loyal partisan rather than as a detached observer.[24] But even if it could be demonstrated that discipline was lax under Oderisius' tutelage, it would still have to be shown that monastic reform motivated Honorius to depose Oderisius. Not only does Honorius not even hint that this was the reason, but everything we know about his character and his relationship with Oderisius points to other causes.

Subsequent events in Montecassino support this conclusion. Peter the Deacon describes the troubles of Montecassino at length, but he maintains that religious order began to break down only after the deposition of Oderisius.[25] He reports that during the administration of Oderisius' unfortunate successor, Nicholas of Tusculum, economic conditions deteriorated to such a degree that monks found it impossible to live according to the *Rule*. Within a year Honorius was forced to step in and order the election of a new abbot. His favor fell upon Seniorectus. After the chaos of the preceding year, Seniorectus appeared as a reformer, but relative to the stringent demands the canons regular and the Cistercians made upon their members, his rule was mild.[26] Moreover, since he supported Anaclet in 1130, reform at Montecassino cannot be equated with the policies of Honorius.

As for Honorius' complaints, and those of the count of Aquino and some dissident monks that Oderisius had dissipated the wealth of his abbey, they cannot be taken seriously. The count of Aquino was Oderisius' enemy and would not have shrunk from defaming the abbot to ingratiate himself with the pope. Likewise, Honorius' criticisms were not careful assessments of Oderisius' administration but charges hurled at the abbot in the heat of the moment after Oderisius had opposed him at almost every turn.[27] No independent source substantiates any of these claims.

---

[24] Hoffmann, "Petrus Diaconus," p. 79. Hoffmann notes that although Schmale claimed that the real problem was monastic discipline, in his analysis he dealt only with the charge of poor administration.

[25] MGH SS 34:555: "Denique ab ipso fere tempore, quo decaniam dimisit, et precipue a morte venerabilis abbatis Gerardi, cum omnes fere priores, qui a Desiderio monachi facti fuerant, ex hoc mundo recessissent, nunc ipsius abbatie ambitione, nunc per fratrum clandestinas seditiones, nunc per abbatum expulsiones, cum fratres ad tantam inopiam devenissent, ut omnium rerum necessitatem permaximan sustinerent, ordinis religio de hoc cepit labefactari. Nec inmerito, cum quamplurimi necessitate coacti arduae vitae tramitem ob paupertatem retinere non possent." Hoffmann, "Petrus Diaconus," p. 79.

[26] Hoffmann, "Petrus Diaconus," pp. 83-84. As further proof that two parties did not already exist during Honorius' reign, Honorius sent Cardinal Priest Gregory of the Holy Apostles to oversee the election. Gregory supported Anaclet, and succeeded him as Victor IV.

[27] See ns. 14 & 15.

Thus, attitudes toward monastic discipline and ecclesiastical reform are not central to understanding the forces that produced the conflicts at Montecassino and the hostility between Honorius and Oderisius. Perched on a mountain guarding valuable plains, Montecassino was a territorial power in the sense that Cluny never was. After the Concordat of Worms, when Calixtus and Honorius could turn to pursuits other than defining their relationship with the emperor, they looked to the south. Calixtus appealed to an ancient agreement with the emperor granting the Patrimonium of St. Peter further territory to the south as justification for his move against the castle of Pico. Honorius wanted to continue Calixtus' initiative but encountered a totally uncooperative abbot, who did not respect him. He managed to rid himself of his adversary, but instead of gaining the help he needed from the new abbot, he had to deal with a Montecassino that had fallen into a state of acute disarray. There was some improvement after the election of Seniorectus, but Montecassino never regained its former splendor or its power. It could not provide Honorius with the military aid he required, and his campaign in the south ended in defeat in 1128. Along with his dream of a greater papal state, his spirit also seems to have broken down.[28]

Innocent, however, did not let the dream die, but attempted to revive Honorius' policies of expansion into southern Italy, and of increasing papal power over Montecassino. Lothar III was his ally, but their interests also conflicted. The bounds of imperial and papal jurisdiction over Montecassino were vague, and they collided in the election in the fall of 1137. Innocent was irate because Lothar dared to arbitrate the election of an abbot while a pope was present, and Lothar was equally furious with Innocent for interfering with the rights of monks to carry on a free election.

Innocent's intervention in Montecassino was a continuation of the policy of Honorius. They both followed the precedent set by Calixtus when he interfered in the liberties of Cluny. Honorius had sent Cardinal Priest Gregory of the Holy Apostles to oversee the election after the deposition of Oderisius, and to command the monks to elect Seniorectus. The monks had stiffly resisted this encroachment on their liberties, but Honorius eventually won after he dispatched Matthew of Albano with the same assignment. The monks, however, balked at swearing an oath of fidelity to the Roman Church, protesting that the abbots of Montecassino had never sworn such an oath.[29]

---

28 For further references to this period see Erich Caspar, *Roger II.* (Innsbruck, 1904), pp. 74-81; Paul Kehr, "Belehnungen der süditalienischen Normannenfürsten durch die Päpste 1059-1192," *Abhandlungen der preussischen Akademie der Wissenschaften*, Phil. Hist. Kl. n. I (Berlin, 1934); Helen Wieruszowski, "Roger II of Sicily, Rex-Tyrannus, in Twelfth Century Political Thought," *Speculum* 38 (1963), 46-78.

29 MGH SS 34:550: "Veniens autem predictus cardinalis ad monasterium fratres convocat et, quod papa preceperat, seriatim enuntiat. Quod dum fratres audissent, murmur inter eos ingens repente exoritur, dicentes non debere Casinensis abbatis electionem in alterius potestate transire et nimis indignum et inconveniens esse, ut Casinensis ecclesia, que sub antecessoribus suis libera semper extiterat, ad sue confusionis obprobrium cardinalibus sub-

Innocent's quarrel with Lothar had its antecedents in the diplomatic skirmishing of the summer of 1137. In May, Duke Henry of Bavaria and Innocent arrived in the Campania. Raynald, elected abbot after Seniorectus, refused to recognize Innocent and to be taken under the protection of the empire. Meeting with the monks in chapter, Raynald and the monks decided that they would remain faithful to Anaclet and Roger.[30] On July 13th Cardinal Gerard of Santa Croce, representing Innocent, and Peter the Deacon debated the question of why the monks at Montecassino would have elected Raynald without consulting the pope. Peter the Deacon defended the liberties of Montecassino. No doubt feeling the precariousness of his position, however, Raynald finally recognized Innocent, and even took an oath to him.[31]

Raynald's late recantation proved to have been a miscalculation, for on September 14th Lothar arrived with a retinue of religious and secular notables to see whether he should remain as abbot. "And if he found Raynald to be unworthy of such an abbey, he [Lothar] would immediately remove him, and place a suitable person on the cathedra of Saint Benedict."[32] While Lothar and his queen, Richinza, proceeded on to Montecassino, Innocent simmered below in San Germano, waiting for an opening to seize the initiative from Lothar. His opportunity came after a group of laymen arrived, infuriating the monks, who wanted to have them ejected. The monks insisted that only they, not laymen could elect an abbot. At this point Innocent sent three of his most effective spokesmen—Haimeric, St. Bernard, and Gerard of Santa Croce—to remind the monks of the faith and obedience they had promised to St. Peter and himself.[33] These men all argued forcefully for Raynald's deposition.

While the debate was raging in Montecassino, Innocent waited for news in San Germano. Lothar and the monks sent emissaries to tell him what was happening, and when he heard, he was so incensed that an emperor would dare to examine an election at Montecassino with a pope present, that he refused to receive them.[34] In his wrath, he even said that all of the archbishops, bishops, and abbots involved in the examination should be deposed. When Lothar's agents reported Innocent's fury, Lothar placated the pope by assuring him that what had been done was not done *studiose*, but *simpliciter*, and not to the pope's injury, but to his honor. In other words, Lothar was simply responding to the situation, and was not carefully considering imperial and papal rights. Mollified, Innocent then sent his three spokesmen back, and they deposed Raynald on September 18th.

---

ieceretur." Ibid., 556: "Et Fratres modis omnibus reniti et contradicere, et hoc Casinenses numquam fecisse dicebant."

[30] Ibid., 566.

[31] Ibid., 589.

[32] Ibid., 593.

[33] Ibid., 593-594.

[34] Ibid., 595.

Gerard of Santa Croce then tried to convince the monks that the election should be in Innocent's hands, and the hard pressed monks once again tried to defend their liberties. Lothar intervened on their behalf. Convinced by his arguments, Innocent agreed that the monks had the right to elect their abbot, the emperor to ordain him, and the pope to consecrate him. But Lothar and Innocent both continued to contend that they had the right to intervene. Obviously attempting to preclude the election of an imperial candidate, Innocent said that he would grant the monks the *licentia eligendi* only if they agreed to select someone from their own congregation. Lothar received the news of Innocent's breach of his agreement gravely, and then threatened to create a schism between himself and the pope if Innocent did not allow the monks to elect whom they wished. The stakes were now too high, and Innocent was forced to back down. The monks then elected the German, Wibald of Stablo, on September 19, 1137.[35] Wibald was an estimable abbot, but he was German, and in the turbulent politics of Southern Italy, he lasted only a few months. In November he fled to Germany.

From this description of events at Montecassino, it is clear that the points of contention were: (1) whether the monks would be able to retain their traditional liberties, and (2) what the limits of papal and imperial authority should be. Accusations of moral decadence and Oderisius' desire to be pope were only ammunition used by the abbot's enemies to get Honorius to take action against him. If there were any substance to the charges, independent sources would have substantiated them. Likewise Honorius' reproach that Oderisius was more of a knight than an abbot was spoken in a moment of anger, and cannot be taken seriously. Moreover, if engaging in military activity were inimical to the priestly office, then Calixtus, Honorius and Innocent would all stand condemned. Even St. Bernard accompanied imperial and papal armies.

Rather than standing as an exemplar of a form of Benedictinism gone soft, and perhaps a bit rotten, Oderisius had the respect of all ecclesiastical reformers before Honorius. His problem with Honorius had nothing to do with a new interpretation of Benedictinism, but rather with money and power. Oderisius was understandably critical of Honorius' election, and was unresponsive to his requests. His disdain elicited the pope's anger, but Honorius bided his time until he could take revenge on the abbot who had treated him with so little respect. This disposition coupled with Honorius' territorial ambitions in the South and his desire to curtail the liberties of the powerful monastery, account for his intervention in Montecassino. Instead of raising the standards of moral behavior at Montecassino, Honorius was instrumental in initiating their long decline.

Innocent's case is slightly more complicated, but again, there is not a whiff of ethical concern. He did not want to get rid of Raynald because

---

[35] Ibid., 596-611; Bernhardi, *Lothar*, pp. 755-759.

Raynald was unreceptive to the new monastic ideals, but because Raynald had supported Anaclet and Roger. St. Bernard was present during the tumultuous proceedings, and there is no report that he ever said anything about the conduct of the monks at Montecassino in the way that he criticized the customs of Cluny. Similarly to Calixtus in Cluny, Innocent wanted to bring Montecassino more directly under papal authority, and he did not want the emperor to stand in his way. Here, he lost out in a power play. Either he would let the monks elect whom they wanted, or Lothar would leave him to the mercies of Roger and Anaclet. Innocent had no choice.

The abbots and monks of Montecassino supported Anaclet for many reasons, none of which had anything to do with attitudes toward ecclesiastical reform. Roger was the most powerful secular ruler in the area, and they were safer allying themselves with him and the pope he recognized than with the distant emperor. They did not like Honorius, who had listened to what they perceived as the scurrilous lies of their abbot's enemies, and who had unjustly excommunicated him. They were therefore predisposed not to recognize the pope chosen by Honorius' chancellor. They disliked Innocent all the more when he interfered in their liberties, and tried to impose more papal authority over them than any pope before Honorius. Anaclet had none of these liabilities. They probably respected him as a learned and cultivated man, and they were relieved that he honored their customs. These reasons more than any conservative ideological affinities account for Montecassino's recognition of Anaclet, and rejection of Innocent.

Chapter VII

THE POPES, THE NORMANS, AND THE EMPEROR

After the papal elections of 1130 there was a wild scramble to gain control of Rome, and to win recognition outside of it. When the dust settled in about seven months, Anaclet was secure in Rome, and had a firm alliance with Roger of Sicily. Although exiled, Innocent nevertheless had gained the recognition of the Western European kings and the emperor. Or did Innocent recognize Lothar, and Anaclet, Roger? The confusion over whether the two popes recognized their secular defenders or the reverse arises out of one of the most widely accepted interpretations of the origins of the schism. The most cogent formulation of the theory goes as follows. The central point at issue prior to the election of 1130 was friendship or enmity towards the emperor. The two attitudes were primarily expressed in a willingness to continue the Investiture Contest, or to resolve it. Anaclet showed his disinclination to accept its resolution in the Concordat of Worms by crowning Roger as king of Sicily, and thus following the traditional papal mentality of relying upon the Normans for support. Innocent's alliance with Lothar, by contrast, proves that he accepted the terms of the Concordat. With the conflict with the emperor behind him, and inspired by the northern religious movements, Innocent then moved forward to concentrate on internal ecclesiastical reform.[1] According to this theory, papal alliances were based upon differences of principle, and did not arise out of political expediency. The view implies that each pope's attitude toward ecclesiastical reform determined his choice of a secular ally.

This argument immediately encounters difficulties, because both popes courted the emperor, and indeed turned to him and the German church before anyone else. Neither pope had any quarrel with Lothar, who had been chosen by churchmen because he would be sympathetic to their views.[2] Even though Lothar opted for Innocent, Anaclet never opposed the emperor, and never objected to any of the terms of the Concordat of

---

[1] Chodorow, *Christian Political Theory*, pp. 39-40. Mühlbacher sees no opposition at all of the Pierleoni to the policy of peace with the emperor. *Die streitige Papstwahl*, p. 74.

[2] Anselm of Gembloux, cont. Sigeberti ad an. 1125, MGH SS 6:380; *Narratio de electione Lotharii*, MGH SS 12:510-512; for a recent discussion of Lothar's election and references see Ernst-Dieter Hehl, "Die Zeit Lothars III. und Innocenz II.," *Kirche und Krieg im 12. Jahrhundert: Studien zu kanonischen Recht und politischer Wirklichkeit*, vol. 19 of Monographien zur Geschichte des Mittelalters, pub. Anton Hiersmann (Stuttgart, 1980), pp. 21-56 at pp. 22-23 & ns. 82-83.

Worms. Losing the contest to gain imperial recognition, Anaclet was forced into a defensive position, in which he had no choice but to rely upon Roger. Since, however, he continued to negotiate with Lothar, and to request that the emperor call a tribunal to examine the papal elections even after he had invested Roger with his kingdom, he presumably saw nothing in his alliance with the Norman King which was inimical to imperial recognition. Like Anaclet, Innocent also recognized Roger as king when Roger's son and namesake defeated him in the battle of Galuccio in 1139, but he too continued to recognize the emperor. Anaclet did not choose Roger over Lothar because he rejected the accommodation reached between *regnum* and *sacerdotium* in the Concordat of Worms, or because his interests were centered on Southern Italy. He invested Roger with his kingdom because he needed him in order to survive.

Although different positions on *regnum* and *sacerdotium* did not lead to the formation of the two parties to the schism, nevertheless each pope had to deal with issues which touched upon that fundamental and delicate relationship. Anaclet's attitudes are more difficult to determine than Innocent's because his interaction with the emperor was so limited, and because of the hostile propaganda and destruction of documents. Still, certain features of each administration are revealed from the evidence we have.

It is highly indicative of the importance that Innocent and Anaclet placed upon imperial recognition that they both turned to the emperor and the German people before anyone else. Anaclet could have expected a warm response from Roger, whose family had had contact with the Pierleoni for some time.[3] Moreover, Anaclet did not have the liabilities that Innocent inherited from Haimeric and Honorius, who had attempted and failed to capture Southern Italy from the Normans. If Anaclet had wanted to initiate an anti-imperial policy to force Lothar to retreat from the Concordat of Worms, and to relinquish imperial investitures of bishops and abbots, this was his opportunity. He did not take it. Rather, as soon as he was able, he wrote carefully drawn up letters to the German people— clergy and laity— and to the emperor and his queen, Richinza.[4]

Even emersed in combatting Innocent's forces in Rome, and with the necessity of organizing a chancery, Anaclet was able to dispatch his letters by February 24th. Innocent bested him by almost a week, however, dispatching two encyclicals to Germany on February 18th, the very week of the election.[5] Haimeric appreciated the advantage to be gained from continuity with the previous regime, and he already had a smoothly running chancery to expedite the letters. While Anaclet concentrated on

---

[3] Deér, *Papsttum und Normannen*, p. 212.

[4] JL 8370; JL 8371.

[5] JL 7403; JL 7404; PL 179:53-54; Palumbo, *Lo Scisma*, pp. 305-307; Hehl, "Die Zeit Lothars," pp. 30-31.

securing Rome, Haimeric coolly announced Innocent's election, mentioning nothing about Anaclet's nor the irregular circumstances under which Innocent's had taken place. He emphasized the emperor's role as the special son of the church and its defender, and thus prepared Lothar for the roles he would be requested to fulfill. He drew attention to Honorius' excommunication of Conrad, the anti-king, and he urged Lothar to come to Rome during the winter to be crowned—a bit of bravado, since Innocent's survival in Rome even for a week was dubious. In his letter to the German people Innocent admonished laymen and clerics alike to be faithful to the king, and to urge him to come to Rome.

Though short, Innocent's letters brought up key issues. They established the fiction of continuity by following immediately after Honorius' death, and by not mentioning any of the circumstances of the two elections. Innocent implied that like Honorius, he too would excommunicate Conrad, and he dangled before Lothar the prospect of being crowned in Rome. In his letter to the German clerics and laymen Innocent alluded to a theme that would characterize his reign. This was the obligation of clergymen to participate in just wars under the leadership of both secular and ecclesiastical leaders. Innocent knew that without the participation of the clergy, Lothar could not possibly give him the aid he needed to establish himself in Rome, and to win back the areas controlled by Anaclet and Roger. This position courted danger from both reform factions of the church and the emperor. One of the objectives of the reform had been to relieve prelates of their feudal obligations so that they could devote themselves to the *cura animarum*. Even the pugnacious Honorius II had criticized Oderisius for being more of a knight than an abbot. While noting how little interest there was among the German prelates of following Lothar to Italy in 1132, Wilhelm Giesebrecht says that it was very significant that in the monastery of Grafenrath near Aachen, the monks strongly disapproved of their abbot's following the king to Rome. This was the main reason they later deposed him.[6]

Of greater concern, Innocent's request for clerical participation in military campaigns on his behalf gave Lothar an opening to demand a redress of the Concordat of Worms, and a return to the customs and practices prior to the Concordat. Since bishops must carry out duties both to God and to Caesar, he argued, then they must be suitable both to God and to Caesar.[7] First at the Council of Liège in March, 1131, and then several

---

6 Wilhelm Giesebrecht, *Geschichte der deutsche Kaiserzeit* 4 (Braunschweig, 1877), p. 76.

7 Although Norbert was unwell, he still acceded to Innocent's request to participate in Lothar's first expedition to Italy. *Vita Norberti Archiepiscopi Magdeburgensis*, MGH SS 12:701: "Ad hanc expeditionem praecepto et obedientia domni Innocentii papae et vocatione domni imperatoris pater Norbertus accessit, corpore quidem invalido, sed spiritu prompto et intrepido." Lothar had called upon the archbishop of Arles to participate in his first expedition to Rome because of the obligation he owed to the empire. Having had no response, on the second expedition he invoked the archbishop's obligation to the church. ". . . cum militia tua nobis occurras daturus tam ecclesia quam imperio debitum consilium et auxilium." MGH D LoIII 8:146-147; cited by Hehl, "Die Zeit Lothars," p. 34 & n. 139; see also ibid., 35, 52; Bernhardi, *Lothar*, pp. 582-583.

times thereafter, Lothar tried to divorce the empire from the conditions placed upon it in the Concordat of Worms.[8] At Liège it took the verbal skills of St. Bernard to rescue Innocent and the Romans from their weak position. A more aggressive emperor might have persevered and won his point, but Lothar was reliant upon the church, and seemed genuinely to want to do his duty toward it. Innocent had many talented advisors who could convince him what his duty was.

Anaclet sent his letters to the German people and to Lothar and Richinza in care of Archbishop Adalbero of Bremen. In these letters he mainly tries to imply the regularity of his election, and he gives little indication of what he thinks the relationship between the emperor and the pope should be. The main clues are the assured authority with which he handles ecclesiastical business, and his allusion to Archbishop Adalbert of Mainz. Adalbert had been instrumental in securing Lothar's election, and the reference to him in the case of the bishop of Halberstadt was a signal of Anaclet's good will toward Lothar.[9]

Independent evidence of Anaclet's wish to bind the papacy to the empire is contained in a letter written to Lothar shortly after the election by members of several Roman families. They state that they frankly are not inclined toward Lothar, and have no desire that he increase his power. Nevertheless, they say, since Anaclet holds him in such high esteem, they consider it their duty to extend respect to him. If he wants the imperial crown, however, they admonish him that he must observe the Roman laws.[10]

In a second letter to Lothar written on May 15th, Anaclet reveals that

---

[8] Otto of Freising, *Chronicon* MGH SS 20:257; Ernaldus, *Vita Bernardi*, PL 185:271-272; Palumbo, *Lo Scisma*, pp. 402-403; Elphège Vacandard, "Saint Bernard et le Schisme d'Anaclet II en France," *Revue des Questions Historiques* 43 (1888), 61-126 at pp. 100-101.

[9] JL 8370; JL 8371. In his letter to Lothar Anaclet emphasizes that he wants the warm relationship, which Honorius had enjoyed with Lothar, to continue. PL 179:691: "Nos siquidem juxta decessoris nostri papae H[onorii] exemplum et vos et honorem vestrum singulari volumnus affectu diligere, vestrosque amicos seu inimicos nostros pariter deputare." The reference to Honorius is a sign of the continuity, which Anaclet saw between his and his predecessor's administration.

[10] This letter is reproduced by Arrigo Solmi in his book dealing with the medieval Roman Senate. *Il Senato Romano nell'alto Medio Evo (757-1143)* (Rome, 1944), pp. 229-234. Solmi also mentions a concession made by the Senate to Montecassino in 1127 dated *Tempore Honorii papae II*. Among the six important personages granting the concession are Petrus Pierleoni's brother, Leo, *consul Romanorum*, and Leo and Cencius Frangipani (pp. 227-228). Chodorow (*Christian Political Theory*, p. 37) is not entirely correct in asserting that after the election of Honorius, members of Petrus Pierleoni's family no longer received important political jobs, and therefore sought to gain control of the city by extra-governmental means. The document is further evidence of the cooperation of the Pierleoni with Honorius and the Frangipani. Solmi (p. 241) mentions how quickly the loyalty of the Roman people for Anaclet dissolved after Innocent and Lothar arrived in 1133. Their fickleness shows that their original support for Anaclet had no ideological significance. Solmi suggests that the factors, which moved them to switch sides were the displays and festivities attendant to Lothar's coronation, and imperial and papal gifts. See also Bernhardi, *Lothar*, p. 322.

he had taken the politically risky step of excommunicating Conrad of Swabia, the anti-king.[11] In the presence of a huge crowd of people at the Lateran Anaclet excommunicated Conrad, and the following day he asked the people to join him in a day of public prayer for Lothar. Anaclet wagered all by this move, committing himself unconditionally to Lothar without any reassurance from the emperor. The act also had the possible consequence of losing the allegiance of Milan, which just at that time was deciding which papal contender to support. Since Milan recognized Conrad, and since Anaclet had excommunicated him and Innocent had not, in that respect Innocent had an advantage over Anaclet. In spite of Anaclet's excommunication of Conrad, however, Milan recognized Anaclet, and Lothar did not.[12]

Besides indicating his support for Lothar against Conrad, in his second letter Anaclet also lays out his position on what he thought the relationship between the emperor and the pope should be. Far from Gregory VII's hierocratic views of the right order between *regnum* and *sacerdotium*, Anaclet identifies himself with the two powers' position of Gelasius expressed in *Duo Sunt*.[13] He states that there should be mutual respect and cooperation between the royal power and the sacred authority of the Roman church. Under such conditions, he says, the condition of the subjects will be secure. It is a position of moderation and accommodation couched in the spirit of the Concordat of Worms. There is no hint here of continuing to do battle with the emperor over investitures or anything else. Rather, it is an invitation to work together to the benefit of the church and the empire.

In his second attempt to win Lothar's recognition, Anaclet used every diplomatic nuance. Conscious of the queen Richinza's influence over the

---

[11] JL 8388; PL 179:706-707.

[12] Other considerations were more important to Milan. It had never readily accepted subjugation to Rome, and Anaclet was willing to acknowledge that Milan had a special status. Rather than requiring the archbishop to come to Rome to receive the *stola*, Anaclet sent it to Milan. Landulphus, the chronicler of Milan, indicates that there was no tension in recognizing both Conrad and Anaclet. *Historia Mediolanenesis*, Ludolfi de Sancto Paulo, MGH SS 20:45: "Honorio defuncto, Anacretus (sic), papa Romanorum secundus, huic Mediolanensi stolam per suos ydoneos nuntios, videlicet Iohanem Palistine episcopum et Beltramum subdiaconum Romanum mandavit. Quam stolam ipse Anselmus pontifex, clero et populo Mediolanensi circumstante et colaudante Anacletum papam eiusque legatos et legationem, reverenter suscepit. Pars vero sibi adversa inde magis detrahere cepit. At plenitudo cleri et populi ad eum concurebat, timorem quoque et reverentiam regi Curado et pape Anacreto ex dilectione portabat."

[13] JL 8388; PL 179:706-707: "Vicissim enim sibi et regalis potestas, et sacra Romana auctoritas mutua debent inter se diligentia respondere. Sane tunc tuta erit conditio subjectorum, si regnum et Ecclesia, diebus tuis, alterutro titulo compassionis arriserint, et ad culmen imperii regni tui moderatio latius extenditur, si ea re Dei gratiam pia fueris devotione sortitus." Palumbo, "La Cancelleria di Anacleto II," p. 17; Palumbo, *Lo Scisma*, p. 315; Hehl, "Die Zeit Lothars," p. 32; for a discussion of *Duo Sunt* see Walter Ullmann, *Medieval Papalism: The Political Theories of the Medieval Canonists* (London, 1949), p. 139, & n. 3 for references; by the same author, *The Growth of Papal Government in the Middle Ages: A study in the ideological relation of clerical to lay power* (London, 1955, 2nd ed., 1962, repr. 1965), pp. 21-26.

emperor, he wrote her a separate letter.[14] He asked her to urge the emperor to express his affection for the apostolic see more concretely, and specifically with regard to himself. He protested that he had loved the emperor for a long time, and he said that his desire was to preserve the emperor's honor, and even to increase it. He closed by asking Richinza for her prayers. By stating that he would like to increase the honor of the emperor, Anaclet was using a common ceremonial expression, but he may also have been hinting that he would be willing to be even more conces- sive than his predecessors. There was little more that he could do short of groveling to show how much he desired to continue the good relations between pope and emperor, which had persisted since the Concordat of Worms.

For the second time Anaclet was beaten by a few days in the competi- tion to win Lothar's recognition. The character of Innocent's letter of May 11th differed markedly from his letter of February 18th. This time he admitted the second election, and he argued, not entirely accurately, that his was the more legal. He said that he had been unanimously elected, and that he was sending Archbishop Walter of Ravenna to describe what had happened. Again he asked Lothar to come to Rome the following winter to receive the *dignitatis plenitudo*. It took Lothar until October to make his decision, which he announced at Würzburg surrounded by a large group of princes, bishops, and abbots, and many of Innocent's supporters. Since none of Anaclet's representatives were present, they must have known beforehand that their attendance would have made no difference to the outcome of the council.[15]

Without examining all of the diplomatic activity on each side to see why Lothar recognized Innocent rather than Anaclet, it is clear that both popes sought his recognition. The letters of Innocent and Anaclet to the German people, Lothar and Richinza demonstrate that Anaclet did not reject Lothar in order to establish an alliance with the Normans. Rather than refusing to accept the compromises at Worms because they worked to the detriment of the church, Anaclet implied that he might be even more flexible. He wanted a mutually beneficial relationship with the emperor in which the prerogatives of each would be respected.

Innocent's and Anaclet's conception of what they thought the authority of the pope and the emperor should be can to some degree be deduced even after the Council of Würzburg. The picture that emerges is not entirely what one might have anticipated. Innocent and Lothar frequently confronted one another over such issues as investitures and papal and imperial rights in Southern Italy. Anaclet, by contrast, demonstrated his

---

[14] JL 8389; PL 179:707-708.

[15] Innocent's letter is JL 7411; PL 179:55-56; for the council of Würzburg see *Annales Palidenses* MGH SS 16:78; see also Hehl, "Die Zeit Lothars," p. 31; Palumbo, *Lo Scisma*, p. 314; Hefele/Leclercq, *Histoire des Conciles*, 5:1, pp. 688-690.

respect for imperial authority by repeated requests to have Lothar call a council to adjudicate the papal elections. To ask Lothar to summon such a council even after the emperor had recognized Innocent was a daring, some might say, foolhardy move, since his decision could be assumed to have been foregone. But since Anaclet was not foolhardy, he must have believed that a council could not avoid recognizing the legality of his election. Another possible interpretation of his intentions is that he cynically made his proposals to gain time, and to delude people into believing that his election must have been legitimate since he was willing to have it examined. Knowing that Innocent would reject the proposal, he had nothing to lose. If by some outside chance, Lothar agreed to it over Innocent's opposition, he could always back down. More probably, he thought that Lothar genuinely wanted to make peace within the church, and that he was not so committed to Innocent that he was unwilling to open the issue again. Lothar's willingness to negotiate with Anaclet's representatives indicates that this was a reasonable calculation.

Anaclet's approach to Lothar during the emperor's march to Rome was not the first time that he had proposed that the elections of 1130 be arbitrated. In November, 1130, he had held a council at Canossa in the presence of the duke of Apulia and a large contingent from the oriental church. On February 25, 1131, he wrote an encyclical to the clergy and laity of Gaul, Burgundy, Aquitaine and Normandy describing what had taken place. He said that after condemning the schismatics, he and his supporters had stated that they were prepared to submit to canonical and ecclesiastical judgment. He called for the schismatics to meet them on an appointed day, but since they did not show up, he was now suggesting that they meet on October 1, 1131. He asked that the recipients of his letter transmit this message, and to declare that if his opponents were unwilling to come to Rome, he would be willing to meet them either in Milan or Ravenna. He promised to submit to the council's judgment.[16]

The council never was held, but Anaclet did not relinquish the hope for a hearing. He sent emissaries to Lothar at San Valentino, just outside of Viterbo, where Innocent and Lothar had met in April 1133 before proceeding to Rome. Norbert's biographer alleges that the emissaries first tried to gain Lothar's recognition by entreaties, arguments, and money, and when that failed, they asked for a tribunal to judge the elections. Some princes and others of the faithful were attracted to this suggestion, and seeing the danger, Norbert reported to Innocent what was happening. After debating the issue with his advisors, Innocent informed Lothar that the proposal was absolutely unacceptable.[17]

---

[16] The letter is edited by Paul Maria Baumgarten, "Ein Brief des Gegenpapstes Anaclet (II)," *Neues Archiv der Gesellschaft für ältere deutsche Geschicktskunde* 22 (1897), 576-578; see Palumbo, "La cancelleria di Anacleto II," p. 25.

[17] *Vita Norberti*, MGH SS 12:701-702.

The account of Norbert's biographer was written thirty years after the incident, and appears to conflate two separate attempts at negotiations. These are distinguished in a manifesto Lothar issued to the world from Rome pronouncing Anaclet's condemnation after the failure of the second attempt. It refers to a delegation sent by Anaclet to San Valentino with the request to receive justice. The delegation claimed the king could not deny justice to someone willing to receive it. Lothar, however, did not feel that he could grant the request without consulting the bishops and cardinals with Innocent. They responded that once the universal church had already made a decision, that decision could not be judged. Anaclet then made a second attempt to persuade Lothar to call a tribunal just before Lothar's coronation in Rome. This time he used the good offices of Peter of Porto and others of his followers. They promised to turn over hostages and fortifications as a guarantee of their intentions. Desiring peace, and wishing to avoid bloodshed, Lothar again asked the cardinals for their opinion. They gave their assent with the proviso that both sides give hostages and put their fortifications in the hands of the king. At this point Anaclet appeared to be stalling for time. Losing patience, Lothar called together his curia, and in their presence solemnly condemned Anaclet.[18]

In addition to Lothar's account and that of Norbert's biographer, there are other more distant sources. Falco of Benevento and Ernaldus, both hostile reporters, claim that the impetus came from Lothar rather than Anaclet. Falco reports that he heard that it was the emperor, who approached Anaclet because he wanted to put an end to the schism, but that nothing ever came of the attempt.[19] Ernaldus says that Anaclet studiously avoided any colloquium with the emperor, and was unwilling to make any concessions. Ordericus Vitalis relied on a source which presented an entirely different account. Ordericus reports that Lothar commanded Petrus either to give way to Innocent or to submit his election to judgment. Petrus gladly accepted the proposal and agreed to appear before Lothar for a trial by just men. Innocent, however, said that he would accede to the request only if the right of the papacy were restored to him. Angry with his response, Lothar handed over everything he held to Petrus. After seven weeks he withdrew, leaving the business unfinished. Marjorie Chibnall, Ordericus' editor, believes that his information was mainly incorrect because Falco and other contemporaries said that Anaclet had rejected the negotiations.[20]

[18] *In Anacletum papam sententia*, MGH Leges 2:81; MGH Const. 1:167; Palumbo, *Lo Scisma*, pp. 494-495; Hehl, "Die Zeit Lothars," pp. 34-35.

[19] Falco says: "Misit [Lothar] namque, sicut audivimus ad Anacletum, ut consilio Religiosorum virorum communicato adesset, & Spiritu Sancto mediante tanti erroris, & homicidi magnitudini finem poneret, quod Anacletus ille, sicut accepimus, facere contempsit." *Chronicon Falconis Beneventani, Rerum Italicarum Scriptores*, ed. Ludovicus Antonius Muratorius 5 (1724), p. 115; discussed by Palumbo, *Lo Scisma*, p. 496; Palumbo attributes Falco's hate for Anaclet primarily to Roger's ambitions in Benevento; p. 468, n. 2.

[20] Chibnall, *Ecclesiastic History* 6, pp. 426-428 & n. l. Anselm of Gembloux had a similar

Out of this tangle of tendentious and conflicting sources, the one which has the ring of reliability is Lothar's. Even though his statement in all probability was drafted by Norbert, it had to correspond to Lothar's perception of the negotiations and why they failed. Since Lothar would have gained no advantage by asserting that he rather than Anaclet had initiated the negotiations, there is no reason to doubt his word that the impetus came from Anaclet. What is open to doubt, however, is Lothar's judgment of why the negotiations failed. It may have seemed to him, or it may have been insinuated to him that Anaclet was negotiating in bad faith, but he could have been wrong.

The main reason for suspecting that he was wrong is that Anaclet would not have benefitted from the delay. The only thing which would have benefitted him was the tribunal itself, in which he thought that he could demonstrate that he was the rightful pope. Moreover, Anaclet had much to lose by making commitments and then not honoring them. His reneging would be proof that he was as duplicitous as his detractors had portrayed him to be. It is also improbable that men of the stature of Peter of Porto and possibly Peter of Pisa would have lent themselves to such a tawdry scheme.

The real reason for the breakdown in the negotiations was more probably the issue of fortifications. It is suspicious that up until this time, and as recently as the last few weeks, Innocent and his advisors had always used legal arguments to demonstrate why a tribunal could not judge the elections. They had asserted that a decision reached by the universal church could not be overturned, and they had reiterated the Gregorian position that a pope could be judged by no man.[21] Why all of a sudden were they willing to enter negotiations as long as both sides put up hostages, and placed their fortifications in the hands of the emperor? Innocent's advisors could have seen the issue of fortifications as a means of appearing to be receptive to having the elections examined, and of making Anaclet look bad at the same time. It is almost impossible to imagine that Peter of Porto and the other negotiators had agreed to turn over all of the fortifications of Rome to Lothar, and thus leave themselves totally vulnerable. Innocent, however, could readily do so, because whatever military support he had in Rome came from Lothar anyway. What

---

point of view, which suggests that there must have been at least one source which transmitted this version. MGH SS 6:384. Palumbo does not lend much credence to either of these sources. *Lo Scisma*, p. 497, n. 1.

[21] *Vita Norberti*, MGH SS 12:701: "summum pontificem hominis iudicio subdi vel tribunalibus assistere non oportere . . ." *In Anacletum papam sententia*, MGH Leges 2:81; MGH Const. 1:167: "Ipse vero, tamquam canonicarum sanctionum et institutionum ecclesiasticarum non ignari, universam Dei ecclesiam iam super hoc promulgasse sententiam. Petrum Leonis ac complices suos damnasse asserentes, quod erat universitatis non debere privatum fieri responderunt." For a description of Norbert as chancellor see Wolfgang Petke, *Kanzlei, Kapelle, und Königliche Kurie unter Lothar III. (1125-1137)* (Cologne, Vienna, 1985), pp. 303-322.

the Anacletians may have had in mind was to put under Lothar's command the fortifications in the area where the tribunal would be held. Lothar could then assure Anaclet's opponents that they could attend in all safety. The arrangement would have been similar to that which the cardinals had tried to work out at St. Hadrian's in 1130 so that the election could take place without pressure. Lothar saw nothing wrong with Innocent's insistence that both sides put all of their fortifications in his hands, but Anaclet could not accept such a condition. The negotiations thus broke down, and the Anacletians appeared to the world as having manipulated the whole process for their nefarious ends.

Lest this scenario prove to be too conspiritorial to be convincing, St. Bernard's letter to the bishops of Aquitaine exhorting them not to support Gerard of Angoulême and Anaclet reveals just how aware people were of the propaganda value to be gained from manipulative behavior.[22] Without defending the claim that the pope can be judged by no man, Bernard devoted a large portion of his letter to a rebuttal of Anaclet's appeal for a tribunal. He pointed out the duplicity and craftiness of the Anacletians in offering to submit to judgment. He reasoned that if Innocent refused, it would appear as though they had right on their side; if Innocent accepted, Bernard speculated that something might turn up which would make their case appear stronger. After advancing several other arguments designed to demonstrate that a council should not be called to adjudicate the election, Bernard concluded by asking to whom the schismatic would entrust Rome after having desired it for so long, and at last of having got it in his clutches. If Anaclet lost his case, Bernard argued, but still refused to give up Rome, the whole world would have been assembled for nothing.

Bernard's last argument may be an oblique reference to the concerns which preoccupied Innocent's advisors in the negotiations in Rome prior to the coronation. They probably reasoned that as long as Anaclet held the fortifications of Rome, there was no way that he could be deposed regardless of what the tribunal ruled. To assure that the one judged to be the true pope would be able to occupy his see and to control Rome, it was necessary that both sides relinquish their military power there. The problem with this reasoning, as Norbert and Innocent's other advisors well knew, was that Lothar was not a neutral party, and Anaclet could not possibly turn over all of his fortifications to him. St. Bernard was right to speak of craftiness, but he should also have suspected his own side. It was Norbert and in all probability Innocent's advisors who worked out the strategy to make Anaclet appear to be dishonest, and it was his reputation which suffered, not Innocent's.[23]

[22] Ep. 126, *Sancti Bernardi Opera*, ed. cit., 7, pp. 309-319.

[23] *Vita Norberti*, MGH 22 12:701-702: "Inde accidit, ut et tergiversatio Petri Leonis circa papatum rugientis frustraretur et ab universis sanum sapientibus de die in diem acceptior Innocentius haberetur." Bernhardi, *Lothar*, pp. 466-468.

Although Lothar questioned whether Anaclet was negotiating in good faith, no one ever asked the same question of him. Yet, if he was willing to reconsider a decision that he had solemnly made with the concurrence of the highest officials in his realm in the Council of Würzburg, it says little for the weight he attached to that commitment. He could hardly have based it on such a serious consideration that Innocent believed in a *modus vivendi* with the empire and that Anaclet did not, or that Innocent held more progressive views on ecclesiastical reform than Anaclet. If this recognition of Innocent was so tenuous, then no profound principle could have underlain it. Many reasons suggest that this was the case, and that Lothar saw no perceptible differences between Anaclet's and Innocent's attitudes toward the empire or ecclesiastical reform. He may even have found Anaclet's to be more compatible, since Innocent had already refused to entertain his propositions on investitures. In his willingness to have Lothar convene a tribunal, Anaclet attributed an authority to the emperor which Lothar could not have helped but to find congenial. It appeared to be a position similar to that accepted at the time of Constantine the Great, where the emperor was the overseer of external matters of the church, and the bishops the overseers of internal doctrine, dogma and faith.[24] This position harmonizes with Anaclet's statement in his second letter to Lothar, in which he emphasizes the cooperation between *regnum* and *sacerdotium*, and has overtones of the future conciliarist movement.

Prior to his arrival in Rome, Lothar had been primarily under the influence of Innocent's very persuasive supporters. Now the Saxon king was in the proverbial city, and he was talking with Anaclet's own eloquent spokesman. Peter of Porto no doubt presented a strong case for a tribunal, probably supported by the counsel of the learned Peter of Pisa. Lothar could observe the authority which Anaclet exercised in Rome, and he was acutely aware of the significance of being crowned in St. Peter's rather than in the Lateran. Moreover, his own military position was weak, and the German church had not strongly supported his expedition to Rome. What did he have to lose by calling a tribunal? It would add to his prestige, and if Anaclet's case were found to be the stronger, there were advantages in recognizing him as pope. These were probably Lothar's considerations, and he may even have been disappointed that the tribunal never was held. Ordericus' report may reflect the disenchantment in Lothar's camp.

Although Lothar is always described as pious, and is considered to have been no match for Innocent, in fact he was not so pusillanimous. He could be insistent upon his rights, as he was, for example, at Montecassino, but on occasion he could also be very deferential to the pope. A notable instance occurred at the Council of Liège in 1131, where he

---

24 Walter Ullmann, "Foundations of Medieval Monarchy," a lecture pub. in *The Sewanee Mediaeval Colloquium occasional papers* (Sewanee, 1982), 27-28.

performed the role of the strator upon Innocent's arrival. The ritual had
its origins in the Donation of Constantine, and thus suggested the acceptance of the principle that the pope held superior temporal authority in the
West. In his confrontations with Innocent Lothar did not concede this
authority, but the symbolism of the ceremony at least had propagandistic
effect, and the precedent later caused great consternation for Frederick
Barbarossa, who understood its implications. The ritual required the
emperor to go out to meet the pope, and, taking the reigns of his horse,
to lead him to their meeting place. Offering his arm, the emperor then
helped the pope to dismount.[25] Characteristically, however, after performing this act of obeisance, Lothar then threw Innocent's camp into a state
of disarray by demanding a return to the conditions preceding the Concordat of Worms.

Lothar's coronation has been seen as another example of his weakness
relative to the pope, but again, the picture is not so clear.[26] In 1133 Innocent was not in a strong position, and it was necessary to extend the
reward of the coronation to get Lothar to come to Rome to help him.
While Lothar was discussing reopening the whole issue of who was the
rightful pope with Peter of Porto, Innocent could only try to dissuade him
from acceding to Peter's arguments. The coronation ceremony itself did
not impugn imperial authority, or suggest that it came from the pope.
Although Lothar swore an oath, it was not an oath of fealty. It was similar
to the oaths which Henry V had sworn in 1111 and 1122, promising to
defend the lands of the church, and to recover those which had been
lost.[27]

After the ceremony, which lasted for several days, Lothar again
demanded the return of episcopal investitures. Norbert's biographer claims
that when Innocent was on the point of conceding, and when no one else
spoke out against the demand, Norbert rose and strode into the midst of
the throng. He delivered an impassioned oration, which convinced both
Innocent and Lothar to step back from a move which would have returned
the church to a state of bondage.[28]

Why then, when Innocent was obviously the vulnerable party, has the
coronation appeared to be a symbol of Lothar's weakness? One of the
main reasons is the depiction of various acts in the ceremony, which Innocent had painted on the walls of a room near the chapel of St. Nicholas in

---

[25] Suger records Lothar's performance of the ceremony at Liége; *Vie de Louis VI*, pp.
260-262. See also Eduard Eichmann, "Das Officium Stratoris et Strepae," *Historische
Zeitschrift* 142 (1930), 16-40; R. Holtzmann, *Der Kaiser als Marschall des Papstes: Eine Untersuchung zur Geschichte der Beziehungen zwischen Kaiser und Papst in Mittelalter* (Heidelberg,
1928); by the same author, "Zum Strator—und Marschalldienst," *Historische Zeitschrift* 145
(1932), 301-350; Palumbo, *Lo Scisma*, p. 400.

[26] Palumbo, *Lo Scisma*, p. 501.

[27] MGH Leges 2:49-50 for Henry's oath; ibid., 82 for Lothar's; also MGH Const. 1:168.

[28] *Vita Norberti*, MGH SS 12:702.

the Lateran palace. To interpret the paintings, he appended the verse:

Rex stetit ante fores, iurans prius Urbis honores:
Post homo fit papae, sumit quo dante coronam.[29]

In this inscription Innocent is boldly asserting that the emperor received the imperial crown in return for becoming his vassal. The verse appears to be a total distortion of what took place, however, for there is no evidence that Lothar became the vassal of the pope in the coronation ceremony, or even days later on June 8th when Innocent invested him with the lands of the Countess Mathilda. Innocent used a ring as a symbol of investiture, and Lothar agreed to pay a yearly tribute of 100 pounds of silver for the use of the lands. Mathilda's castellans and rectors were required to perform homage and to take an oath of fealty to the pope. Innocent extended the concession to Duke Henry of Bavaria and his wife with the stipulation that they also present homage and swear fealty. Lothar pointedly did not submit to these conditions, and therefore did not become a vassal of the pope.[30] The ceremony was an echo of an earlier age when investiture with a fief and becoming a vassal through homage had not yet coalesced into the institution of feudalism.

By these murals and the explanatory verse Innocent was claiming that the church holds both spiritual and temporal authority, and that through the act of coronation the emperor receives the empire as a fief from the papacy. Since it is obvious from his relations with Innocent that Lothar did not share this conception of the relationship between the empire and the papacy, the murals must have been painted after his death in 1137. By that time Innocent was much more secure, and was using imagery of every sort to portray his power. By blurring the ceremonies of 1133, he could plausibly insinuate that Lothar received his crown in return for becoming his vassal.

To show how much at variance this boast was from the actual situation in 1133, on the same day that Innocent invested Lothar with the lands of the Countess Mathilda, Innocent issued a clarification of the Concordat of Worms, generally referred to as the *Innocentianum*.[31] Lothar had complained that contrary to the agreement of the Concordat of Worms, German prelates had been taking possession of the *regalia* before they had been invested by the emperor. Innocent admonished them not to usurp

---

[29] Gerhart B. Ladner, *Die Papstbildnisse des Altertums und des Mittelalters* 2 vols. (Vatican City, 1941-70), vol. 2, pp. 17-22; Christopher Walter, "Papal Political Imagery in the Medieval Lateran Palace," *Cahiers archéologiques* 20 (1970), 166-169; ibid., 21 (1971), 123-133; Krautheimer, *Rome*, p. 151; Palumbo, *Lo Scisma*, p. 501 & n. 2; Ernst Kitzinger, "The Arts as Aspects of a Renaissance: Rome and Italy," *Renaissance and Renewal in the Twelfth Century*, ed. Robert Benson & Giles Constable with Carol Lanham (Cambridge, Mass., 1982), p. 644.

[30] MGH Const. 1:169; Bernhardi, *Lothar*, pp. 481-482; Palumbo, *Lo Scisma*, p. 503.

[31] MGH Const. 1:168-169; Robert Benson, *The Bishop Elect: A Study in Medieval Ecclesiastical Office* (Princeton, 1968), pp. 251-263.

the *regalia*, but to receive them from the emperor. Lothar had not always been so successful in his demands, but this time he was only insisting that the compromise between the papacy and the emperor already agreed upon be honored. Nevertheless, the recognition of imperial rights represented a victory for Lothar. He had now strengthened his position in Germany and Central Italy. What remained was to impose his authority in Southern Italy.

Here, he was less successful, but more because of Roger than because of Innocent. As a spur to coming to Innocent's aid, St. Bernard had written to Lothar that it was an insult to Caesar that a Norman occupied his lands.[32] Yet, the question of whose lands they were was still contentious, and once Lothar had conquered them both he and Innocent laid claim to them. Just as he did not back down at Montecassino, Lothar stood his ground in Apulia in 1137. He and Innocent agreed that Rainulf of Alife should be made the duke of Apulia, but each insisted that he had the right to invest Rainulf with his duchy. Since neither of them would capitulate, and since neither wished to push the affair to an open confrontation, they arrived at the novel solution of sharing the ceremony of investiture. The pope held one side of the banner, and the emperor the other.[33] Thus, the determination of who held authority over this land was left ambiguous.

Roger's claims to authority in Southern Italy were primarily the rights of the conqueror supplemented by the rights of inheritance. His main opponents were his powerful vassals, such as Rainulf of Alife and Robert of Capua. Both Honorius and Innocent allied themselves with these lords to extend the lands of St. Peter, but with minimal results, for these Normans just as much as Roger, wanted to extend their power.[34] Moreover, even though these vassals were occasionally victorious, in the long run Roger defeated them.

Although the Pierleoni had had good relations with Roger's family, Anaclet nevertheless waited until the end of March or the beginning of April 1130 even to write to Roger. It was not until September, well after Anaclet's second letters to Lothar and Richinza, that he met Roger at

---

[32] Ep. 139 to Lothar in 1134, *Sancti Bernardi Opera*, ed. cit., 7, pp. 335-336.

[33] *Chronicon Falconis Beneventani*, ed. cit., p. 122; Paul Fridolin Kehr, "Die Belehnungen der süditalienischen Normannenfürsten durch die Päpste (1059-1192)," *Abhandlungen der preussischen Akademie der Wissenschaften* Phil. Hist. Kl. Nr. I (Berlin, 1934), 41; Deér, *Papsttum und Normannen*, p. 222; Palumbo, *Lo Scisma*, pp. 572-573; Hehl, "Die Zeit Lothars," p. 40.

[34] For the lands of St. Peter see Peter Partner, *The Lands of St Peter: The Papal State in the Middle Ages and Early Renaissance* (Berkeley, Los Angeles, 1972). As an example of this unstable relationship, in 1127 and 1128 Honorius formed a coalition with Robert of Capua and Rainulf of Alife against Roger. The campaign failed, and Honorius accused his allies of *dolosas machinationes*. Rainulf had not fought aggressively against Roger because he had aspirations to Apulia, whereas Honorius regarded it *que iuris beati Petri est. Lib. Pont.* 2, p. 379; Deér, *Papsttum und Normannen*, pp. 199-200.

Avellino to work out the final terms for the coronation. Deér argues convincingly that the initiative came from Roger rather than from Anaclet, and that Roger dictated the terms of the agreement.[35] If Deér is correct, then it is further proof that Anaclet did not turn to the Normans as the traditional defenders of the pope because he did not accept the Concordat of Worms. He turned to Roger because his two overtures to Lothar had born no fruit. Lothar had not yet publicly declared his recognition of Innocent, but Anaclet knew that Norbert had Lothar's ear, and he knew the direction in which the winds were blowing in Northern Europe. Besides, he obviously did not consider Roger's coronation to be a bar to Lothar's ultimate recognition, since he continued to negotiate with him and to call for a tribunal. The reverse is also true, since Lothar considered holding a tribunal.

The bull of Roger's investiture of September 27, 1130 is unusual in that it was witnessed by only two cardinals, Matthew of St. Eudoxia and Saxo, the chancellor. The other witnesses were all members of the Pierleoni family. To some historians—Peter Partner and Josef Deér, for example— the arrangement between Anaclet and Roger appears to have been dynastic.[36] This view finds support in the famous purple diploma, which Roger issued to members of the Pierleoni family in January, 1134.[37] John Pierleoni approached Roger because Anaclet needed help in restoring order after Lothar's departure following the coronation in 1133. In return for becoming Roger's vassals, and putting their fortifications at his disposal, Roger gave them 240 pounds of gold, seven horses trained for war, and two Ethiopian slaves.

The purple diploma shows that like Anaclet, the Pierleoni family depended upon Roger. The coronation bull seems to indicate a direct family connection with the papacy, but it does not necessarily imply that the papacy had become the pawn of another Roman family in the way that characterized the papacy before the reform. Anaclet's cardinals were too independent to allow themselves to be coöpted by the Pierleoni, and since they continued to witness other bulls in large numbers, presumably they found nothing offensive about the witnessing of the coronation bull. Moreover, there is a direct parallel in the oath which Lothar swore to Innocent and his successors outside of the walls of the Lateran on the day of the coronation. Cencius Frangipani administered the oath, and his nephew and other noble Romans witnessed it.[38] None of Innocent's

---

[35] Deér, *Papsttum und Normannen*, pp. 203-204; the text of the agreement between Roger and Anaclet is recorded by Josef Deér, *Das Papsttum und die süditalienische Normannenstaaten 1053-1212* (Göttingen, 1969), Nr. XVII, pp. 62-63; see also Anaclet's letter, JL 8411; Partner, *The Lands of St Peter*, p. 169.

[36] Partner, *The Lands of St Peter*, p. 169; Deér, *Porphyry Tombs*, p. 121.

[37] Paul Kehr, "Diploma Purpureo di Re Roggero II per la Casa Pierleoni," *Archivio della R. Società Romana di Storia Patria* 24 (1901), 253-259.

[38] MGH Leges 2:82; MGH Const. 1:168: ". . . domino Cencio Fraiapane iuramentum computante, et Octone nepote suo ac ceteris nobilibus Romanis ibi existentibus."

cardinals objected to the secular involvement, and no one suggested that the papacy was in the hands of the Frangipani.

In the fall of 1137 St. Bernard requested that Roger set up a tribunal to decide which candidate should be pope.[39] Bernard had entertained the hope of achieving the more ambitious objective of peace between Roger and Innocent, but failing that, he settled for the tribunal. After his sharp arguments against Lothar's calling a tribunal, he was now willing to appear before one presided over by the ruler he usually dubbed "the tyrant." There was a difference between the two tribunals, however, in that the former would have been making a decision for the whole church, whereas Roger's was confined to his kingdom. Bernard and Innocent may also have been more receptive to a tribunal at this time, for things had not been going well for them. There had recently been a mutiny in the German army directed at Innocent and the cardinals, and Lothar had just marched home on less than amicable terms. For Anaclet, it was the first time that he had had an opportunity to state his case publicly, and he chose his most able spokesman. The tribunal will be discussed more fully below, but briefly, the outcome was that Bernard convinced Peter of Pisa to come over to the side which was supported by all of the notable monastic orders and church leaders. For his own reasons, Roger steadfastly continued to support Anaclet. The main thing to note about it in this context is that it implied recognition of Roger's sovereignty by all parties, and it showed that Innocent and his party were willing to submit a papal election to a temporal ruler for his approval. Just as St. Bernard feared that Anaclet would be unwilling to acquiesce in a negative ruling by a council summoned by the emperor, Innocent rejected Roger's ruling in favor of Anaclet.

Lothar died on the way home in 1137, and Anaclet in January of 1138. Innocent celebrated the Second Lateran Council in March, 1139, in which he excommunicated the king before whom his representatives had so recently stated their case. Rainulf of Alife died the following month, and Roger immediately invaded Apulia.[40] By June Innocent had organized a huge army, and headed toward San Germano. Roger sent legates to talk peace with him, and although Innocent received them, negotiations broke down over the disposition of the principality of Capua. Fighting erupted, and Innocent's army was badly beaten by Roger, the king's son, at the battle of Galuccio. Innocent, Haimeric, and many cardinals were captured. Like Paschal II in 1111, Innocent had to negotiate as a prisoner. In the treaty of Mignano of July 25, 1139, he and Haimeric did the best they could, avoiding investing Roger with Sicily, Capua and Apulia as a single fief, but nevertheless recognizing his sovereignty. More important than

---

[39] Ernaldus, *Vita Bernardi*, PL 185:294-295; *Chronicon Falconis Beneventani*, ed. cit., 5, p. 125; Palumbo, *Lo Scisma*, pp. 580-585.

[40] The main source for the following account is Falco of Benevento, op. cit., pp. 127-129.

any diplomatic nuances, Innocent could not avoid granting Roger the principate of Capua, belonging to Robert of Capua, who had just fought at his side. He reaped a bitter harvest from this concession, for the principate of Capua carried claims to Naples and to many counties of the Abruzzi, which were crucial to Rome's defense. Innocent suffered in future years when Roger came to the Abruzzi to make good his acquisitions.[41] Innocent also was forced to overlook his and Lothar's joint investiture of Rainulf of Alife, even though Rainulf's brother, Riccardo, had shared his defeat at Galuccio.[42] In the power politics of Southern Italy rights counted only if you could enforce them. Just as Anaclet helped to further Roger's ambitions when he failed to get support from the emperor, so now Innocent sacrificed his allies when his only other choice was indefinite captivity.

Innocent had no opportunity to insinuate graphically that Roger's office was conferred by the papacy in the way that he did with Lothar, even though in Roger's case there was more justification, since as king, he did become a papal vassal. Roger outlived Innocent, and would have made a mockery of any misrepresentation of their relationship. Like Innocent, Roger himself used art as propaganda. In the church of the Martorana in Palermo there is a mosaic in which Christ, not the pope is placing the crown on Roger.

In retrospect both popes helped to consolidate Norman power in Sicily and Southern Italy, but neither of them did so entirely willingly. Had there not been a split election, and had Anaclet been regularly elected, there is little doubt that Lothar would have recognized his election, and that he and Anaclet would have been on good terms. Because Innocent lost the battle for Rome and had to go North into exile, where his supporters had the confidence of the king, there was almost no possibility that Anaclet could obtain imperial recognition. Under the circumstances it is amazing that Lothar remained as independent as he did, and considered adjudicating the election after he had recognized Innocent, and Anaclet had invested Roger with his kingdom. The whole situation was radically changed from the days before the Concordat of Worms when a defenseless pope had to seek protection from the Normans in the face of a hostile emperor. The Normans at that time were not united, and they had not established a state which might threaten the papacy. By 1128 Roger was consolidating that state, and popes could either oppose it, or gain whatever advantage they could from it. Honorius did the former, and Anaclet the latter. Had Lothar recognized Anaclet, it is improbable that Anaclet would have been the pope responsible for bringing the Norman Kingdom into existence.

---

[41] Partner, *The Lands of St Peter*, pp. 174-177.

[42] Kehr (*Die Belehnungen*, p. 41-42) thinks that Innocent was totally cynical in ignoring his and Lothar's joint investiture of Rainulf. Deér, (*Papsttum und Normannen*, p. 222), however, emphasizes the fact that Rainulf had already died.

Chapter VIII

LEGALITY AS A FACTOR IN DETERMINING
THE OUTCOME OF THE ELECTION

PART 1: THE ELECTION

Both Innocent's and Anaclet's supporters claimed that the election of their candidate was legal. Anaclet's partisans obviously thought that they had the stronger case, because they continued to emphasize its legality until the tribunal held before Roger II in 1137 shortly before Anaclet's death to determine which contender was the rightful pope. Peter of Pisa presented the case for Anaclet, but then capitulated to St. Bernard's entreaties to recognize Innocent, not because he had been canonically elected, but in order to restore unity to the church. By contrast, although Innocent's backers never ceased to protest the validity of their candidate's election, knowing that they had a weak case, they quickly shifted to other criteria to demonstrate that he should be acknowledged as pope. St. Bernard's introduction of personal worthiness as a superseding criterion ultimately proved to be decisive. Even though Innocent's partisans minimized legal considerations, some scholars have nevertheless argued that Innocent was the legally-elected pope.[1] More have come to the opposite conclusion,[2] but probably most would agree with Klewitz that of the two not wholly canonical elections, that of Anaclet was the more legal.[3]

Haimeric had wanted the election of Innocent to be legal. In order to get Honorius elected in 1124 he had had to use the Frangipani to break up the election of Celestine, and then he had to bribe key people to agree to vote for Lambert (Honorius) in a mockery of canonical proceedings. He did not want to resort to similar measures again, and besides, such tactics might not have worked a second time. The cardinals were now alerted to the possibility of violence, and would probably not have been moved by bribes, since Haimeric had not made good on those of 1124. His most promising course of action was to secure the appointment of a sufficient number of sympathetic cardinals during the reign of Honorius to assure

---

[1] E.g., E. Amélineau, "Saint Bernard et le schisme d'Anaclet II (1130-1138)," *Revue des questions historiques* 30 (1881), 47-112.

[2] E.g., Bernhardi, *Lothar*, p. 301.

[3] Klewitz, "Das Ende," p. 212. For a brief description of the elections and an analysis of their legality see Bernard Jacqueline, *Episcopat et Papauté chez saint Bernard de Clairvaux* (Saint-Lo, 1975), esp. pp. 71-72.

the regular election of the next pope. He and Honorius did their best, but they were unable to create an adequate number to form a majority.

There is less disagreement over what actually happened in the elections than one might expect. The main differences lie in the comprehensiveness of the accounts; the Anacletians offered far more specific data than the Innocentians. To see what each side wanted to reveal I shall summarize their best statements—the letter to Diego of Compostella by an unknown writer—probably Pandulphus—for the Anacletians, and the letter to Norbert of Xanten from Bishop Hubert of Lucca for the Innocentians.[4]

The letter to Archbishop Diego of Compostella is dated April 10, 1130. It states that certain people advised that the dying pope be moved from the Lateran to the monastery of St. Gregory, and that their advice was followed. The cardinals and bishops who were present there agreed that since there was so much agitation within the city, they ought to consult with the pope about his successor. Some felt that the canon should be observed that while the pope was still living and had not been buried according to the traditions, no discussions should be held. Others felt that under such threatening circumstances, the canons should be tempered. Eventually the former opinion prevailed—"ut insepulto Papa nulla de personae alicuius electione mentio penitus haberetur."

Since the city continued to be rife with rumors, and agitation increased, the cardinals and bishops at St. Gregory's met and decided to elect eight cardinals who would discuss the election and then elect a new pope. If they could not agree on a candidate, others should join them so that there would be concord on one person. There were also long discussions on where the election should be held. They agreed that St. Hadrian's would be a suitable location if they could gain control of the fortifications. Two cardinals from the committee of eight were dispatched to secure them, but they were thwarted by certain bishops accompanied by guards. Both cardinals regarded the incident as a signal of bad intent, and the "pars maior et sanior ad praedictum monasterium non sunt amplius ausi redire."

On February 13th, with the pope sinking, the doors to the monastery were closed, and no other cardinals were permitted to enter. Within, another meeting was held at which were present very few cardinals and four bishops "quibus nulla vel minima est in electione potestas." Again it was agreed that until the pope was buried with the proper funeral rites, and until the other brothers, especially the committee of eight, had been

---

[4] J. M. Watterich has collected the major sources describing the two elections. *Gesta pontificum Romanorum* 2 (Leipzig, 1862), pp. 174-192. The letter to Diego is on pp. 187-190, and that to Norbert pp. 179-182. Watterich thought that Peter of Pisa wrote the letter to Diego, but it is now thought that it was Pandulphus. For a detailed comparison between the letters see Luigi Pellegrini (Mario da Bergamo), "La duplice elezione papale del 1130: I precedenti immediati e i protagonisti," vol. 2 of *Contributi dell'Istituto di Storia Medioevale; Raccolta di studi in memoria di Giovanni Soranzo* (Milan, 1968), pp. 265-302. The article concludes with a list of the cardinals who supported Innocent, and those who supported Anaclet, divided into electors and non-electors.

summoned, the election could not be discussed. But then, to the astonishment of the writer, while those surrounding the pope proclaimed that he was still living, his body was wretchedly borne away by a group of laymen. He was not even placed on a bier, nor were obsequies observed. Rather, he was lowered into the most mean grave as though he were a vile beast.

The writer then both describes and judges the election by his choice of words. He says that with the body uncovered, and in contempt of their oath, Haimeric and his followers, drunken with malice and craftiness, fraudulently gathered together. Without summoning the other cardinals, and in excessive haste, they elected Gregory of St. Angelo as pope. Peter of Pisa, who was present, and who is thought by some to have been the writer of this letter, objected to the shady proceedings. Then Innocent, who is characterized as an idol, hurried to the Lateran accompanied by a few laymen bearing Honorius' body: "ibique corpore Pontificis non sepulto, immo in vilis tumuli angustia sine cooperimento et obsequio male deposito," the pope/idol was taken swiftly to a palace. There he was concealed by the Frangipani until they came over to Anaclet.

Turning to Petrus' election, the writer says that with the exception of the five cardinals who wanted Gregory to be pope, the *priores* cardinals along with the other cardinals to whom the election pertained, gathered together with the clergy and people of Rome at St. Mark's to await the death of Honorius. They had expected to bury him according to the ancient Roman customs, but when they heard that Honorius had already died and been buried, "deliberato consilio, expetente populo cum honoratorum consensu pari et communi voto," they unanimously elected Petrus Pierleoni. Peter of Porto consecrated him in St. Peter's on February 23rd.

The writer contends that the Roman church recognized that Anaclet had been canonically elected, and regularly installed, and that it rejected Innocent. In conclusion, he asserts that what he has said is true, and that his readers should not be misled by the lies of the schismatics, who have been excommunicated.

The orientation and emphasis of the letter of Bishop Hubert of Lucca to Norbert of Xanten are consciously and markedly different from the letter to Diego. Without mentioning any of the preliminary meetings or their decisions on the procedures to be followed in electing a new pope, Hubert says that the cardinals at St. Andrea (a small church next to St. Gregory's where the discussions took place) agreed that a committee of eight persons should be constituted to elect the new pope. The members were two cardinal bishops: William of Palestrina and Conrad of Sabina; three cardinal priests: Peter of Pisa, Peter Rufus, and Petrus Leonis; three cardinal deacons: Gregory of St. Angelo, Jonathan, and the chancellor, Haimeric. When Honorius died, the person, "quae ab eis communis eligeretur vel a parte sanioris consilii" would be accepted by all as pope.

Then the bishop of Palestrina with the others decreed that if anyone should not accept such an election, he should be subject to anathema.

Moreover, if anyone attempted to elect another, they said that the election should not be recognized. Petrus Leonis consented to this ruling, and added that he would rather be submerged in an abyss than that he should be the cause of any offense to the church. With the discussion thus concluded, the electors agreed to reconvene later.

However, Petrus Leonis and Jonathan left the monastery "ut corvus ille vel submersus vel carnium ingluvie detentus," and they scorned returning to the others. They gathered together their supporters and insisted that Honorius, whom they believed to be already dead, show himself at a window to prove otherwise. Honorius was propped up in front of the window, but died that night. Because of the tempests brewing around the church, the funeral rites were celebrated, and then four members of the committee elected a fifth—Gregory of St. Angelo—who accepted the honor reluctantly. Other clergy also participated in the election, but Peter of Pisa along with Petrus and Jonathan, who were not there, did not. The group around Petrus and Jonathan elected Petrus, who, Hubert contended, had long coveted the office, and who had gained allies toward that end by distributing largess. Peter of Porto "proh dolor!" enmantled him with the red cape.

Thereafter, there was a terrible shedding of blood, much destruction, and the seizing of sacred images to pay the fighters even though Petrus' brother, Leo, and Leo Frangipani had sworn not to cause trouble, and to accept whomever the church elected. Innocent's followers, however, accepted the counsel of religious and orthodox catholics from Tuscany, Lombardy, and the ultramontane. They declared Petrus Leonis to be a villain, a schismatic, and a heretic, and embraced Innocent as their father and highest pontiff.

The tone of the two letters became typical of the propaganda disseminated from each side. While the letter to Norbert minimized legal aspects of the proceedings, that to Diego emphasized them. And while the letter to Diego was highly critical of actions—e.g., the burying of Honorius—the letter to Norbert concentrated on character. Anaclet was corrupt and ambitious, while Innocent was humble and self-effacing. The treatment of the committee of eight is especially indicative. Neither letter reveals who originated the idea, but both sides accepted what they stated were its functions and constraints. There they differed, however, for the letter to Diego said that there must be unanimity among its members, while the one to Norbert said that the vote of the *sanior pars* was sufficient. The proviso has all the earmarks of something constructed after the fact, since it is highly improbable that being in the minority, Petrus and Jonathan would have agreed to such a condition.

The proposals of William of Palestrina mentioned only in the letter to Norbert also have the ring of justification created after the fact. They anticipate that there would be some who would not be satisfied with the election, and more pointedly, that those who were not might even attempt to elect another. But why would William have foreseen such a contingency? One possibility is that he doubted that Haimeric could improvise a legal election of his candidate. If people objected to it, they would ipso facto be struck with anathema. If they nevertheless proceeded to elect another, that election would be invalidated in advance. Another possibility is that Hubert of Lucca simply fabricated William's proposals to support the legitimacy of Innocent's election. The letter to Diego would not have mentioned them because they never were made. In either case the proposals were not formulated to ensure a regular election, but only to vindicate Innocent's. It is ironical that the same forces which contrived a second election in 1124, insisted on the priority of the first in 1130.

The description of the departure of Petrus and Jonathan in each letter is particularly revealing. Hubert neglects to state that the two cardinals had been dispatched to find a safe place in which to hold the election, and that they encountered threats. He implies that they went out to gorge themselves, and that they did not feel like returning. The choice of *corvus* to describe Petrus was particularly apt because the name was based on the fable of an originally white bird which had been changed to black as punishment for treachery. The description of the incident both conceals the obstacles to an open election interposed by Haimeric and his followers, and casts aspersions on Petrus' character.

Hubert describes the dramatic window scene, while the other letter does not. The latter, however, states that the doors of St. Gregory's were closed as the pope's life was ebbing away, while the former does not. It also omits mention of another resolution that the pope must be properly buried before discussions could be held, and of the allegation that those surrounding Honorius continued to proclaim that he was living even after he had died. Likewise, Hubert does not describe Honorius' undignified burial, the hasty and fraudulent election without notification of the other cardinals, Peter of Pisa's objection, and the unseemly proceedings at the Lateran. Vague at this point, Hubert simply states that the funeral rites were celebrated. The sketchiness could be attributed to lack of information since Hubert was not present, but if there were nothing to hide, Haimeric or someone else who had been there could have informed him about such important proceedings.

The letter to Diego is obviously based on an eyewitness account, almost certainly that of Peter of Pisa. One might therefore argue that the description was distorted to Anaclet's advantage. Against this contention is the overwhelming evidence of Peter of Pisa's integrity, recognized to the end even by St. Bernard. At the final session of the tribunal before Roger II held in Sicily Ernaldus, the biographer of St. Bernard, reports that the abbot said, "Scio, Petre, te virum sapientem et literaturm esse et utinam sanior pars et honestiora te occupassent negotia."[5] Bernard considered it

---

[5] Ernaldus, *Vita Bernardi*, Lib. II, PL 185, pt. 1, c. 7, pp. 294-295; Watterich, *Gesta 2*, p. 246.

to be a great boon to the church to bring Peter back into the fold. Thus, there is a presumption of truth in the letter to Diego.

Not surprisingly, Hubert only refers briefly to Anaclet's election, and instead concentrates on the violence which ensued. By-passing Innocent's lack of support in Rome, Hubert specifies that his strength lay in the North. The letter to Diego, as would be expected, describes Anaclet's election in detail, stressing the great number of persons present, and their disposition to observe all of the correct procedures. The reason that they did not do so had nothing to do with their volition, it claims, but with the quick burial of Honorius.

Summing up the intent of the two letters, the letter to Norbert wanted to show that Innocent had been legally elected because the majority—and indeed the *sanior pars*—of the committee of eight voted for him. Their haste was justified by the threatening conditions. Anaclet was an ambitious and corrupt man who had paid his followers to fight in order to bring to fruition his long campaign to become pope. The letter to Diego reveals that the Anacletians believed that the Innocentians had resorted to the most iniquitous acts to impose Innocent as the head of the church. They regarded his clandestine election as a farce, and accentuated their belief that Anaclet's election was canonical, and that their position could be verified because the proceedings had taken place in the open.

These, then, are roughly the two positions. There are many other descriptions of the elections, a great number of which have been collected by Watterich. Most of them are brief notations, but the following illustrate some of the issues which will be raised concerning the elections. The life of Innocent from the early fourteenth century manuscript of Bernard Guidonis is notable for its inaccuracies. It claims that Innocent was elected by a majority of the cardinals, and Anaclet by a minority, a point which St. Bernard would make at least once, even though he knew that it was false. It also lays all of the blame for the violence following the election on Anaclet and his family.[6] The cardinal of Aragon, using different papal registers, books from the apostolic camera, and other books and chronicles, expressed the position usually maintained by Innocent's supporters. He said that Innocent was elected not by the majority, but by the better and sounder part.[7] Falco of Benevento, who showed no signs of hostility toward Anaclet at this time, mentions that Anaclet's electors went through the formality of declaring Innocent's election to be null before proceeding

---

[6] ". . . Hic prius dictus est Gregorius, fuitque Diaconus Cardinalis S. Vincentii, qui a majori parte Cardinalium, & Petrus Leonis a minori ad Papatum dispariter eleguntur; Gregoriusque Innocentii, Petrus Leonis Anacleti nomine alterantur. Sed Petro Leonis apud S. Petrus, ob parentelae suae fortitudinem, commorante, ipsam Ecclesiam cum manu armata, & per violentiam habuit, & aureum Crucifixum & pendentes coronas cum toto thesauro auri & argenti & lapidibus preciosis tollens, expoliavit . . ." A. L. Muratori, *Antiquitates Italicae medii aevi* 3 (Milan, 1783-1742), pp. 433-434.

[7] "Sed melior & sanior eidem Innocentio, qui majoribus studiis et meritis juvabatur, adhaesit." Muratori, op. cit., 3, p. 434.

to a new one. He also asserts that it was Leo Frangipani who started the violence after the election, and that Petrus' family only responded to this provocation.[8]

The annals of the Grande Chartreuse are particularly interesting because Guigo, its abbot, knew Innocent and Anaclet, at least by reputation, before they were elected. Guigo was fearless and incorruptible, even criticizing Innocent's administration after he had recognized it, but his relationship with St. Bernard was so close that he could not be dispassionate in his judgment of the election. Haimeric visited the monastery shortly after Innocent went into exile, so that he had the opportunity to tell the monks his version of what happened directly. Nevertheless, the annals reflect some attempt to weigh other reports heard at Chartreuse. For example, the author states that Innocent was elected before Honorius' death was announced, and he notes that although some say that the election took place on the day of the pope's death, others assert that it was not until two days later. Other notable features of the account are: (1) It states that Anaclet's electors declared Innocent's election to be null. (2) It mentions the council called by Bishop Hugh of Grenoble soon after the election, in which Anaclet was anathematized. (3) It quotes the part of Guigo's biography of Bishop Hugh of Grenoble in which Guigo mentions that both Anaclet and his father had shown great respect to Hugh. However, because justice demanded it, Guigo continues, Hugh did not allow himself to be influenced by this friendship.[9]

The points brought up in these and other sources describing the elections will be discussed in different contexts, but for an understanding of what happened at the election and why, the letters to Norbert and Diego are still the most revealing. An analysis of their contents suggests the following account. Haimeric did not relinquish his ambition to select the new pope, even though he did not have a majority of supporters among the

---

[8] "Deinde, Innocentii illius electionem damnantes, Anacleti Pontificis electionem confirmabant. Cumque Leo Frangenspanem, qui partem Innocentii sequebatur, electionem Anacleti audivisset, coepit Romanos cives fideles suos et amicos exhortari, ut ejus faverent auxilio. Inde Leo germanus praefati Anacleti, aerario aperto, totum fere populum Romanum rogavit, ut juxta vires fratris electionem tueretur: quod et factum est. Sicque ab utraque parti graviter civile bellum saevissimum incoeptum est." Bouquet, *Recueil* 15, pp. 344-345.

[9] D. Carolo Le Couteulx, *Annales Ordinis Cartusiensis ab Anno 1084 ad Annum 1429*, 1 *1084-1141* (Monstrolii Typis Cartusiae, S. Marie de Pratis, 1888), pp. 332-335. The part quoting Guigo's life of Hugh is as follows: "'Defuncto Honorio, cum per tyrannicam et schismaticam rabiem, non suis meritis sed cognatorum et fratrum fultus praesidiis, Petrus Leonis adversus vestram Innocentiam (scribebat Hugh ad Innocentium II Papam) quae beatae memoriae Honorio successerat, emersisset; . . . Et certe tam Petrus quam pater ejus, sancto viro multas olim venerationes et obsequia praestiterant, sed beatus homo in tali negotio, id est ubi periclitabatur justitia, nec amicitia flectebatur nec potentia terrebatur.' Haec Guido." Concerning Haimeric, p. 335: "Interea vero cum Innocentius Papa peregrinans esset in via, et Valentinae, ut diximus, a sancto Hugone visitatus fuisset, Haymericus cardinalis et S.R.E. cancellarius sanctum Episcopum usque Gratianopolis forsan comitatus, ad Majorem tunc potuit Cartusiam ascendere, ad quam constat ipsum aliquando ascendisse Guigonem invisendi gratia, cujus prudentiae et sanctitatis fama longe lateque tunc diffundebatur."

cardinals. He used the agitation which had arisen throughout Rome as news of Honorius' illness spread as an excuse to bring the moribund pope to the monastery of St. Gregory. There, in the Frangipani preserve, he would be safe. Next, Haimeric convinced the cardinals present to agree to the formation of the committee of eight cardinals to act for the full college, ostensibly to insure that the election would take place quickly without outside interference. By sending Petrus Pierleoni and Jonathan out to secure the fortifications of St. Hadrian's, only one member of the committee was left who was not solidly in his camp—Peter of Pisa. Peter had at first not objected to the highly irregular proceedings in 1124, and it was hoped that he would not object to those which would be less so now.

St. Hadrian's was on the borderline of the area dominated by the Frangipani, and the guards were under their orders to frighten Petrus and Jonathan away. No one at St. Gregory's would know why they did not return, so that the remainder of the committee of eight would have no qualms about going ahead without them. The other expedients such as the hasty burial of Honorius and the neglect of summoning the other cardinals would be accepted because the volatile situation necessitated quick action. The only thing that went wrong with the plan was that Peter of Pisa objected, and left to tell the others gathered at St. Mark's about the debasing scene he had just witnessed.

In the meantime, Gregory of St. Angelo was rapidly led to the Lateran where he was acclaimed Innocent II. Immediately thereafter he returned to Santa Maria in Pallara on the Palatine to the protection of the Frangipani. Even though the plan had not worked out completely, at least Haimeric had ensured that Innocent would have some legal advantages. It is estimated that seventeen cardinals supported him, and that four of the six cardinal bishops had voted for him.[10]

At St. Mark's Petrus and Jonathan rallied the cardinals in the vicinity— the majority. They had become convinced because of their reception at St. Hadrian's and by past experience that the Frangipani would not allow a free election to take place at St. Gregory's, so they decided to hold one elsewhere. St. Mark's was in the center of the city at the foot of the Capitoline. It was close both to the Frangipani and Pierleoni strongholds, and was therefore a reasonably neutral and safe location.

When the cardinals, their numbers greatly augmented by the secular and religious clergy of the area and by the notable laymen, heard that Honorius had died and that Innocent had already been secretly, and therefore illegally, elected, they held their own election. They had wanted to observe the customary three-day interval during which the obsequies of the dead pope would be performed, but Honorius' quick burial gave them no choice. With or without declaring Innocent's election to be null and

---

10 See n. 28, ch. I. The cardinals were never specified, and there have been various estimates of their identity and number. Palumbo has determined that there were 17.

void (disputed) Petrus Pierleoni nominated an unidentified cardinal, who, it is suggested, may have been Peter of Porto. This person humbly declined the honor, and then the cardinals unanimously elected Petrus as Anaclet II.

Anaclet was consecrated in St. Peter's by Peter of Porto, and Innocent was consecrated by Cardinal bishop John of Ostia. Since it was traditionally the function of the cardinal bishop of Ostia to consecrate popes, Innocent had the advantage over Anaclet in that respect. The impact of the magnificence of a consecration in St. Peter's would not compensate for this deviation in the procedure of Anaclet's installation in the subsequent debates. Thus, the formalities of the election were completed, and each side then began the struggle by force and by word to have its candidate accepted by the church at large. Anaclet won the battle for Rome, but Innocent would win the battle for most of the rest of Europe in spite of what appeared to be irreparably undermining weaknesses in his legal position.

Chapter IX

LEGALITY AS A FACTOR IN DETERMINING
THE OUTCOME OF THE ELECTION

PART 2: THE BATTLE OF THE WORD

Although the letter to Diego tried to minimize the special competency of the cardinal bishops in the election of a pope, the Innocentians had some ground for emphasizing that four of the six bishops had voted for Gregory. The intent of the electoral decree promulgated by Nicholas II in 1059 was not that the bishops alone should choose the candidate, but it clearly states that they should have a special role.[1] The situation in 1130, however, was complicated by the existence of a corrupted text which stated that the cardinal bishops only had the right of approving the election at the demand of the cardinal clerics and of the Roman people. This text, which accentuated the role of the emperor, had found its way into such Italian collections as those of Deusdedit, Anselm of Lucca, Bonizo of Sutri, and the abbey of Farfa.[2]

In practice, by the beginning of the twelfth century the cardinal priests had transformed their right of ratification into the right of election, and the role of the cardinal bishops had been reduced to that of approving or rejecting the choice made by other cardinals. Peter of Porto, himself a cardinal bishop, emphasizes this limited function in his letter to the four bishops who voted for Innocent. In demonstrating why the election in which they had participated was not legal, he says: "Finally, it was neither for you nor for me to elect, but rather to reject or approve him who had been elected by our brethren.[3] It is clear from chapter 1 of *Distinctio* 79 of

---

[1] MGH Const. 1:537: (end of the *Narratio*) "Unde, si placet fraternitati vestre, debemus auxiliante Deo futuris casibus prudenter occurrere et ecclesiastico statui, ne rediviva —quod absit—mala prevaleant, in posterum providere." (*Ordo electionis*) "Quapropter instructi predecessorum nostrorum aliorumque sanctorum patrum auctoritate decernimus atque statuimus: ut, obeunte huius Romane universalis ecclesie pontifice, inprimis cardinales episcopi diligentissima simul consideratione tractantes, mox sibi clericos cardinales adhibeant; sicque reliquus clerus et populus ad consensum novae electionis accedant, ut—nimirum ne venalitatis morbus qualibet occasione subrepat—religiosi viri praeduces sint in promovendi pontificis electione, reliqui autem sequaces."

[2] For analysis of the papal decrees see Jacqueline, *Episcopat et Papauté*, pp. 72-73; Hans Georg Krause, *Das Papstwahldekret von 1059 und seine Rolle im Investiturstreit*, Studi Gregoriani 7 (Rome, 1960); R. Holtzmann, "Zum Papstwahldecret von 1059," *Zeitschrift der Savigny-Stiftung für Rechtsgeschichte* KA 27 (1938), 135-153; Elphège Vacandard, "Saint Bernard et le Schisme d'Anaclet II en France," *Revue des questions historiques* 43 (1888), pp. 69-70, n. 3.

[3] Peter of Porto's letter written in Anaclet's defense is recorded by William of Malmes-

Gratian's *Decretum* that Peter was not denying episcopal rights only to strengthen his own case. Gratian, who was writing his important collection of canon law during the period of the schism (it was published about 1140), reflects what the interpretation of the decree of 1059 had become by that time. He does not attribute any special prerogatives to the cardinal bishops, but only states that a pope must be elected by the cardinals.[4]

Although St. Bernard and other supporters tried to make the vote of the majority of the bishops for Innocent an issue, and emphasized the discrepancies in Anaclet's election—that he was elected second, that the conclave had allegedly failed to declare Innocent's election to be null and void before proceeding to a new one, and that he had not been consecrated by the cardinal bishop of Ostia—even they knew that their arguments carried little legal weight.[5] No one believed that the electoral decree of 1059 sanctioned carrying on an election in secret without announcing the death of the previous pope no matter what the cardinal bishops did. It was only by suppressing the true nature of Innocent's election that any sort of legal case at all could be made for him. The divergences in the procedures of Anaclet's election were all products of the extraordinary proceedings of Innocent's. Anaclet was elected openly by the majority of the cardinals, and his election was approved by the Roman people. In spite of the vagueness of the decree, those factors appeared to encompass its intent.

Both sides initiated a campaign to convince the church and secular leaders that their candidate was the true pope. Innocent's supporters were somewhat quicker to act, and were ultimately far more successful. Anaclet may have yielded the advantage of precedence to Innocent because he thought that the first order of business was to secure Rome. His chancery was also less experienced than Innocent's, even though his chancellor, Saxo, was competent, and had been involved in such curial business as the negotiations resulting in the Concordat of Worms. Haimeric, however,

---

bury in his *Historia Novella*. *The Historia Novella by William Malmesbury*, tr. K. R. Potter (London, Edinburg, Paris, Melbourne, Toronto, New York, 1955), p. 8. It is also edited in MGH SS 10:484-485 and PL 179:1397-1399.

[4] *Corpus Iuris Canonici*, ed. Aemilius Friedberg (Graz, 1959), p. 276, Dist. 79, c. 1: "Si quis apostolicae sedi sine concordi et canonica electione cardinalium eiusdem ac deinde sequentium clericorum religiosorum intronizatur, non Papa uel Apostolicus, sed apostaticus habeatur." In the *Polycarpus*, a collection of canons compiled by Gregory, Cardinal priest of St. Grisogono c. 1111, Gregory emphasizes the role of his own order, the cardinal priests, in papal elections. Since Gregory was functioning in Rome, and was involved in the turmoil there during the Investiture Contest, his collection would have been well known to the participants in 1130. The collection was disseminated into Italy and France, influenced various canonical collections, and finally was incorporated in the *Decretum*. See Uwe Horst, *Die Kanonessammlung Polycarpus des Gregor von S. Grisogono: Quellen und Tendenzen* (Munich, 1980), pp. 2-7, 58-59.

[5] Palumbo suggests that in the opinion of the conclave the formality of declaring Innocent's election null and void seemed unnecessary because there was no legally elected pope. *Lo Scisma*, pp. 212-213; as already mentioned, the *Annales Ordinis Cartusiensis* state that Anaclet's electors did declare Innocent's election to be null.

was a seasoned adminstrator with broad contacts, and with many church-men in his debt for past favors. Moreover, since he had been Honorius' chancellor, his continuity in office seemed to imply legitimacy to the pope he served.

Anaclet's major assets were the active support of the most distinguished members of the college of cardinals, especially Peter of Porto and Peter of Pisa, and the allegiance of most of the clergy and laity of Rome.[6] Within a short time Anaclet was able to subdue the violence, and to gain control of the city. The Frangipani abandoned Innocent and came over to his side.[7] To Anaclet and his supporters, it must have seemed as though he had triumphed. He occupied St. Peter's, and he controlled Rome. Innocent was forced to flee, first to Pisa, and then to France. Even there, where Innocent had his chief support, monasteries and bishoprics were bitterly divided, and Anaclet had a "multitude" of adherents.[8] Rallied by the redoubtable bishop Gerard of Angoulême, Aquitaine remained loyal to Anaclet until 1135 when Duke William IX capitulated to the irresistible emotional appeal of St. Bernard.

The semblance of victory was fleeting, however, as Anaclet slowly lost the battle for recognition. Outside of Rome, rather than dissipating, the schism deepened. Although Roger II of Sicily was never moved by the oratory of the formidable abbot of Clairvaux, and Scotland remained intransigent, Milan succumbed to it. In the councils of Étampes, Würzberg and Liège Louis VI and Lothar III recognized Innocent, and Henry I of England also reluctantly joined the groundswell. Later, I shall analyze in greater detail why Innocent was so successful; here I simply wish to determine the effect of legal factors.

Whether men of authority thought that the legality of the election should be decisive, or even weighed heavily, is still disputed. Schmale does not take Peter of Porto's legal grounds for recognizing Anaclet seriously, and in general he belittles the legal aspects of the election of 1130 as well as those of 1124. As long as the election was suitable, he contends, the reform papacy did not worry too much about legal procedure. The fulfillment of the "letter of the law," he contends, was less important than the man and the good he could do for the church.[9] Both White and Palumbo disagree. White asserts that the pope was thought to hold his power directly from Christ, not by virtue of his personal worthiness, but on the basis of his legal election to the episcopal see of Rome. One of the fundamental tenets of the Gregorian program, he avers, was the idea that the papal office stood above criticism from any human source on the basis

---

[6] See Peter of Porto's letter, *The Historia Novella*, ed. cit., pp. 7-9; for the reputation of Peter of Pisa as a theologian as well as an expert on canon law see Palumbo, *Lo Scisma*, p. 205.

[7] Bernhardi, *Lothar*, p. 311.

[8] Palumbo, *Lo Scisma*, p. 337.

[9] Schmale, *Studien zum Schisma*, pp. 58, 123, 147, n. 4, 226.

of the morality of the occupant.[10] Bernhardi agrees that the legality of the
election was critical, and thinks that by his clever maneuvering Haimeric
forced a double election which presented him with the opportunity for
reproaching his opponents with the charge of having acted illegally and
arbitrarily.[11] In spite of the fact that both sides defended their candidates
on legal grounds, however, Bernhardi believes that in the double election,
as in other really important cases concerning the church and the state,
power more than law became the deciding factor.[12]

Though power may, in fact, have turned out to be the final arbiter,
those scholars who argue that the church regarded the legality of the election to be of the utmost importance are correct. The leading figures of the
reform papacy realized that if the selection of the pope were to be determined by the church rather than by the emperor, powerful Roman families or any other interest, and if the best man were to be chosen rather
than he who could afford to buy the office, there must be a prescribed
procedure to insure that control. This is the fundamental reason why the
decree of 1059 was drafted. It was deficient in that it did not deal with
such contingencies as a divided vote or a split election, but clearly its
objective was to assure that the cardinals would elect the pope without
outside interference or manipulation. As the *Narratio* of the decree of
1059 says, the church must provide for the ecclesiastical state in order to
prevent the recurrence of evils which have arisen in the past.[13]

Ivo of Chartres delineates more specifically what procedures are acceptable if a candidate is to be recognized as pope. In his *Decretum* he says
that if anyone by money or by human favor, or by popular or military
tumult, without the concord and canonical election and benediction of the
cardinals, bishops, and then of the following religious orders will have
been enthroned in the apostolic see, he shall be held to be not the pope or
apostolicus, but an apostate.[14] Here Ivo states both what factors a candidate
must satisfy, and what he must avoid if he is to be accepted as pope. A
canonical election is a necessary criterion; bribes and the use of force

---

[10] White, "Pontius of Cluny," p. 199; Palumbo, *Lo Scisma*, p. 383; for an excellent
analysis of the papal office in relation to its occupant see Brian Tierney, *Origins of Papal Infal-
libility 1150-1350* (Leiden, 1972).

[11] Bernhardi, *Lothar*, p. 294.

[12] Ibid., 298-303.

[13] See n. 1 above.

[14] PL 161:325: "Quod si quis pecunia aut gratia humana, aut populari seu militari tumul-
tu, sine concordi et canonica electione et benedictione cardinalium episcoporum ac deinde
sequentium ordinum religiosorum, apostolicae sedi fuerit inthronizatus, non papa vel apostolicus, sed apostaticus habeatur: liceat que cardinalibus, episcopis cum religiosis et Deum
timentibus clericis et laicis invasorem, etiam cum anathemate et humano auxilio et studio a
sede apostolica repellere, et quem dignum judicaverint praeponere. Quod si hoc intra urbem
perficere nequiverint, nostra auctoritate extra urbem congregati in loco quo eis placuerit, eli-
gant quem digniorem et utiliorem apostolicae sedi perspexerint, concessa ei auctoritate re-
gendi et disponendi res ad utilitatem sanctae Romanae Ecclesiae, secundum quod ei melius
videbitur, juxta qualitatem temporis, quasi jam omnino inthronizatus sit."

must be shunned. But this was law, not practice. Gregory VII, for example, was acclaimed by the people and the clergy, and the cardinals voted only thereafter. More flagrantly, in the election of 1124 Haimeric and the Frangipani used both force and bribes. Nevertheless, in each case the backers of the candidate felt constrained ultimately to satisfy the legal requirements. These instances show that the observance of the law was held to be a necessary condition for recognition as pope.

Innocent himself recognized the binding power of the canons, even though he had profited from their manipulation. In his address presented before the Lateran Council of 1139, and reported in the *Chronicle of Morigny*, he says: "Therefore, because the precepts of divine law and the inviolable sanctions of the holy canons have been implements in the peace of the church, they ought to be arms in the time of war." He then argues that because Petrus Leonis made himself the equal of the pope not *aliorum assentatione, imo rapina*, and was therefore not the pope, his decrees and appointments had no validity.[15] In essence, then, Innocent concurs that a legal election is essential to become pope. Petrus was not pope because he gained his office through force rather than through a canonical election. But Innocent's judgment is the word of the victor. Peter of Pisa's testimony defending the legality of Anaclet's election before Roger II two years earlier must be given much greater credence.

In his *Invectiva* against Gerard of Angoulême concerning the schism of Petrus Leonis, Arnulf of Séez equivocates about the force of law. He says that Innocent was the pope both on the basis of his character, which was greatly superior to Anaclet's, and also on the basis of his election. He calls attention to the fact that it preceded Anaclet's, and that the most distinguished men of the Roman Church participated in it. Petrus, he claims, bought the papacy. Tacitly admitting that Petrus did have a case, however, Arnulf says that even if he could have defended his election as having some sort of form, he could still not be accepted as pope because of the quality of his life and reputation.[16]

The law, then, to Arnulf, is not sufficient in its own right to determine who should be pope. It is simply a tool to be used or ignored in supporting a contender. A few paragraphs later he does both. Since the electoral decree of 1059 does not stipulate what procedures should be followed in a case where the vote is divided, Arnulf cites a decree of Leo I. Leo says that in such a case, "visus est illis iure canonico praeferendus is, qui maioribus studiis iuvabatur et meritis."[17] In Arnulf's estimation, Innocent clearly was that man.

What is interesting about Arnulf's argument here is that although he does not say where he obtained Leo's statement, it was almost certainly c.

---

[15] Watterich, *Gesta* 2, p. 252.

[16] Ibid., 268.

[17] Ibid., 269.

6 of Book III of the *Panormia* of Ivo of Chartres. In this book dealing with papal elections, Ivo lays down guidelines which, if followed, could have prevented the schism. In c. 1 he repeats the statute of Nicholas II of 1059 which stresses that if a pope is elected in any other way, he and his followers shall be subjected to anathema. In c. 2 he deals with the question of what should happen if a pope died unexpectedly without the opportunity to discuss the election of his successor. The procedures outlined in the decree of 1059 should be followed, and if there is agreement on a given person, he should be consecrated. However, Ivo points out, such unanimity is rare, so that when opinions differ *convincat sententia plurimorum.*[18] Anaclet had the votes of the majority and therefore according to Ivo should have been pope. Arnulf fails to mention any of this discussion, and skips directly on to c. 6 where Ivo cites the decree of Leo I.

Even here Arnulf cites only that part of the chapter which appears to support his case. Ivo goes on to state that no one should be thrust upon the people whom they reject because such an imposition might result in making them less religious.[19] Anaclet, as all writers acknowledge, had the support of the people.

Although Arnulf, Bernard, and other followers of Innocent focused on Leo's decree that emphasized the good character of the pope as the criterion for resolving a disputed election, it was not the condition which became authoritative. In *Distinctio* 79 on papal elections Gratian totally ignores it, and instead includes Ivo's solution that when opinions differ, the judgment of the majority should prevail.[20]

Yet, the strategy worked out by St. Bernard and Haimeric secured Innocent's acceptance as pope in spite of his manifestly illegal election. In 1130 Haimeric cleverly feigned compliance with the electoral decree, while at the same time undermining it and creating a situation which permitted other criteria to be adduced. St. Bernard then glossed over Innocent's weak legal position, and emphasized the defects of Anaclet's. The technique he inspired was to stress that Innocent's election came first, and to remain silent about how this priority had been achieved. Then, by demonstrating that Anaclet's election had not been wholly legal, he in effect neutralized legality as the determining criterion. While never acknowledging that Innocent was not the legally elected pope, he shifted to more promising grounds for demonstrating that Innocent more than Anaclet deserved

---

[18] PL 161:1127-1130: "Si tamen, ut fieri solet, studia coeperint esse diversa, eorum de quibus certamen emerserit, convincat sententia plurimorum, sic tamen ut sacerdotio careat qui captus promissione non recto judicio de electione decreverit." p. 1130.

[19] Ibid., 1130: "tamen ut nullus invitis et non petentibus ordinetur, ne plebs invita episcopum non optatum aut contemnat, aut oderit et fiat minus religiosa quam convenit, cui non licet habere quem voluit."

[20] *Corpus Iuris Canonici*, ed. cit., p. 279, c. 10: ". . . Si uero, ut fieri solet, studia ceperint esse diuersa eorum, de quibus certamen emerseit, conuincat sententia plurimorum: sic tamen, ut sacerdotio careat, qui captus promissione non recto iudicio de electione decreuerit."

to be pope. Perhaps influenced by Ivo, he argued that the personal worthiness of each candidate must be assessed, and that on those grounds, there was no comparison. Innocent was far superior to Anaclet.

One can ask whether St. Bernard consciously developed such a strategy, whether his distortions were intentional or whether he was simply ill-informed, and was laying out the situation as he saw it. The answer is that informed or not, he really did not care. He heard Peter of Pisa's description of the two elections in the tribunal before Roger II in 1137, and disregarded them. For his own reasons he wanted Innocent rather than Anaclet to be pope, but because the reform church had taken such a strong position on the canonicity of elections, he had to put the best construction he could on Innocent's.

In at least one case St. Bernard seems willfully to have misrepresented what happened in Innocent's election. Writing to Geoffrey of Loreto, who probably knew little about the politics of the curia, he stated that Innocent had been elected by the majority of the cardinals.[21] It is clear, however, that he knew better, for when he wrote to the more knowledgeable Archbishop Hildebert of Tours, who did know something about the conditions in Rome, he said only that Innocent had been elected by the better people, and approved by the majority. But even more importantly, Bernard immediately added, Innocent's good character commended him to be confirmed as pope.[22] In both of these letters Bernard treats the legal issues only after he has carefully prepared his reader by picturing Anaclet, whom he never dignified by naming, as a monster. He associates him with Antichrist and the beast of the apocalypse, and makes evocative puns on his name (Leonis).

St. Bernard formulated his legal arguments in greater detail in a long letter to the bishops of Aquitaine in which he attempted to convince them to relinquish their allegiance to Anaclet's legate, Gerard of Angoulême. Bernard opens his letter by castigating Gerard, accusing him of being vain and ambitious, and charging him with first having approached Innocent with the request that he become his legate, and then, having been rejected, of approaching Anaclet with the same request.[23] The letter is the

---

[21] Ep. 125, *Sancti Bernardi Opera*, ed. cit. 7, pp. 307-308: "Merito autem illum recipit Ecclesia, cujus et opinio clarior, et electio sanior inventa est, nimirum eligentium et numero vincens, et merito." See Bernhardi, *Lothar*, p. 330, & n. 104. Bernhardi cites other sources, which picked up Bernard's claim that Innocent had been elected by the *maior et sanior pars*.

[22] Ep. 124, *Sancti Bernardi Opera*, ed. cit., 7, pp. 305-307: "Electio meliorum, approbatio plurium, et, quod his efficacius est, morum attestatio, Innocentium apud omnes commendant, summum confirmant pontificem." See Bernhardi, *Lothar*, p. 331, n. 106.

[23] Ep. 126, ibid., 309-319; Watterich, *Gesta* 2, pp. 196-198; for an analysis of this letter see Bernhardi, *Lothar*, p. 328, n. 101; for descriptions of Gerard see ibid., p. 331, n. 107. Gerard was a learned canonist, who was highly respected until the attacks made on him by Bernard, Arnulf, the Cluniacs and other supporters of Innocent. Perhaps one reason that they attacked him so viciously was that he wrote a report of the election, which was devastating to Innocent. Part of the report may be contained in c. 6 of the *Invectiva in Girardum Engolismensem Episcopum*, MGH Ldl 3:81-108; Watterich, *Gesta* 2, p. 270. The following excerpt from Arnulf's summary of what he claims were Gerard's very partial impressions of

sole piece of evidence that Gerard turned to Anaclet only after Innocent
had repudiated him, and it should be regarded with caution since the allegation probably came from Haimeric. St. Bernard says that the volte-face
was revealed in an intimate letter written to the chancery, and since
Haimeric was his chief contact there, it was probably he who passed the
information on to St. Bernard. To accept it unquestioningly, therefore,
would be to rely upon the word of a notoriously unreliable reporter.[24]

But whether or not Gerard was a chameleon, it was less he than the
pope he represented who was at issue. As usual, blackening the character
of his adversary before he proceeded to the charges against him, Bernard
says that it would have been better if Anaclet had never been born. Who,
he asks, but a man of sin would have striven after the papacy, and
invaded it after another had already been canonically elected? Moreover,
he contends, Anaclet coveted the place not because it was holy, but
because it was the highest. Emphasizing the word "invasit" by using it
three times in quick succession, he implies that Anaclet used force before
the election and then went through a sham ceremony afterwards to con-
ceal his craftiness and that of his supporters. They say that it is an election, Bernard states, but they are lying. Becoming technical, he notes that
canon law states that after an election, there cannot be a second. Even if
the first one was carried out with less solemnity and order than was usual,
nevertheless a second cannot be held unless the first has been reasonably
discussed and then declared to be invalid.[25]

Bernard then dispenses with the last attempt to decide the dispute on
the basis of law—Anaclet's request to Lothar to submit the case to arbitra-
tion. He accuses Anaclet's followers of making the proposal for tactical
purposes. If their offer were refused, he reasons, it would seem as though
they were the just ones; if it were received, time would be expended on
litigation while they were devising other means of triumphing over Innocent. Moreover, Bernard claims, when they protest that they are seeking a
hearing to review what has been done up until now, and they affirm that
they are prepared to submit to judgment, they are really only trying to

---

Anaclet explains why many rejected Anaclet: "Asseverare multos, ipsum non iustitia, sed
potius invidia reprobatum, eo quod perspicax eius ingenium et amplitudinem animi et ir-
refragabilem potentiam reliqui vererentur."

[24] Cf. White, "Pontius of Cluny," p. 213, n. 105, 219.

[25] Ep. 126, *Sancti Bernardi Opera*, ed. cit., 7, p. 315: "Quis vero ille, nisi HOMO PECCA-
TI, qui super electum a catholicis catholicum, et canonice, locum sanctum invasit, quem tamen, non quia sanctus, sed quia summus est, affectavit? Invasit, inquam, invasit armis,
igne, pecunia, non vitae merito vel virtutum; pervenit in quo stat, et stat in quo pervenit.
Nam illa quam iactat iuratorum suorum, non electio, sed factio, umbra tantum fuit, et oc-
casio, et velamentum malitiae. Dici potest electio, sed impudenter, sed mendaciter. Stat
quippe sententia ecclesiastica et authentica, post primam electionem non esse secundam.
Celebrata proinde prima, quae secundo praesumpta est, non est secunda, sed nulla. Nam etsi
quid minus forte sollemniter minusve ordinabiliter processit in ea praecessit, ut hostes uni-
tatis contendunt, numquid tamen praesumi alter debuit, nisi sane priore prius discussa ratione, cassata iudicio?"

seduce the simple, and to arm the malevolent. But they are wasting their efforts, Bernard implies, because God has already made his judgment. Would human temerity dare to retract the judgment of God, he asks? He follows this rhetorical question with a list of a large number of ecclesiastical and secular leaders, and religious orders which, he says, were not influenced by money, power, or other blandishments, but accepted the judgment of God.

Then, surprisingly returning to the subject of the elections after he has alleged that God has already made his decision, he asserts that Innocent's election was the more honest, the more creditable, and the first in time. The first two statements are established, he argues, by the virtue and dignity of Innocent's electors. Since in addition Innocent was consecrated by the proper person, the cardinal bishop of Ostia, he concludes that Innocent was both the more worthy of the two candidates, and the more regularly elected.[26]

The fact that Bernard felt compelled to reaffirm the legality of Innocent's election even after he had invoked the arguments of Anaclet's depravity and Innocent's worthiness, and of God's recognition of Innocent shows the weight which he attached to that criterion for acceptance as pope. But the fact that he introduced other arguments also suggests that Bernard was not confident enough of his case to let it rest on that support alone. This was not true of the Anacletians, who believed that Petrus Pierleoni had been canonically elected, and that he should therefore be recognized as pope.

The two main presentations of the legal case for Anaclet are the previously mentioned letter to Diego, and the one written by Peter of Porto to the four cardinal bishops who voted for Innocent—William of Palestrina, Matthew of Albano, Conrad of Sabina, and John of Ostia.[27] Peter asks them how they could possibly call the travesty they had engaged in an election. He calls attention to its secrecy, and asks why they resorted to such unseemly subterfuge as proclaiming the pope still to be living after

---

[26] For a discussion of the consecration see Palumbo, *Lo Scisma*, pp. 226-227. In ep. 127 of the Cistercian edition, St. Bernard, or someone of his persuasion, adds the refinement to the above argument that even if all of the scandalous things said about Anaclet were not true, the mere fact that they were said means that Anaclet's reputation had been besmirched. That fact alone, he claims, is enough to prevent his becoming pope. Ep. 127, *Sancti Bernardi Opera*, ed. cit., 7, pp. 320-321. The letter is written to Duke William of Aquitaine. In his English translation of Bernard's letters Bruno Scott James says that he doubts that Bernard wrote ep. 127. *The Letters of St. Bernard of Clairvaux* (London, 1953), p. 199. For a discussion of ep. 127 see Bernhardi, *Lothar*, p. 328, n. 101. In a recent article Hans Grotz compares the legal arguments St. Bernard adduced in the papal elections of 1130 with those he advanced in the schismatic election of 1133 in the archdiocese of Tours. Noting that he used the same legal principles to draw different conclusions in the two cases, Grotz concludes that Bernard arbitrarily used legal arguments to support a preconceived position. Hans Grotz, "Kriterien auf dem Prüfstand: Bernhard von Clairvaux angesichts zweier kanonisch strittiger Wahlen," pp. 237-263 of *Aus Kirche und Reich: Studien zu Theologie, Politik und Recht im Mittelalter*, Festschrift für Friedrich Kempf, ed. Hubert Mordek (Sigmaringen, 1983).

[27] *The Historia Novella*, ed. cit., pp. 7-9.

he had died. And after the pope had died, he admonishes them, it was neither their right to elect a new pope, nor his own, but that of their brethren. Summarizing the reasons why that tiny number of recently elected cardinals could not claim with any credibility to have elected a pope, Peter enumerates that they ignored procedure, despised canon law, and showed contempt for the interdict which they themselves had drawn up. Moreover, they did not so much as summon or wait for himself and the other senior cardinals, much less consult them.

Peter then shifts to the election of Anaclet, stating that God showed them the way of dealing with the false election. Again, Peter emphasizes that it is his brother cardinals who have the chief power to elect. He says that they came together with the entire clergy at the request of the people and with the agreement of the nobles, and in the light of day, openly and unanimously elected Petrus as Anaclet. Peter testifies that he saw the election performed according to canon law, and that he therefore ratified it.

He then goes on to defend Anaclet from the allegations made against him. He says that he sees religious and lay people paying court to Anaclet, and observes that they are received with kindness and depart with even greater kindness. He pleads with the bishops who voted for Innocent to return to understanding, and not to create a schism. "Let the fear of God hold you, not the stench of the world." Then he asks them to desist from their lies, noting one that the bishop of Tivoli told about him. The bishop said that Peter believed that the Deacon of St. Angelo alone was fit to be pope. In closing, Peter says that it had always been his opinion that until the pope was buried, no discussions should be carried on about his successor. He then utters an oath all the more noble by comparison with the vituperative rhetoric being bandied about: "I have held and I shall hold the unity of the church. I shall take care to adhere to truth and justice, confidently hoping that justice and truth will free me."

To see whether Anaclet's or Innocent's claim to be the legally elected pope is stronger, Peter's arguments can be compared with Bernard's. The contest is not even close. Bernard's arguments are convincing only to those who had been misinformed about the two elections, or who knew little about them. For a fraudulent election to precede another gave it no legal advantage. Although the electoral decree of Nicholas II gave priority to the bishops, it did not stipulate that a majority of bishops had the power of deciding the election. It says only that the bishops should first come together to discuss the selection of the new pope, and that soon they should call other cardinals to participate in the discussions. By 1130 the bishops' prerogative was interpreted to mean the authority to instigate the process for choosing a new pope, not that their votes should be weighed more heavily than those of the cardinals from other orders. The judgment of who constitutes the *sanior pars* is by its very nature subjective, but to apply it to the *cardinales novitii*—the novice cardinals who voted for Innocent—is stretching the meaning of the expression. It could more credibly be argued that it described the men with long and distinguished records who supported Anaclet. And finally, consecration by the archbishop of Ostia was customary, but not constitutive. No canon ever stipulated, nor did custom dictate, that only he who was consecrated by the archbishop of Ostia was the pope.

Peter of Porto, on the spot, and informed of the proceedings at St. Gregory's by Peter of Pisa, is a far more reliable reporter. He had no animosity toward Innocent, whose record he admired, so that he was judging the situation on procedural rather than personal grounds. He goes to the heart of the problem—the election itself—which Bernard never touches. No rationalization could make legal the election which was carried out under the circumstances he describes—in secret without announcing the death of the pope or burying him according to tradition, and without summoning or consulting with the other cardinals. However men in 1130 may have understood the electoral decree of 1059 or its subsequent interpretations, they would not have found these proceedings to be in accordance with it. Innocent's supporters were wise to make only a passing feint at defending his election as canonical, and then to concentrate on the worthiness of each candidate. This masterstroke, with what could be argued as support from the *Panormia* of Ivo of Chartres, gave much more latitude to the opinions of religious leaders with dedicated followings like St. Bernard, Norbert of Xanten, Peter the Venerable, and Guigo of Chartreuse.[28]

---

[28] Bernhardi deals with the question, which Schmale will later raise, that perhaps it was better that the letter of the law be sacrificed so that the papacy would not again become the private preserve of a Roman family. He points out, and I believe correctly, that there is no evidence that the Pierleoni family would control Anaclet, and that on the other side, there was a serious possibility of pressure from the Frangipani. Thus, from both perspectives the form of the election was of overwhelming importance. Bernhardi, *Lothar*, pp. 301-302.

Chapter X

CARDINALES NOVITII

To those who see the papal elections of February 1130 as the result of opposing views on ecclesiastical reform, the reason why the election of Anaclet was the more legal is obvious. The progressive cardinals, as they see them—those who owed their promotion to the last years of Calixtus, to Honorius, and to Haimeric—were still in the minority. Even though little is known about their attitudes, their identification with the enlightened tendencies in the church appears to these scholars to be beyond dispute. Did they not come from the areas north of Rome, where the new, spiritual religiosity held sway? Was Haimeric not so intimately associated with the very incarnation of this religiosity—St. Bernard—that the ascetic abbot once declared that the chancellor was like a mother to him?[1] And did not the other most prominent leaders of the movement—monks like Peter the Venerable and canons regular like Norbert of Xanten and Gerhoh of Reichersberg—support Haimeric and Innocent?[2] How much more clear could it be, they ask, that the novice cardinals espoused the ideals of these inspiring churchmen?

The circumstantial evidence is imposing, but as in some celebrated criminal cases, under deeper probing it proves to be misleading. Even if it were demonstrated that the cardinals broke down into factions based upon provenance and age, and that their religious convictions were determined by these factors, it still would not necessarily follow that religious convictions prompted them to vote for one candidate rather than the other. They could have been motivated by political or personal considerations. Or even if they were influenced by the reformers of the North, those men might have known little of the religious ideals of the candidates, and not improbably, they might have been misinformed. But if in addition, it is not even certain that the curia was divided into two parties along the lines

---

[1] Ep. 144, *Sancti Bernardi Opera*, ed. cit. 7, p. 346. St. Bernard also dedicated his tract, *De Diligendo Deo*, to him; ibid., 3, 118-155; see Schmale, *Studien zum Schisma*, p. 169.

[2] Gerhoh states his position in a long letter to Innocent in which he defends the regular against the secular canons; MGH Ldl 3:202-239; on p. 227 he says: "Nonne complices et fautores illius nuper damnati, immo iam olim predampnati Petri Leonis, Romanae aecclesiae invasoris, manifeste sunt ministri Pharaonis?" Schmale thought that Innocent and Haimeric were canons regular, but more recent scholars are less sure. Schmale, *Studien zum Schisma*, pp. 39-40, 185, 242; Werner Maleczek, "Das Kardinalskollegium unter Innocenz II. und Anaklet II.," *Archivum Historiae Pontificiae* 19 (1981), 33 & n. 22.

indicated, then the effect of that split on the papal schism becomes even more tenuous.

Helene Tillmann's analysis of twelfth century cardinals from the environs of Rome throws open the question of whether most of Anaclet's support did come from Rome and southern Italy. She concludes that of the nineteen members of the college of cardinals under Paschal II, whom Klewitz concluded were Roman, in only four cases is the evidence concrete enough to justify his conclusion. Her own opinion is that of the eighty two cardinals during the reign of Paschal, five definitely were Roman, five probably were, and others may have been.[3] Tillmann also cites other statistics, which cast doubt on the North/South antithesis. She notes that Calixtus II created only one Roman cardinal—Gregory of Sts. Sergius and Bacchus—and that his appointment was made about the same time as Haimeric's (March 1123).[4] This was the time, according to the Klewitz/Schmale thesis, that Calixtus' orientation was supposed to have shifted toward the new reform and the North. Moreover, this Roman cardinal voted for Innocent. Honorius created no cardinals from Rome, but Innocent created three.[5] These statistics appear to show that Innocent had more of a penchant for selecting Romans than either of his predecessors, but they could indicate that being Roman was simply not an important consideration.

Besides the provenance of the cardinals, the inference that there was a correlation between age and ideology is still not established. The Anacletians first used the term, *cardinales novitii*, as an expression of derision for the inexperienced cardinals, who had co-operated with Haimeric in staging what they believed to be a parody of an election. They were novices, who still had not been entrusted with the higher tasks of church governance. Yet, even though it is admitted that they had accomplished little, they still are held to have been notable for their spiritual tendencies.[6] They held more progressive views, and the Anacletians showed themselves to be conservative by calling them *cardinales novitii*, it is speculated. These idealistic younger men were impatient to achieve their goals, this reasoning continues, and their impetuosity made them act so aggressively in electing Innocent. Their unbridled zeal explains why the older men resented them so much, and why the senior cardinals identified with Petrus Pierleoni. The more basic reason why Peter of Porto wrote his powerful letter defending the legality of Anaclet's election, the view concludes, is not that

[3] Helene Tillmann, "Ricerche sull'origine dei membri del collegio cardinalizio nel XII secolo: I. La questione dell'accertamento delle origini dei cardinali," *Rivista di Storia della Chiesa in Italia* 24 (1970), pp. 442-444.

[4] Helene Tillmann, "Ricerche sull'origine dei membri del collegio cardinalizio nel XII secolo: II/1. Identificazione dei cardinali del secolo XII di provenienza romana," *Rivista di Storia della Chiesa in Italia* 26 (1972), 335; Hüls, *Kardinäle*, p. 242.

[5] Ibid., 336-344.

[6] Klewitz, "Das Ende," p. 219.

Peter was so concerned with legal procedure, but that as an older member of the curia, he espoused the same philosophy as Anaclet.[7]

One of the weaknesses of this reasoning is its lack of discrimination between age, time of appointment, and experience. The Anacletians did not brand the cardinals who voted for Innocent as "new" or "young," but as novices. They never referred to differences of opinion on any issue, but stressed the inexperience of the *novitii*. These unseasoned cardinals, the Anacletians felt, were not in a position to override the judgments of the cardinals, who not only were in the majority, but who also had acquired wisdom and perspective after participating in the administration of popes of various ideological persuasions. Without time to develop their own stature, and beholden to Haimeric and Honorius for their appointments and whatever influence they could exert within the curia, the *cardinales novitii* were susceptible to pressure to vote for the candidate of their patrons. Even without pressure their self interest dictated that they support Haimeric's candidate, for their authority was bound to Haimeric's, and with a new chancellor, they would be on their own. These factors rather than any youthful revolutionary fervor more plausibly account for why the *novitii* voted for Innocent.

They also had reasons for opposing Anaclet. As an esteemed member of the curia, and as a very powerful man in Rome, he was not dependent upon their support.[8] Also, his Jewish descent might have been offensive to some of them, especially since many of them were not from the environs of Rome and southern Italy, where people tended to be more tolerant of ethnic and religious diversity. Or they could have feared that the Frangipani might once again resort to violence, either because the family did not want to live under a pope from a family of converts, or because it thought that the Pierleoni would gain power at its expense. If this had happened, it would have been inauspicious to have been caught on the other side. There may have been still other reasons why the *cardinales novitii* voted against Anaclet, but at least it is clear that different religious convictions are not the only possibility.

Indeed, I suggest that ideology is one of the less likely possibilities because neither Gregory of St. Angelo nor Haimeric is known to have written or done anything, which distinguished their views from those of the rest of the cardinals. The only confrontations within the curia had been political, and there had been no issues involving either ecclesiastical reform or the relationship between *regnum* and *sacerdotium* over which the

---

[7] Schmale, *Studien zum Schisma*, pp. 32-34; 57-58.

[8] In a conversation between Bishop Guido of Arezzo and a papal nuncio, "Nuncius vero episcopo respondit, 'eius gratia Petrus Leonis est Romae, ut ad illius nutum tota Roma taceat, et tota loquatur. . .'" This text was found and published by S. Löwenfeld, "Kleinere Beiträge. 2. Ueber Anaclets Persönlichkeit," *Neues Archiv der Gesellschaft für ältere deutsche Geschichtskunde* 11 (1885-86), 596-597. The text is frequently cited, e.g. Palumbo, *Lo Scisma*, p. 198 & n. 1. I will discuss it in greater detail below.

electors of Anaclet had differed with those of Innocent. The joint legate-ship of Petrus Pierleoni and Gregory of St. Angelo to France after the signing of the Concordat of Worms, and Peter of Porto's letter describing Gregory as a reputable cardinal are indications that there were no major ideological rifts.

Moreover, the fact that many of the *cardinales novitii* came from Central and Northern Italy, and from France can be explained on grounds other than ideology. Since Haimeric was a Frenchman, and had been educated in Bologna, and Honorius was from Bologna, many of their contacts would have been from those areas.[9] Southern Italy, by contrast, would have been a poor recruiting ground because Honorius spent much of his reign involved in military campaigns there, and he incurred the hostility of the monks of Montecassino by interfering in their affairs.

Since the *cardinales novitii* had such scanty records in 1130, one way of deducing the traits for which they were chosen is to observe those of members of the pope's inner circle. Starting with Honorius himself, there is little to link him with the new northern spirituality. One need not rely on Pandulphus' assessment that he had the character of a swine to con-clude that his virtues were other than spiritual.[10] Even the annals of Char-treuse describe him as grave and severe, and his acquiescence in the power play, which brought him to office, shows that he had his feet firmly planted in the clay of the politics of the day.[11]

One of the cardinals about whom much is known, and who was very active during Honorius' reign, is John of Crema, cardinal priest of St. Grisogonus. Elevated to the cardinalate by Paschal II before 1116, John is one of the exceptions to the theory that for the most part the younger, more recently appointed cardinals voted for Innocent.[12] Klewitz concedes that his character was among the most dubious (*zweifelhaftesten*) in the college of cardinals, but he nevertheless believes that John was one of its most gifted members. He notes that John began to come to people's attention under Gelasius, and that he was used by Calixtus as his spokes-man in the Council of Rheims of 1119. He observes, however, that John was extremely ambitious, and that his way of living was "unspiritual." He alludes to problems, which emerged during John's legateship to England, which caused him to lose favor with Honorius, but he points out that the

---

9 Schmale (*Studien zum Schisma*, pp. 47-48, 56) emphasizes the shift in provenance of the cardinals, but the shift is not that radical. Of the cardinals appointed since 1123 two were from Rome, three from Pisa, one each from Bologna, Florence, Venice, Crema, and Castel-lo, and three from France.

10 *Lib. Pont. Dert.*, p. 203: "Hic [Honorius] de uili plebe comitatus Bononiensium gen-itus, litteratus tamen, homo porcini moris et in specie bubalus, quoniam videbatur aliquando rigidus in iustitia, a domno papa Pascali receptus est et in episcopum Bellitrensem promotus, siquidem episcopus habitu uidebatur. Sed quamvis subdole fecerit, exitus approbauit."

11 *Annales Ordinis Cartusiensis*, ed. cit., p. 332.

12 Zenker, *Die Mitglieder*, pp. 59-62; Hüls, *Kardinäle*, pp. 176-178; see n. 8, ch. II for references to John.

pope soon forgave him, and appointed him legate to Northern Italy in
1128-1129.[13] The Anacletians hated him, and probably with good reason,
Klewitz believed, since he let personal interests influence decisions concerning fundamental principles.[14]

Klewitz' evaluation of John is measured, but he glosses over the magni-
tude of the charges made against him as a result of his legateship to England; he does not emphasize John's loss of favor with Honorius, but its
short duration.[15] What happened during John's visit to England is difficult
to piece together, not because of a shortage of sources, but because of the
difficulty of interpreting these sources. The English church traditionally
had been removed from Rome, and papal intervention was rare. By custom, no papal legate could interfere in its affairs unless the king requested
his presence to settle a particular dispute or to deal with a matter, which
the archbishop of Canterbury and the bishops could not settle on their
own. But during the reign of Henry I—the time in which the papacy was
beginning to expand its authority—these interventions became more frequent.[16] Henry tried to maintain the barrier which his father, William I,
had interposed between England and Rome, but three of the five *legati a
latere* (papal legates from Rome) succeeded in reaching England. The first
was Guy, when he was archbishop of Vienne (1100), the second was
Petrus Pierleoni (1121), and the third was John of Crema (1125). The
first two failed to perform any legantine act, making John of Crema's success in holding a Council at Westminster in 1125 stand out all the more
starkly. The canons of the council introduced some novelties derived from
the Lateran Council of 1123, but the holding of the council itself was a
landmark, breaking a tradition going back to the beginning of the reign of
William the Conqueror.[17]

---

[13] *Lib. Pont. Dert.*, p. 208: "Hic Iohannem Cremensem, hominem litteratum et proui-
dum, sed turpis fame magis quam opus sit, suspendita cardinalatus officio; sed ipse scit et
Deus qualiter eum postea restituerit."

[14] Klewitz, "Das Ende," pp. 220-221. In a letter written to the Cluniacs in May 1130
Anaclet expresses his opinion of John and some of the other supporters of Innocent. JL
8376; PL 179:696-698: "Quorum caput est Aimericus quondam cancellarius, avaritiae
servus, histrionum et scurrarum delirus incentor, ecclesiarum expoliator, servorum Dei im-
probus exactor, alter Giezi, qui simoniis publicis et privatis lepram Naaman, et maledicionem
Dei haereditatio est jure sortitus. Huic Joannes de Crema, homo miserabilis et vere Nicolai-
ta, et inter biothanatos aliquando per papam Honorium et cardinales damnatus, promis-
sionibus vanis inductus, alludit. De Petro cardinali Sanctae Anastasiae, quod thesauri Cluni-
censis assuetis tergiversationibus insatiabilis exstitit praedo, et Gozelmo Sanctae Caeciliae,
silere dignius diximus, quam de eis et de eorum turpissima servitute vobis scribere." It is indicative that Anaclet begins with the archcriminal in his eyes, and proceeds progressively to
lesser villains. In this hierarchy John ranks second.

[15] Zenker (*Die Mitglieder*, n. 47, pp. 60-61) cites the large number of English sources,
which transmit reports of John's sexual improprieties. She questions whether these reports
have any validity, speculating that John intervened so aggressively on behalf of the pope in
England, that one of the ways of attacking his position was to attack his character.

[16] Martin Brett, *The English Church under Henry I* (Oxford, 1975), pp. 34-47; Z. N.
Brooke, *The English Church and the Papacy from the Conqueror to the Reign of John* (Cambridge, 1952), pp. 167-169.

The interesting question, of course, is why John succeeded while Guy and Petrus, both capable and experienced prelates, failed. The answer appears to be primarily political. Although Calixtus sent John to England to resolve a primacy struggle between Archbishop Thurstan of York and Archbishop William of Canterbury, and to deal with a dispute between Thurstan and some Scottish bishops, Henry was far more concerned with another issue—securing a divorce between his nephew, William Clito, in Normandy, and the daughter of the count of Anjou. Petrus and Gregory of St. Angelo had probably discussed the problem with its vast dynastic implications at a synod they held at Chartres on March 12, 1124, but it was John acting as Calixtus' special legate in June, who recommended the divorce, which received Calixtus' approval. The divorce had profound repercussions for Henry's authority on the continent, so that John greatly raised himself in the king's favor by his ruling. That good will smoothed the way for John's permission to enter England in time to chant the Easter High Mass at Canterbury cathedral on March 29, 1125. With renewed authority from Honorius, John set out on a mission to English bishoprics, met with Kind David of Scotland, and ended his tour with the Council of Westminster in September.

Although probably not a first hand witness, Bishop Gilbert Foliot of London cites John's legation as a model for judicial reform, while acknowledging that the legate had acted contrary to the customs of the country.[18] But if Gilbert's account of John's visit to England is mainly favorable, comparing his methods with those of Thomas Becket, other reports are more critical. Gervase of Canterbury sniffs that although John was only a priest, and not even a bishop, he presided at the Easter mass at Canterbury adorned with pontifical insignia, and thereby causing great offense.[19] Henry of Huntingdon goes even further. He transmits a tale relating that while John called a council which stressed clerical celibacy, he himself was dallying with a whore.[20] With some irreconcilable differences, the Winchester Annals transmit a similar story.[21]

The problem is to determine whether the stories are true. In the case of the Easter Mass at Canterbury Cathedral the issue does not arise. John did conduct himself ostentatiously, and with what the monks considered to be superbia. His offense may not have been great, perhaps, but it was

---

[17] *Councils and Synods with other Documents relating to the English Church*, pt. II, 1066-1204, ed. Dorothy Whitelock, Martin Brett, & Christopher N. L. Brooke (Oxford, 1981), pp. 733-741. Petrus Pierleoni's legateship will be discussed in a following chapter.

[18] *Councils and Synods*, p. 732; Brooke, *The English Church*, n. 4, p. 169.

[19] *The Historical Works of Gervase of Canterbury*, ed. William Stubbs, Rolls Series 73 (1879-80), vol. 2, pp. 381-382: "eminenti cathedrae praesidens et insigniis pontificibus utens, licet non episcopus sed simpliciter . . . presbyter cardinalis . . ." Brett, *The English Church*, p. 44.

[20] *Henrici Archidiaconi Huntendunensis Historia Anglorum*, ed. T. Arnold, Rolls Series 74 (1879), p. 245; *Councils and Synods*, p. 732.

[21] *Annales Monastici*, ed. H. R. Luard, 4 vols., Rolls Series 36 (1864-69), vol. 2, pp. 47-48.

inconsistent with the ideals of the new reform. In the case of the two scurrilous tales, Martin Brett suggests that their origin came from the ire John raised by infringing the ancient liberties of the English church. The clergy of the old school took revenge by spreading stories of the discovery of the pompous legate in *flagrante delicto*, he speculates.[22] But since the English clergy seem to have helped to formulate the decrees of the Council of Westminster, it is improbable that they were offended by them. Moreover, rather than being allowed to slip into desuetude once John had departed, the decrees were uncommonly widely distributed.[23] For these reasons one must be cautious in accepting the infringement of English liberties as an explanation for the genesis of the stories.

Given these uncertainties, the possibility persists that the charges were true, and Honorius' suspension of John from his cardinalate dignity increases the suspicion that they were.[24] Honorius was not a hermit like Celestine V, who would have been shocked at the mere rumor of an impropriety. For him to have taken such a radical step as the suspension of a powerful figure in the curia must have required major provocation. If John's legateship in England did not provide this provocation, then something equally offensive must have. Any favor John may have exhibited towards the canons regular, and any good words St. Bernard may have had for him are not sufficient reasons to demonstrate that he was a new reformer.[25] His support of Innocent in no way identifies the pope with progressive attitudes toward ecclesiastical reform.[26]

---

[22] Brett, *The English Church*, pp. 44-45.

[23] *Councils and Synods*, pp. 733-736.

[24] See n. 13 above.

[25] Schmale associates John with the new reform for these reasons; *Studien zum Schisma*, pp. 37-38.

[26] To see how John could be identified with the ideals of the new reform, and used as a paragon to determine the ideology of the *cardinales novitii*, who voted for Innocent, it is instructive to observe how modern historians have evaluated these sources. While sympathetic to Innocent, Zöpffel admits that John neither enjoyed a good reputation with his contemporaries nor with subsequent writers. But he emphasizes that the stories spread about John in England and by the Anacletians cannot be verified, and concludes that a cardinal asked by popes to perform such important functions could correspond little to the picture created by the poisonous pens of the Anacletians. Zöpffel also argues that because John stood close to Haimeric, he must have supported the policy of peace with the emperor. Zöpffel contrasts John with the Pierleoni, who, he asserts, had long represented the Gregorian position. *Die Doppelwahl*, pp. 310-313.

Bernhardi finds it significant that the complaints made about John came from many different sources, some of which had absolutely nothing to gain by defaming him. For this reason he concludes that there is a strong presumption of truth in their charges. He also reasons that although Anaclet was an avowed opponent of John, he nevertheless depicted him honestly in his letter to the monks at Cluny. He reasons that because other charges made in the letter could be verified, particularly those made against Peter of St. Anastasia for plundering the treasury at Cluny, that he would not say anything about John, which could not be verified. Bernhardi, *Lothar*, p. 319; Hüls, *Kardinäle*, p. 149

Historians writing after Zöpffel and Bernhardi line up behind one or the other. Palumbo (*Lo Scisma*, n. 1, p. 266) cites Bernhardi, but not Zöpffel. Conversely, Klewitz and Schmale (*Studien zum Schisma*, n. 6, p. 34) cite Zöpffel, but not Bernhardi or Palumbo. Thus, no one has attempted to grapple with the arguments inconsistent with his point of view. Schmale

The Anacletians had abundant reasons for criticizing the cardinal of St. Grisogonus without speculating that their animus originated from anger generated from a presumption that as an older cardinal, John should have voted for Anaclet. The probability that John cast off the ideological accretions accumulated through his long tenure as a cardinal and voted for Innocent because they both espoused the younger ideas—although neither of them was young—strains credulity. It is equally dubious that Peter of Porto, the dean of the cardinals, voted for an allegedly ambitious, corrupt, and morally lax Anaclet because as older men they held similar views on ecclesiastical reform.

Similarly to John of Crema, Peter of St. Anastasia has been linked to the new piety.[27] The reasoning goes as follows:[28] Although Anaclet accused Peter of plundering the treasury of Cluny, no other source mentions the charge.[29] If there were any substance to it, then it must have concerned the turmoil in Cluny in 1126 when Peter was sent in to restore order. If Peter did take some action against Pontius at that time, it would have been interpreted by Pontius' supporters, including Anaclet, in a negative light. Accordingly, Peter might have done something perfectly appropriate to his commission from Honorius, but which Anaclet characterized as plundering. Having attenuated the seriousness of Anaclet's charge, and omitting any reference to Pandulphus' allegation that Peter

---

claims that John not only was a man of brilliant gifts, capable of performing the most difficult tasks, but also that he was *ein durchaus reformtreuer Mann*, who represented the papal policy with zeal and energy. (ibid., 35) He describes John's active role in the curia, ending with an invidious comparison between John's success with Henry I of England, and Petrus Pierleoni's failure. (ibid., 36)

But Schmale admits that the English sources describing John's legateship to England cast a shadow over the cardinal's previously brilliant image. (ibid., n. 17, p. 36) He reasons, however, that since the sources do not present a consistent picture, Zöpffel is right not to place too much weight on them. Besides, he says, the question of John's character is not terribly relevant to his thesis. For understanding the direction in which the church was moving the degree of moral excellence of the two papal contenders is far more important than that of the cardinals who elected them, he states. In other contexts, where there is no evidence to impugn the character of the electors of Innocent, however, he does regard their presumed virtue as an indication that Innocent represented the finer and more progressive elements in the church. The admission that John's character is not directly relevant to his thesis not only shows some ambivalence in his reasoning, but it also weakens his theory by implying that the convictions of the electors could be separated from their behavior. By contrast, Carlo Servatius, speaking of the cardinal bishops in his biography of Paschal II, notes that: "Der Kandidat musste den strengen moralischen Anspruchen der Reformer genügen." *Paschalis II. (1099-1118)*, vol. 14 of *Päpste und Papsttum* (Stuttgaart, 1979), p. 45.

Clearly uneasy with accepting the implications of this reasoning, Schmale attempts to neutralize the negative reports about John by citing sources such as Gilbert Foliot, and by explaining the Anacletian's hatred for John not out of his unethical behavior, but out of his zeal in carrying out the policies of Haimeric and Honorius. Like Klewitz, he thinks that the older cardinals thought that John, as their contemporary should have supported Anaclet, and that when he did not, they felt betrayed.

[27] Hüls, *Kardinäle*, pp. 149-150; Zenker, *Die Mitglieder*, pp. 70-71; L. Spätling, "Kardinallegat Petrus im Pontifikat Honorius II," *Antonianum* 38 (1963), 162-192.

[28] Schmale, *Studien zum Schisma*, pp. 54-55.

[29] JL 8376.

was derisively called *Boccaruncione*, the reasoning then purports to establish Peter's credentials as a new reformer.[30] It notes St. Bernard's commendatory words for him, and emphasizes that he functioned as a legate in northern Italy with John of Crema.

As with his co-legate, the attempt to link Peter with the new piety fails. Working with John is hardly evidence of Peter's spiritual inclinations, and St. Bernard was more effusive than discreet in lavishing his praise. One of the most frequent recipients of his plaudits, for example, was Arnulf of Séez, who wrote some of the most intemperate and scurrilous prose during the schism. Moreover, since we do not know what position, if any, Anaclet took on the dispute at Cluny, his accusation that Peter plundered the treasure is not an automatic defense of Pontius.

More than some of the other seasoned cardinals, who voted for Innocent, Peter and John exemplify a seeming immunity to the ideals of the new reform. John, especially, appears to have been a political diplomat, thrown into the breach when something crucial was at stake. When neither Petrus nor Gregory of St. Angelo could decide what to do about the divorce of William Clito, John made the decision in order to curry favor with Henry I, and to gain leverage over the English church. When Calixtus needed someone to cover up the breakdown of the negotiations with Henry V at Mouzon during the Council of Rheims of 1119, John was his man. And it was John, who captured the antipope at Sutri in 1121. He was neither a new reformer nor an old. He merely carried out his orders, and probably was not unduly fastidious about his personal life.

This is not to say that all of the *cardinales novitii* were like John or Peter. Many of them went on to have distinguished careers. But it does suggest that Haimeric and Honorius did not select their new cardinals because they exemplified the more spiritual tendencies in the church.[31] The linchpin in the theory that the Innocentians represented the new piety developing in the North, however, is Haimeric, and it is his career, which substantiates or invalidates the theory.

---

[30] *Lib. Pont. Dert.*, p. 207: "Petrum sancte Anastasie, quem satis conuenienter boccaruncionem clamabant . . ." Klewitz ("Das End," p. 219) does not mention this passage. "Boccaruncionem" is neither Latin nor Italian. "Runcione" may have been an alternative spelling of "ronzio," meaning a buzzing or humming. Thus, the whole word would mean a buzzing mouth. The word is usually translated as "slanderer." Whatever its precise meaning, it was negative.

[31] Timothy Reuter concurs that we know too little about the new cardinals to assert that they represented a new policy. There may have been tensions between a younger and an older generation, he says, but there is no evidence that they were of a programmatic nature. Timothy Reuter, "Zur Anerkennung," pp. 395-416.

Chapter XI

HAIMERIC AND DIEGO OF COMPOSTELLA

Haimeric is the most controversial of all of the Innocentians. As the dynamic leader of a faction determined to keep control of the papacy, he operated more as a prime minister than as a papal functionary. It was he, rather than the pope, who determined the outcome of the papal elections of 1124 and 1130. He corresponded widely under his own name, and during the reigns of Honorius and Innocent he participated in all of the major negotiations. Bernard and other leaders of the new reform praised him, and he in turn has been assumed to have been the driving force for their program in the curia.

But at the same time he is known to have used force to overthrow the election of a legally-elected pope, to have bribed the prefect and Petrus Pierleoni's father to obtain their acquiescence in the coup, to have engaged in deception and intrigue in bringing about the election of his candidate in the next election, and to have accepted money in return for favors.[1] Can one reconcile the contradictory sides of his character, and see

---

[1] Haimeric's part in the papal elections of 1124 and 1130 has already been noted. See *Lib. Pont. Dert.*, p. 205 and the letter of Peter of Porto (n. 4, ch. VIII) among other sources. Mühlbacher (*Die streitige Papstwahl*, p. 70 and n. 3) acknowledges that Haimeric had his hands open to gold, but says that in doing so he was merely following the customs of the curia, which regarded the plundering of Christianity as its hereditary right: "Wenn er [Haimeric] seine Hände auch wirklich dem Golder geöffnet, so folgte er nur der allgemeinen Sitte der ganzen römischen Curie, welche die Brandschatzung der Christenheit als ihr Erbrecht betrachtete." For the lax moral state of the curia during the papacies of Calixtus and Honorius see Gerhoh of Reichersberg, *De Investigatione Antichristi*, lib. 1, c. 52, MGH Ldl 3:358-359.

Mühlbacher accepts the general view that Haimeric was associated with the moral reform of the church because of his close connections with people like St. Bernard and Guigo of Chartreuse, but he also concedes that he succumbed to the Roman corruption by engaging in an act of nepotism. Haimeric wanted to impose his nephew, Peter, as the archbishop of Bourges against the will of the French king. This act of nepotism, Mühlbacher notes, resulted in the interdict's being leveled over France. For further references to the venality of the Romans see Mühlbacher, p. 80.

Innocent acted well within the tradition of his predecessors, according to Peter the Deacon. He says that Innocent bought the support of his former opponents after the death of Anaclet. MGH SS 34:607: " Innocentius autem immensa in filios Petri Leonis et in his qui eis adherebant, pecunia profligata illos ad suam partem attraxit, sicque cardinales qui iam dicto filio Petri Leonis communicaverant, omni auxilio destituti Innocentii vestigiis advoluntur;" for secondary sources mentioning the corruption of Haimeric see Schmale, *Studien zum Schisma*, pp. 94-95; for general primary sources see Hüls, *Kardinäle*, p. 236; Zenker, *Die Mitglieder*, pp. 142-144.

Haimeric as the leader of a spiritual reform of the church? Can one see him leading the charge for a more international church based upon a *modus vivendi* with the emperor?

Yes, says one school of thought, which adduces Haimeric's ideological conditioning to support its point.[2] While admitting that his origins, education, and professional life are almost completely unknown, adherents of this view are at least convinced that Haimeric was a Burgundian. On this basis, they reconstruct Haimeric's heritage as follows: Because Cluny was located in Burgundy, the area had been the center of religious reform for a century. Calixtus and St. Bernard both stemmed from its soil, showing its continued religious vitality. Largely because papal rule was uncontested there, no investiture contest ever developed. By implication, therefore, Haimeric grew up in an atmosphere where churchmen did not worry primarily about papal and royal prerogatives. Rather, Burgundy was the spawning ground for the new monasticism, concentrating on the restoration of purity, discipline, simplicity, and piety, and exemplified by Cîteaux. As a product of this ambience, Haimeric worked to spread its values to the church at large once he was in a position of authority.

The main problem with this reasoning is that it is shaped like an inverted pyramid, resting wholly on the point that Haimeric was a Burgundian. Here the evidence is at best slight. Peter Classen argued that the only hard evidence of Haimeric's association with Burgundy was his connection with Calixtus.[3] Calixtus, however, came from the imperial Kingdom of Burgundy, where conditions were far different from those as the French Duchy. As the archbishop of Vienne, he had been deeply enmeshed in problems between the church and the empire both on an international and a local level. Vying with Henry V to be the chief power in the Kingdom, he fought the emperor at every turn. They had one memorable battle, for example, over the status of the churches of St. John and of St. Stephen in Besançon.[4] Moreover, not every Burgundian, either French or Imperial espoused the views of St. Bernard, or even those of Peter the Venerable. Pontius, most notably, was a Burgundian. For these reasons, extrapolating Haimeric's religious ideology from his background is too hypothetical to be anything more than suggestive.

Once Haimeric became chancellor, and more information becomes available, it is easier to argue that he championed the new ideology. The same school notes that his arengas emphasize *charitas*, which they see as betokening his spiritual orientation.[5] Timothy Reuter disputes this

---

[2] Schmale develops this theory, op. cit., pp. 96-102.

[3] Peter Classen, "Zur Geschichte Papst Anastasius IV.," *Quellen und Forschungen aus italienischen Archiven und Bibliotheken* 48 (1968), 48, n. 14; Chodorow, *Christian Political Theory*, n. 49, p. 51.

[4] See Mary Stroll, "The Struggle Between Guy of Vienne and Henry V," *Archivum Historiae Pontificiae* 18 (1980), 97-115 at pp. 109-110.

[5] Schmale, op. cit., pp. 100-102, 108-118.

contention, however, arguing that the arengas bear no relationship to an Augustinian idea of *charitas*, and therefore to an identification with a more spiritual/moral idea of reform.[6] Likewise, the increasing number of privileges granted to the new houses does not mean that Haimeric favored the new ideology against the old. Since the older style Benedictine houses were not being founded, it was impossible to grant them the same privileges. Haimeric certainly did not deny them any privileges, and his participation in ousting Pontius and Oderisius was politically rather than ideologically inspired.

The school makes no attempt to demonstrate that the elections of 1124 and 1130 were legal, but suggests that like St. Bernard, Haimeric probably looked to the good which a man could do for the church rather than unreflectively fulfilling "the letter of the law." Besides, one scholar points out, none of the previous papal elections had been absolutely legal either. It is understandable that the Anacletians would emphasize the illegality of Innocent's election, he says, but that does not mean that the issue was a very serious one. Although he does not believe that the aphorism, "the end justifies the means" quite accurately characterizes the thinking of the period, he nevertheless concludes that it would be correct to say both for members of Haimeric's party and that of his opponents, that their goals justified their behavior.[7]

But in fact twelfth-century churchmen were not tolerant of actions so long as they were performed in a good cause. Even before the reform had developed its momentum, Henry III removed Gregory VI from office, not because the erstwhile pope's objectives were not good—they were—but because he had bought his office. Likewise, as we shall see below, churchmen criticized the resort to abusive behavior to secure Innocent's election because the behavior in itself was offensive. Whether Innocent was a worthy candidate or not had nothing to do with their criticisms. Procedure was important, and Haimeric's flagrant disregard of it elicited strong disapproval. It was, most prominently, the reason why there was a second election.

Haimeric's relationship with Archbishop Diego of Santiago de Compostella provides other insights into his character and objectives.[8] The years in which Diego flourished were turbulent ones in the history of northern Spain. Both he and the papacy were involved in the local infighting—

---

[6] Reuter, "Zur Anerkennung," pp. 408-412.

[7] Schmale, op. cit., p. 124: "für Haimerich und seine Anhänger, aber genauso auch für seine Gegner dürfte gelten, dass ihr Verhalten von den Zielen her seine Rechtfertigung erhielt."

[8] For Diego see Servatius, *Paschalis II.*, pp. 119-143; Ludwig Vones, *Die 'Historia Compostellana' und die Kirchen Politik des Nordwestspanischen Raumes 1070-1130: Ein Beitrag zur Geschichte der Beziehungen zwischen Spanien und dem Papsttum zu Beginn des 12. Jahrhunderts* (Cologne, Vienna, 1980), pp. 363-522; R. A. Fletcher, *St. James' Catapult: The Life and Times of Diego Gelmirez of Santiago de Compostela* (Oxford, 1984), pp. 192-222.

secular as well as ecclesiastical—and in the attempts to drive back the Muslims. In the wake of the Muslim retreat the papacy struggled to reestablish the Spanish church under its leadership, and both Haimeric and Diego participated in this struggle.

In 1101 Diego became bishop of Compostella, and under his guidance the previously unnoteworthy see achieved great eminence. Emphasizing the alleged possession of the relics of St. James, he intimated that because James was the equal of Peter and Paul, Santiago should be the equal of Rome. He referred to its bishops as the "episcopi apostolice sedis," and himself as "summus pontifex." Paschal granted him an exemption from the jurisdiction of the archbishop of Braga as well as other privileges, and allowed him to attach cardinals to his cathedral. One measure of the degree of Santiago's distinction is that three of its cardinal priests were external prelates, including Archbishop Gerald of Braga. In 1102 Diego visited his possessions in Braga, but not confining himself to asserting his control over the clergy of the city churches, he also plundered their treasure, and secretly transmitted venerated objects to Santiago. Archbishop Gerald never retrieved them, but Paschal did accede to his request to have Diego return the two plundered churches.

Diego believed that as a logical consequence of Santiago's special position, Compostella not only should be an archbishopric, but also the Primatial See of Spain, a position Toledo held. The attainment of these honors became his primary, and almost sole occupation. But although he claimed preeminence over the churches of Western Spain, the curia reasoned that since the archbishoprics of Toledo, Braga, and Tarragona already existed, there was no need for another. Diego's solution was to transfer the metropolitan rights of Merida to Santiago, but the papacy responded that it was impossible to withdraw the administration of Merida, still under Moslem occupation, from Toledo.

Diego persevered, however, and found an ally in Pontius of Cluny, who forcefully represented his interests in the curia. Eventually, primarily on the basis of many political considerations, Calixtus granted Diego his all consuming desire to become archbishop. The new archbishop had been well known to Calixtus long before he became pope. Diego had been the notary of the future pope's brother, Count Raymond of Galicia, when Calixtus was still in Burgundy. The two men became joint guardians of Raymond's son, who would become King Alfonso VII of Leon and Castille (1126-1157). Diego had tried to rob him of the wealth of his kingdom, and one of the new archbishop's obligations in return for his promotion was to treat his charge in ways befitting his guardianship.[9]

How had Diego achieved such great success? Besides whatever advantages he could offer Rome for increasing its influence in Spain, his other chief means of obtaining favorable responses to his petitions was the

---

[9] *Historia Compostelana*, ed. cit., p. 275.

paymemt of "benedictions."[10] Benedictions theoretically were gifts given to defray the expenses of actions taken by the curia, but frequently the distinction between benediction and bribe was evanescent. In Diego's case there was scarcely any pretense. He learned very quickly that the lavish use of the wealth of his bishopric was a powerful inducement. Calixtus was particularly open to Diego's benedictions, and especially at the beginning of his reign when he needed money to establish himself in Rome. Moving very slowly, granting Diego only limited privileges, he received gold and other treasure at each transaction, at times in huge quantities.[11] Haimeric and other members of the curia also benefited from the archbishop's largess. In a letter written to Diego in 1136 requesting that he grant a benefice with a prebend to the bearer of the letter, Haimeric reminds Diego that he has aided the church of Santiago from the time of Calixtus.[12] In another letter Cardinal Deacon Guido says that Haimeric especially wished Diego to grant the request. The implication of the invocation of Haimeric's name is that it carried special weight with the archbishop.[13]

There are signs indicating that the curia became adept at exploiting Diego's readiness to pay for every privilege. In the fall of 1123 Diego sent emissaries to Rome to attain further confirmation of his legateship. In support of their cause they produced letters from Alfonso VII and his mother, Uracca, and the usual benediction, in this case 400 gold pieces.[14] On November 29th Calixtus confirmed the legateship to Compostella.

---

[10] For the concept of the "benedictio" see Karl Jordan "Zur päpstlichen Finanzgeschichte im 11. und 12. Jahrhundert," *Quellen und Forschungen aus italiaenischen Archiven und Bibliotheken* 25 (1933-1934), 82-88.

[11] Among the many references in the *Historia Compostelana* (ed. cit.) are the following: After the Council of Toulouse in 1119, when Calixtus had deferred a decision on Diego's request to make Santiago an archbishopric: "Haec atque alia postquam Papa Calixtus nobis aperuit, ne eo insalutato reverteremur, viginti uncias auri, ei attribuimus, arcam vero auream cum praedictis morabitinis, & cetera, Cluniacensi Abbati ad reservandum commendavimus" (p. 275). When Calixtus made Diego a legate of the Holy See in 1120 Diego presented a huge benediction (pp. 290-291). In one case (1120) Diego's emissaries were embarrassed because a part of the treasure they delivered to the curia was adulterated or even false. In order to pacify the pope and the curia Hugo, the emissary, had to make up the sum from his own pocket: "Praeterea quarta pars auri quod receperat Stephanus de Bisontio Camerarius Papae, scilicet ducentas uncias, falsa esse comperta fuerat. . . . Nempe Romano Pontifici, Romanis Cardinalibus, ceterisque in Romana Curia, necnon Canonicis, atque amicis suis, ad haec iterum laborantibus, saepius magna atque innumera distribuendo ad quod diu anhelaverat effectui mancipaverat: plurima quoque ut adepta possidere & cetera adhuc adipiscenda valeat adipisci, praedictus Archiepiscopus & S.R.E. Legatus frequenter distribuit. Utinam vita diutius comite per Dei misericordiam utpote fidelis dispensator, in opus simile plurima dispenset atque distribuat: quatenus ejus temporibus Compostella B. Jacobi Ecclesia ad majorem sublimetur dignitatem" (p. 300).

[12] Ibid., 584: "A tempore Dni Papae Calixti ex quo praestante Dno Romanae Ecclesiae militavi, quae ad honorem Compostellanae Ecclesiae spectare cognovi, gratanter peregi."

[13] Ibid., 585: ". . . pro nostrae intercessionis precibus & praecipue Dni A. Cancellarii, qui pro eo rogat . . ."

[14] Ibid., 394; Vones, *Die 'Historia Compostellana'*, p. 451.

The following year (1124) Diego wanted to be assured that Compostella's status as a metropolitan would extend in perpetuity. Again the same emissaries distributed a benediction, and again it was 400 gold pieces.[15] Calixtus received the major part, and the curia and the most important cardinals the minor. In consultation with the curia and other high cardinals Calixtus granted the request, but in a most surprising form. Without appending a seal, he handed the emissaries the draft to be emended as Diego and his advisors saw fit. The astonished Diego did make some corrections, added a few embellishments, and then returned the document to Calixtus. Once more the emissaries were directed to distribute gold, this time 300 ounces. But fearing that they might be attacked enroute, Diego sent the money with men dressed as pilgrims. One of them was nevertheless robbed of 27 ounces of gold, and the completion of the transaction had to be delayed for a month until two other canons of Santiago could produce the missing gold.[16]

What this unusual transaction suggests is that Calixtus and his advisors devised this unique procedure, not to insure Diego's concurrence on the final wording, but to receive another benediction. If Diego's representatives were satisfied with the terms, there was no reason to obtain the archbishop's imprimatur. Further, Calixtus would never have allowed the initiative to pass from his hands if he had anticipated any substantive changes. It was an attractive stategem for extracting a few more hundred ounces of Santiago's gold, and Diego had left himself open to it by routinely offering magnanimous benedictions. The pope and the curia expected them, and they demanded the full amount if the favor were to be granted.

After Calixtus' death on December 13, 1124, there was a major shift in the attitude of Rome toward Santiago. Rather than honoring Calixtus' privilege made in perpetuity, Diego was immediately asked to come to Rome to renew his privileges. Even before he received the summons, he had sent emissaries who learned that his stock in Rome had drastically diminished. Honorius did not grant him a broad-ranging privilege, and the curia became unresponsive. Diego realized that the only way he could improve his position was by identifying himself more closely with the Kingdom of Leon and Castille.[17]

Diego also continued to practice his old technique of distributing gold, but even this inducement no longer proved to be effective. Archbishop Raymond of Toledo and Bishop Gonzalo of Coimbra had provoked too much distrust of the ambitious archbishop. In a clear tilt toward Toledo Honorius confirmed Raymond's election and the privileges of his church without mentioning the restrictions in favor of the rights of Santiago.

[15] Ibid., 397.

[16] Ibid., 400-402; Vones, op. cit., pp. 452-455.

[17] Vones, op. cit., pp. 472-473.

When a legation arrived somewhat later from Compostella the curia was negatively disposed, and Honorius did not renew the privilege of Santiago. On the contrary, he wrote a stiff note dated January 10, 1126, warning Diego not to misue his pallium.[18] Another legation distributed the usual gold, but succeeded only in eliciting a reserved letter from Honorius on July 13, 1126. Haimeric seems to have been almost embarrassed by the hostility emanating from Rome. About the same time, along with Leo Frangipani, he wrote a placatory note thanking Diego for his gifts, and promising to work for him in the future.[19]

Haimeric presumably did a good job, for by 1130 Santiago not only had recovered its original position, but had become the most powerful bishopric in Galicia.[20] Given the chancellor's loyal support, even in the face of Honorius' reservations, one would expect that Diego immediately would have taken a strong stand for Innocent, but he did not. He dispatched two emissaries to Rome to determine what had occurred, and they were told that the *major et melior* part of the clergy and people of Rome had congregated, and *communi assensu & unanimi voluntate*, they had elected Innocent. The emissaries were further informed that after Innocent's election, Petrus was elected pope because his family had distributed money and favors. This allegation may not have daunted the representatives of the worldly Diego, but for whatever reason, the *Historia Compostelana* reports that the church of Santiago branded Anaclet as a schismatic.[21]

Yet, Diego's position must still have been ambiguous, for in 1134 Innocent and Anaclet dispatched nuncios—on the same day according to the *Historia*—to Diego. Each of them entreated the archbishop to declare himself for the pope he represented, and presumably Diego must have opted for Innocent, for there are no further communications from Anaclet.[22]

From this brief description, there is is no obvious connection between

---

18 *Historia Compostelana*, ed. cit., p. 442; Vones, op. cit., p. 481.

19 Ibid., 442-443: "Charissimo amico suo Didaco Dei gratia venerabili Compostellano Archiepiscopo A. Ecclesiae Romanae Diaconus Cardinalis & Cancellarius & L. frui pane salvete. Gratias vobis, tamquam patri & amico referimus pro exeniis nobis a vestra paternitate collatis. Pro honore & servitio vestro laboravimus, & usque ad terminum quem postulatis juxta posse quod nobis Deus dederit laborare nullatenus desistemus. Valete." Vones (op. cit., n. 13, p. 481) points out that Schmale dated this letter a half year too early.

20 Vones, op. cit., p. 513.

21 *Historia Compostlana*, ed. cit., p. 512: "Compostellanus autem eum schismaticum & non canonice electum sciens, literas ejus omnino vilipendit, nec visis ipsis literis a tramite veritatis deviare voluit."

22 Ibid., 549-551. Innocent says: "Miramur autem, quoniam elapso tanto tempore de statu & incolumitate tua nullam nobis certitudinem reddidisti. Ut igitur tuae dilectionis affectus erga Matrem tuam Ecclesiam Romanam magis apparet, per exhibitionem operis id ipsum studeas demonstrare." Similarly, Anaclet says: "Verum tu frater in Christo carissime nescimus quo torpore detentus nulla a te aliquando suscipere rescripta meruimus: proinde nos licet in his plurimum admirantes aliquantulum doleamus, non tamen desistimus quin & iterato te nostris literis visitemus, & de his que penes nos acta sunt vel aguntur, certiorem reddamus."

Diego and the new reform as it has been interpreted. He was associated with Pontius, and was received cooly by Honorius. He robbed the churches of Braga, and was accused by Alfonso VII of appropriating the wealth of his kingdom. He distributed money to the pope and the curia in a way that could best be described as simony, and he was involved in numerous political squabbles. If he was interested in the *cura animarum*, it escaped the notice of those around him. His overriding interest was to increase the power and authority of his bishopric.

Haimeric's intense involvement with Santiago is not a sign that Diego's relationship with the reform party was good.[23] The chancellor's interest in the archbishopric stemmed from his desire to control the Spanish church rather than from any ideological identification with Diego. Besides, it was a lucrative association. But even though Diego was conspicuous more for his benedictions than for his austerity of life, it is still argued that he evinced a desire to promote the spiritual and moral improvement of his clergy by introducing canons regular into his church.[24] This emphasis is misleading, however. From the end of the eleventh century the canons regular had begun to make inroads into Spain, mainly under the *Rule* of Aachen, but also under the Augustinian.[25] Paschal favored them, and put them to good use. They frequently performed military functions against the Moors and helped to resettle and rechristianize the conquered lands. As part of this movement, Diego took his lead from the French—the France of the time of Hugh and Pontius, not that of St. Bernard—and instituted reforms among the canons of his church. But there was no particular association between Diego and the new reformers.

Indeed, in at least one case it is clear that his political objectives overrode any possible spiritual concern. In 1125 Bishop Gonzalo of Coimbra and Archbishop Bernard of Toledo complained to the curia about Diego's incursions, and their complaints fell on receptive ears. Honorius was only mollified after Diego sent two more emissaries bearing a benediction, and

---

[23] Vones, op. cit., p. 479: "Entgegen der Ansicht von Franz Josef Schmale waren die Beziehungen des Erzbischofs von Compostela zu dieser sich weiter formierenden Reformpartei nicht von Beginn an günstig, sonder bis zum Ende der 20er Jahre eher zweispältig." Schmale (*Studien zum Schisma*, p. 127) thinks that the relationship must have been good since Haimeric was so intensely involved with Santiago. For this reason he believes that it is understandable that Diego ignored the letters from Anaclet's electors and recognized Innocent.

[24] Schmale, op. cit., pp. 128-129. The canons are not specified as regular, but Schmale (n. 34) argues that they were. On pp. 255-256 the *Historia Compostelana* says simply: "Fuit namque in Ecclesiasticis & in saecularibus negotiis vir perspicacissimi ingenii, & quoniam Ecclesia B. Jacobi rudis & indisciplinata erat temporibus illis: applicuit animum ut consuetudines Ecclesiarum Franciae ibi planataret. Quod nimium laboriosum fuit ei, ut bonus tamen agricola spinas & tribulos extirpando, silices atque urticas evellendo utilia plantarum semina collocat. Constituit Canonico praetaxato numero, scilicet septuaginta duos, qui non ingrederentur chorum B. Jacobi nisi superpelliciis, & in capis, cum prius non rasis barbis, capis dissutis & variatis, rostatis pedibus, & hujusmodi ad modum equitum Clericos Ecclesia B. Jacobi haberet." See also Fletcher, *St. James' Catapult*, pp. 163-191.

[25] Servatius, *Paschalis II.*, p. 143.

aroused his friends in the curia to intervene on his behalf. As opposed to
Diego, Gonzalo did have ties with the new reform.[26] His archdeacon,
Tello, founded the monastery of Santa Cruz in Coimbra, which adopted
the customs and *Rule* of the canons regular of St. Rufus of Avignon.
Santa Cruz developed into a center of the new reform in Portugal.

The great preponderance of evidence, therefore, indicates that Diego
was not an exponent of the new reform, and Haimeric's association with
him is not a sign of the spiritual inclinations of either of them. On the
contrary, they both continued the abuses which reformers like Ivo of
Chartres specifically tried to eradicate.[27] Diego's tardy support of Innocent
must be seen in political, not ideological terms.

Perhaps the best indication of what Haimeric represented comes from
Guigo of Chartreuse, because Guigo was not a hostile, but a friendly witness. Guigo wrote to Haimeric shortly after the chancellor's visit, probably
in 1132. The letter conveys the impression that Guigo was reluctant to
speak out, but that out of his zeal for the good of the church, he felt that
he must do so. He speaks in general of the sins of pride, indulgence, and
living in opulence, and then turns specifically to the Roman court. Calling
attention to its abuses, he emphasizes the use of precious vestments, the
holding of banquets, and the resort to the use of arms. He says that either
he must say that what is bad is good, or he must be silent—which, he acknowledges, would be safer—or he must reprehend the apostolic see for its
excesses. Nothing, he asserts—not the fervor of princes, the brightness of
ornaments, the multitude of affairs, the glory of solemn ceremonies, the
delicacy of banquets, nor magnificent gifts—should be allowed to damage
one's soul. Recommending that these worldly delights be eschewed,
Guigo advises Haimeric to give himself over to prayer and good works.[28]

In spite of these admonitions, Haimeric and Innocent did not initiate a
program of reform substantially different from those of the recent past,
and the Roman curia continued to function as Guigo described it.[29] St.

---

[26] Vones, *Die 'Historia Compotellana'*, p. 480.

[27] *Decretum*, c. 85, PL 161:353: *"Ut nullus pro gradu sacerdotii conferendo, nec antea, nec
post munus sine periculo exigat.* (1, q. I c *Qui per pecuniam*) Quicunque pro conferendo cui-
quam sacerdotii gradu, aut munus quodcunque, aut promissiones muneris antequam ordinetur acceperit, vel etiam postquam ordinatus fuerit, in aliquo se pro hoc ipso praesumpserit
munerari, sive ille qui dederit, sive qui acceperit, juxta sententiam Chalcedonensis concilii
gradus sui periculum sustinebit." Schmale (op. cit., p. 134) applauds Haimeric's bribing of
the opposition in 1124 because he believes that it was done in a good cause. "Bei der Wahl
von 1124 war man im Grunde nur sehr hart an einem Schisma vorbeigekommen, dank der
Umsicht des Kanzlers, der die Schwäche des Gegners ausnutzen wusste." For the use of
money to obtain ecclesiastical offices during this period see also Noonan, *Bribes*, pp. 144-151.

[28] *Lettres des premiers Chartreux*, 1, *S. Bruno, Guiges, St. Antheleme* (Sources Chretiennes,
88), ed. un Chartreux (Paris, 1962), pp. 183-195: "Numquid Ecclesia romana conviva
respuit, exercitum non conducit, bella non conficit? Non est autem discipulus supra magistrum, neque apostolus major eo qui misit illum; sed potius perfectus omnis erit, si sit sicut
magister ejus."

[29] Maleczek, "Das Kardinalskollegium," p. 34.

Bernard's recommendations to Eugenius III in *De consideratione* reflect what the reformers saw as its ongoing excesses. Even though St. Bernard may have had kind words for Haimeric, contemporary historians are hard put to reconcile the chancellor's actions in 1130 with the ideals of the saint. One suggests that in contriving Innocent's election Haimeric might even have been acting legally. His actions, the argument goes, could have been justified under the medieval concept of the right of resistance because the Pierleoni forced him to take such drastic steps. He also wonders whether if Christ had been in the same position, he might not have acted similarly. As in the case of Christ, he reflects, there are times when one is forced to resort to revolutionary measures to achieve what is right. If the choice were between complying with the moral and legal conventions, and having Anaclet as pope on the one hand, and doing what was necessary to assure the election of Innocent on the other, the choice was obvious.[30]

But, of course, the choice was not obvious, and that is why there was such a profound split within the church. Haimeric's behavior as well as his history of good relations both with entrepreneurs like Diego of Compostella and monks like St. Bernard suggests that differences in attitude toward the reform did not cause the split. Innocent's record substantiates this hypothesis.

---

[30] Schmale, op. cit., p. 163 & n. 5.

Chapter XII

INNOCENT II

In spite of his highly irregular election, his rejection by the most distinguished members of the curia, and his banishment from Rome, Innocent defied the odds, and became the recognized pope. To understand the politics of the curia as well as the forces operating in the church at large, it is critical to understand how he achieved this remarkable turnabout. Was it because of his own outstanding qualities, because he represented the new tendencies in the church, because he was the pawn of his chancellor, or because of some combination of these factors? In general he has been seen as Haimeric's creation, an electable vehicle who was sympathetic to the policies originated by the more creative and aggressive members of his party.[1] He was an experienced diplomat with a decent reputation. As an elder cardinal he could have been expected to have the support of the senior as well as the junior generation within the curia, and as a Roman, he should have had no trouble maintaining himself within the city.

The restraint Anaclet and his cardinals showed in criticizing Innocent by comparison with the shrill accusations raised against him by Innocent's protagonists is often interpreted as an indication that Anaclet was vulnerable to such attacks, while Innocent was not. If Innocent had not lived a morally upright life, it is assumed, his opponents would have used his liabilities as ammunition against him. This conclusion may be true, but the reverse is not. Unscrupulous opponents might well have invented charges against Anaclet which had no foundation in fact. Rather than taking the contrast in accusations against each candidate as a measure of his presumed virtue, Peter of Porto's letter provides a more judicious assessment. The dean of the cardinals says that prior to their election, both Anaclet and Innocent had lived wise and honest lives.[2]

Once elected, however, a new Innocent emerged, whom Peter of Porto would hardly have recognized. Far exceeding any of the displays his predecessors had put on, he used pageantry and the majesty of his office to awe those who were fortunate enough to see these brilliant spectacles. Even Calixtus, who entered Rome for the first time wearing a jewel-encrusted garment, and riding a white horse, seems pallid by comparison. Innocent allowed himself to be regally received at Cluny, and later he

---

[1] Klewitz, "Das Ende," p. 228.

[2] William of Malmesbury, *The Historia Novella*, ed. cit., p. 7.

consecrated its huge basilica.[3] In the Council of Liège in 1131 he impressed the Northerners with Roman pomp, and accepted gifts from Lothar and the clergy. At the celebration of the Lord's supper, he also distributed some of his own largess, which Suger describes as sumptuous in the Roman tradition. Suger appears to have been very impressed with the whole scene, and describes it in minute detail—the procession of Innocent and his court riding white horses covered with white blankets; the jewels; Innocent's use of the *frigium*, an *ornamentum imperiale*, as Suger points out; and finally approaching apotheosis, the pope's head surrounded by a golden diadem. Barons and vassals of the church performed the functions of the *strator*, and coins were thrown to the crowd to keep them from crowding in too closely. The royal way along which the procession moved glistened with precious fabrics hung from trees.[4]

After the overwhelming impression he created at Liège, Innocent went on to St. Denis to celebrate Easter. There, he did no less. He arrived at the basilica wearing a golden crown, with silver, precious gems, and pearls which glowed even more brilliantly. After mass, there was a great feast, and then the following day the same procession wended its way to St. Remi. The third day after Easter Innocent and his entourage set off on a tour of the churches of Gaul, asking them to supply from their riches the deficits of his own.[5]

Not everyone was favorably impressed with this display, however. Anselm of Gembloux seems to have been negatively disposed toward Innocent from the beginning, mentioning that Gregory had usurped the privilege of election from Honorius with the concurrence of certain cardinals. In describing the Council of Liège, he compares Innocent's entry into the city with the he-goat (*hyrcus caprarum*) in chapter eight of the Book of Daniel.[6] The he-goat produces many horns, the last of which the Book of Daniel says was:

---

[3] Chibnall, *Ecclesiastic History* 6, pp. 418-420: " . . . Cluniacenses, ut eius aduentum cognouerunt, lx equos seu mulos cum omni apparatu congruo papae et cardinalibus clericis destinuauerunt, et usque ad suam basilicam fauorabiliter conduxerunt."

[4] Suger, *Vie de Louis VI*, p. 262: "Summo mane vero extrinseca via ad ecclesiam Martirum in Strata, cum multo collateralium collegio quasi secreto commeavit, ibique more romano seipsos preparantes, multo et mirabili ornatu circumdantes, capiti ejus frigium, ornamentum imperiale, instar galee circulo aureo circinatum imponunt, albo et palliato equo insidentem educunt, ipsi etiam palliati equos albis operturis variatos equitantes, odas personando festive geminati procedunt." For other sources on the council see Watterich, *Gesta* 2, p. 202; Mühlbacher, *Die streitige Papstwahl*, p. 134, n. 3; Bernhardi, *Lothar*, pp. 356-357 & notes. Bernhardi and Mühlbacher draw attention to the pomp. Palumbo (*Lo Scisma*, p. 369) mentions the good living of Innocent and his curia. Rather than an increase in simplicity and parsimony in the curia during the reigns of Honorius and Innocent, Palumbo contends that the popes after Paschal and Gelasius no longer stressed these values.

[5] Suger, op. cit., p. 264: "Parveniens vero ad sanctorum basilicam, coronis aureis rutilantem, argenti et plus cencies auri preciosarum gemmarum et margaritarum splendore fulguantem divina missa celebrans . . . Exinde Galliarum ecclesias visitando et de earum copia inopia sue defectum supplendo, . . ."

[6] *Sigiberti Gemblacensis chronica*, cont. Anselmi a. 1112-1135, ed. D. L. C. Bethmann, MGH SS 6:383: "Dominica in medio quadragesimae Gregorius, sicut hyrcus caprarum in

a little horn, which waxed exceedingly great, toward the south, and toward the east, and toward the glorious land. And it waxed great, even to the host of heaven; and some of the host and of the stars it cast down to the ground, and trampled upon them. Yes, it magnified itself, even to the prince of the host; and it took away from him the continual burnt offering, and the place of his sanctuary was cast down. And the host was given over to it together with the continual burnt offering through transgression; and it cast down truth to the ground, and it did its pleasure and prospered.

Daniel asks a holy man to interpret this vision, and the holy man identifies the he-goat and each of its horns with a king of Greece. Of the last king he says:

And in the latter time of their kingdom, when the transgressors are come to the full, a king of fierce countenance, and understanding dark sentences, shall destroy wonderfully, and shall prosper and do his pleasure; and he shall destroy the mighty ones and the holy people. And through his policy he shall cause craft to prosper in his hand; and he shall magnify himself in his heart, and in their security shall he destroy many: he shall also stand up against the prince of princes; but he shall be broken without hand.[7]

Using this simile, Anselm says that Innocent approached St. Lambert's for the coronation as if he were celebrating a Roman triumph.

It was a daring text for Anselm to use because it evoked allusions of craftiness, the will to power, resistance to God, and finally a fall. But the *Glossa Ordinaria* and the gloss of Nicolas de Lyra reveal that the passage generated even more emotive images. Commenting on the *hircus caprarum* in the *Moraliter*, the *Glossa Ordinaria* calls it a foul animal signifying a tyrannical prince detested for the stench of infamy. *Et non tangebat* refers to lovers of earthly things, whom the tyrant does not harm, but rather favors. Of *porro hircus* he says, that is a very great power, notable because of its wicked adherents. In the text itself the *Glossa Ordinaria* explains the symbols of the passage. Again speaking of the *hircus caprarum* it says that the expression refers to the kingdom of the Greeks, signified by a goat because the Greeks were extravagant, just as a he-goat is a foul and extravagant animal. Nicolas of Lyra, writing about 1300, goes even further. By a *hyrcus* is meant the power of the evil ones because the 25th chapter of Matthew states that (on the day of the last judgment) the sheep will be on the right hand, and the goats on the left.[8] Anselm's brief simile thus

---

Daniele, qui pedibus terram non tangebat, cum curribus et redis ab aecclesia sancti Martini in publico monte, quasi Romae via triumphali, usque ad capitolium sancti Lamberti ascendit . . ." See Bernhardi, *Lothar*, p. 358.

[7] *The Modern Reader's Bible*, ed. Richard G. Moulton (New York, 1945), pp. 675-676.

[8] *Biblia Sacra cum Glossa Interlineari, Ordinaria, Nicolas Lyrani expositionibus, Burgensis Additionibus & Thoringi Replicis* 4 (Venice, 1588), p. 313.

carried overtones which were as hostile as any that Innocent's followers invented for Anaclet. Either Anselm must have been disgusted by the extravagance and papal display, or one of Innocent's critics must have revealed things which inspired the comparison between the pope and the he-goat.

Although Innocent shared the stage with Lothar in Liège, he laid great stress on his own *dies coronae*, which were performed with Roman splendour on certain feast days even within the French villages where he spent his exile. St. Bernard observed his triumphal procession to the Lateran palace after his return to Rome, and this, no doubt, was one of the spectacles the abbot had in mind when he wrote his famous contrast between the apostle Peter and Peter's successors. Peter did not dress in garments ornamented with precious jewels, cover himself with a roof of gold, ride a white horse, and surround himself with knights and ministers, Bernard pointed out in *De consideratione*. For Peter it was enough to obey Christ's command: "If you love me, feed my sheep."[9]

But Innocent was an imperial, not a pastoral pope. In Panegyrics he was addressed as "Caesar and ruler of the whole world," and as "true emperor." Cardinal Gerard of Santa Croce, the future Lucius II, said of him in 1137 that the "*ecclesia te in caesarem totiusque orbis dominatorem et elegit et consecravit.*"[10] Innocent not only acted the part in rituals and ceremonies involving *regnum* and *sacerdotium*, but in others as well. A notable example is the scene when the aged abbot, Hariulf, of the abbey of Oudenburg in Holland came to Rome to plead his case against the abbey of St. Médard of Soissons. After prior conversations with Haimeric, the chancellor led Hariulf to Innocent, who was sitting in the consistory of the Lateran palace surrounded by his cardinals and noble Romans dressed in ceremonial clothing. Hariulf performed the Romano-Byzantine act of *proskynesis*, kissing the feet of the pope seated on a raised tribunal. In return, the pope raised him and gave him the kiss of peace.[11] This ceremony was an exact repetition of the old imperial ceremony, which carried overtones of the pontiff as the eastern godlike basileus.

As his final statement to the world Innocent chose as his resting place what no other pope had used—a porphyry sarcophagus.[12] The symbolism

---

[9] *De consideratione*, lib. 4, III, *Sancti Bernardi Opera*, ed. cit., 3, p. 453; Deér, *Dynastic Porphyry Tombs*, pp. 146-147.

[10] Krautheimer, *Rome*, p. 151; Percy Ernst Schramm, *Kaiser, Könige und Päpste* 4 (Stuttgart, 1979), pp. 183-184, n. 26.

[11] *Chronicon Aldenburgense Majus, Appendix ad Hariulfum*, PL 174:1544-1554; Ernst Müller, "Der Bericht des Abtes Hariulf von Oudenburg über seine Prozessverhandlungen an der römischen Kurie im Jahre 1141," *Neues Archiv der Gesselschaft für ältere deutsche Geschichtskunde* 48 (1930), 97-115; Maleczek, "Das Kardinalskollegium," pp. 66-67; Deér, *Dynastic Porphyry Tombs*, pp. 148-149.

[12] Deér, *Dynastic Porphyry Tombs*, pp. 149-152. Benedict, a canon of St. Peter's, reveals this bit of information incidentally to identify the emperor Hadrian's tomb in the *Mirabilia urbis Romae*. The *Mirabilia* was the first guide to the antiquities of Rome, and was written in the period of Innocent's undisputed power between the death of Anaclet and the revolt of

was not lost, for porphyry had a long, and well-known monarchical and liturgical tradition. In earlier times porphyry sarcophagi had been used for the burial of saints and martyrs in imitation of imperial ceremonial practices. Although the ecclesiastical-liturgical usage paralleled the monarchical, it did not signify any rivalry between church and state. Innocent was the first pope to break with this tradition by using an imperial sarcophagus. He himself made all of the arrangements, ordering the emperor Hadrian's sarcophagus to be removed from the Castel St. Angelo. Anticipating the practices of the Renaissance popes, he first had it placed in the open near the Lateran. Later he had it transferred inside the basilica, where it served as his tomb until it was destroyed in a great fire in 1308. His remains were then moved to Santa Maria in Trastevere, where they still are kept.

Innocent's imitation of Roman imperial practices took many other conscious forms. One was the writing of the *Mirabilia urbis Romae*, the first guide to the ancient monuments of Rome.[13] It was composed during Innocent's years of undisputed power—after Anaclet's death, and before the revolt of the Roman commune in 1143. This revival of antiquity was a glorification of empire, and the divergence between it and the ideals of the reform can be seen by contrasting two different churches built in, and within the vicinity of Rome about the same time.[14] The two churches are those of Ss Vincenzo ed Anastasio alle Tre Fontane, located a few kilometers outside of the gates of Rome, and Santa Maria in Trastevere. In 1138, after Anaclet's death and before the Lateran Council of 1139, Innocent conceded the church at Tre Fontane to the Cistercians. Except for its nave, the church is representative of French Cistercian architecture at its most austere. This style of architecture did not attract Innocent, and it did not serve as inspiration for his own works. The new form of architecture spread elsewhere in Italy, but not into Rome.[15]

By contrast, within Rome Innocent rebuilt Anaclet's old cardinalate church—Santa Maria in Trastevere—into a splendid monument, using

---

the Roman commune in 1143. It was later incorporated into the *Graphia Aureae Urbis Romae*, a composite work compiled in 1155. Its most recent edition is ed. by Roberto Valentini & Giuseppe Zucchetti, *Codice Topografico della Città di Roma*, vol. 90 of *Fonti per la Storia d'Italia* (Rome, 1946), pp. 17-65; it is also edited in the *Liber Censuum*, 1, pp. 262-283; Percy Ernst Schramm, *Kaiser, Könige und Päpste* 3 (Stuttgart, 1968), pp. 322-338. For recent discussions of the *Mirabilia* and its significance for Innocent's reign, see two articles in *Renaissance and Renewal in the Twelfth Century*, ed. Robert L. Benson and Giles Constable with Carol D. Lanham (Cambridge, Massachusetts, 1982): Robert L. Benson, "Political *Renovatio*: Two Models from Roman Antiquity," pp. 339-386 at p. 353; Ernst Kitzinger, "The Arts as Aspects of a Renaissance: Rome and Italy," pp. 637-670 at p. 648; see also Ingo Herklotz, "Der Campus Lateranensis im Mittelalter," *Römisches Jahrbuch für Kunstgeschichte* 22 (1985), 1-43, esp. 3, 11.

[13] See the preceding footnote.

[14] Kitzinger, "The Arts as Aspects of a Renaissance," p. 648.

[15] Ibid.; Hanno Hahn, *Die frühe Kirchenbaukunst der Zisterzienser* (Berlin, 1957), pp. 171-173; Vincenzo Golzio and Giuseppe Zander, *Le Chiese di Roma dall'XI al XVI Secolo*, vol. 4 of *Roma Christiana*, ed. Carlo Galassi Paluzzi (Bologna, 1963), pp. 67-68.

classical and early Christian motifs. Not a "building pope," Innocent obviously picked his one show case with care. As if to erase the very memory of his antagonist, he had the Santa Maria of Petrus totally destroyed and replaced by a bigger, more majestic building, using the latest Roman style. In an unmistakable analogy, he modeled it after the old St. Peter's, the church Constantine had erected to commemorate his victory over Maxentius.[16] Santa Maria became the new symbol of the church triumphant.

The opulence of the basilica and the richness of its decorations far exceeded anything else built during the *renovatio* in Rome in the first half of the twelfth century. Although the use of Roman columns and capitals was not unusual, nowhere else was there another series of modillions so rich and diverse as those in Santa Maria. The columns were taken from the baths of Caracalla, and in the popular imagination, the palace of Caracalla was recomposed in Santa Maria.[17] Innocent also used porphyry lavishly, and in the *ciborium*, jewels of ancient carving.

But if the columns conveyed majesty, the most striking expression of grandeur in the church was the brilliant apse mosaic. The scene is the enthronement of the Virgin, who is seated on a golden throne next to Christ. In other compositions of the Roman *renovatio* Christ stands, but here he is seated in a more regal pose. The Virgin is crowned and richly dressed as an empress in a beautifully embroidered, jewel-studded garment. There are figures standing both at the right and at the left of the Virgin. At her right are the martyrs, Calixtus I and San Lorenzo, and next to them stands Innocent carrying a replica of the basilica he had remodeled. The entire scene is set against a background of gold mosaics.[18] A dedicatory inscription reads:

> This royal palace, in your honor, O radiant Mother of honor,
> Shines with the splendor of divine grace;
> In which [palace], O Christ, your seat remains forever.
> Worthy of His right hand is she whom the golden robe envelops.
> As the old structure was about to collapse
> Pope Innocent II, thence to be born, renovated it.[19]

---

[16] Kinney, *S. Maria in Trastevere*, p. 311.

[17] Ibid., 325; the sumptuousness of the church is revealed in the *Acta Consecrationis* of 1215: "Igitur decimo anno sui Pontificatus eam [basilicam] ex tot dirui fecit . . . eam pulchri operis columnis capitalis, sumptuosisque fabricis decoravit et pavimento marmoreo tam affabre composito stravit ut vix ei simile reperiri alicubi possit . . ." Filippo Mallerini, *Memorie istoriche della sacrosanta Basilica di S. Maria in Trastevere*, 1891; Kinney, n. 76, p. 216.

[18] *Lib. Pont.* 2, p. 384; *Liber Politicus*, ed. *Liber Censuum* 2, p. 169; Golzio and Zander, *Le Chiese di Roma*, p. 187; Kitzinger, "The Arts as Aspects of a Renaissance," p. 648; Gerhart Ladner, *Die Papstbildnisse des Altertums und des Mittelalters 2 Von Innocenz II. zu Benedikt XI.* (Vatican City, 1970), pp. 9-11; Onophrio Panvinio, *De praecipuis urbis Romae sanctioribusque basilicis quas septem ecclesias vulgo vocant* (Rome, 1570), pp. 64-65; Nilgen, "Maria Regina," pp. 24-32; Philippe Verdier, *Le Couronnement de la Vierge: Les origines et les premiers développements d'un thème iconographique* (Montreal, Paris, 1980), pp. 32, 40-47.

[19] Kinney, *S. Maria in Trastevere*, p. 326.

The mosaic is symbolically rich, but certain themes stand out. The royal emphasis is not fortuitous, but refers to Innocent's imperial pretensions as the emulator both of Christ and of Constantine. By placing the papal throne directly beneath the depiction of the enthroned Christ, surrounded by his bishops during a stational mass, he would appear as the counterpart of the image above his head. Other architectonic features of the mosaic also accentuate Innocent's stature. Like Mary, Innocent positions himself on the right side of Christ, and like Mary, he is worthy of Christ's embrace. By accentuating Mary's worthiness, Innocent implicitly raises the opposite possibility—that she as the symbol of the church might be unworthy. What he seems to be insinuating is that under Anaclet, Santa Maria in Trastevere representing the *Ecclesia Romana* was unworthy of Christ's embrace. When the church in both senses was about to collapse, Innocent rebuilt it, and made it worthy again unto eternity. It is to Innocent in a secondary sense that Christ utters the words printed on the scroll that Mary holds, "Come, my elect, and I will place you on my throne."

On casual observance, there is nothing unusual about the way Innocent depicts himself. There are numerous mosaics and frescoes in Roman churches portraying papal donors standing at the side holding a model of the church they are presenting. There is one significant difference, however; Innocent portrays himself as a saint rather than as a living, humble donor. He is the same size as the saints, stands on the same level, has the same stylized unearthly expression, and is not differentiated from them by wearing the square halo—the symbol of a living pope. By omitting halos for all but Christ and Mary, and possibly Peter—whose halo is lightly sketched, and may have been added later—Innocent takes on the aura of saintliness of those around him. It will be the last time in medieval iconography that a pope will be depicted on the same level as the saints standing in heavenly glory.

Innocent's implicit elevation of himself to sainthood is understandable, since he had just emerged from his bruising struggle with Anaclet when he began his reconstruction of the church. He needed a dramatic medium to proclaim that the papacy not only had returned to its former stature, but had transcended it. It was optimal propaganda for his victory over his foe and the reunification of the church. What it was not was a statement of papal humility associating Innocent with the spirituality and asceticism of the religious movements of the North. A decade earlier Guigo of Chartreuse had admonished him to set a different example. Just as in this visible world light is contrary to darkness and heat is to cold, Guigo said, so also ought your innocence to be contrary to the sins of the whole world, your wisdom to errors, your temperance to luxuries, (my emphasis) your tolerance to adversities and objective justice to vices.[20]

---

[20] *Lettres des premiers Chartreaux*, ed. cit., p. 170; Innocent also did not go out of his way to set an example of simplicity by the way he dressed; rather, Arnulf of Séez says that he dressed in a fashion suitable to his time. "Vestitus autem apostolatus tempore sane con-

Like his predecessors, Innocent gathered funds where he could, and he had the added aggravation of having been forced to spend most of his reign either on military campaigns or in exile. France bore many of the expenses of the itinerant pope, and it has been speculated that one of the reasons why Louis VI was reluctant to allow French prelates to attend the Council of Pisa in 1135 was that he did not want them to be further requisitioned. Even Peter the Venerable complained about these financial burdens.[21] Without being unduly fastidious in complying with canon law, Innocent met emissaries of Diego of Compostella in Pisa, and in return for a benediction of forty marks of silver, he lent a sympathetic ear to their petition.[22] Similarly to Calixtus, Innocent became dependent upon the gifts from Santiago, and when he found them to be inadequate, he indicated his continuing need.[23] Just as Diego's petitions received hearings correlated with his benedictions, so also petitioners to papal courts were successful in proportion to the amount of money they paid.[24] Toward the end of his reign, however, Innocent instituted reforms in the curia, paying wages to cardinals as recompense for their judicial services.[25] When the abbot, Hariulf, came to Rome to plead his case in 1141, Haimeric told him that although in the past people had spoken of the venality of Rome, now the city would be known for its justice. For this reason he admonished Hariulf not to make any payments or give any gifts to anyone in the Roman palace. Hariulf agreed, but then asked Haimeric how much he should give to the pope. He was greatly surprised when Haimeric told him that he should not give Innocent anything.[26]

But just two years previously Innocent reputedly had been unable to resist what must have been a much greater blandishment offered by King

---

veniens," PL 201:183. Some scholars think they detect a note of defensiveness when Arnulf also says: "Quibus enim impresentiarum vestibus induatur, iam non ex ipsius pendent arbitrio, sed sanctorum patrum antiqua constitutione decretum est."

[21] In a letter to Haimeric; Constable, *The Letters of Peter the Venerable* 1, p. 112: "Non se putabant nostri tale apud dominum suum meritum reposuisse, pro cuius obaedientia et seruito dicuntur se suaque pene omnia expendisse." Bernhardi, *Lothar*, pp. 634-635. Another cause of the disaffection between Louis VI and Innocent may have been the murders of two members of the French clergy in which Louis might have been implicated. See Palumbo, *Lo Scisma*, pp. 525-526.

[22] *Historia Compostelana*, ed. cit., p.521: "ibique primum Compostellani Archiepiscopi nuntii benedictionem spontaneam, scilicet XL. Marcas puri argenti deferentes, ei cum gaudio occurrerunt: quos honorifice susceptos, eorum petitionibus benignam aurem accommodans, jocunde remisit."

[23] Ibid., 561-562; JL 7665.

[24] *Bertholdi Zwifaltensis Chronicon*, c. 44, MGH SS 10:119; Bernhardi, *Lothar*, p. 637 & n. 12.

[25] The oath which an advocate had to take is dated to the last years of Innocent's reign (1138-1143): "Pretium exinde non suscipiam, nec per summissam personam, nec suscipi permittam. . . . Hec omnia observabo bona fide, sine fraude et malo ingenio, quamdiu domnus papa Innocentius vel successores sui C libras vel valens denarium papiensium nobis advocatis et judicibus annis singulis solvent." *Liber Censuum* 2, p. 127; *Lib. Pont.* 2, p. 383.

[26] PL 174:1545.

Stephen of England. John of Salisbury reports this transaction in a case brought before Innocent at the Lateran Council of 1139 by Henry I's daughter, Matilda.[27] She and Stephen of Blois contested the English throne after her father's death, and although Innocent had confirmed Stephen's election at once, he nevertheless agreed to hear her appeal. John presents a graphic description of the enquiry. Bishop Ulger of Angers, whom he describes as the leading bishop of Gaul, and outstanding for his learning, good repute, unbending justice, and most pertinently, for his freedom of mind, presented Matilda's case. As Stephen's advocate, Arnulf of Séez used the sorts of scandalous charges he had polished against Anaclet in the papal schism. He argued that Matilda was not entitled to succeed her father because she had been born of an incestuous union, the daughter of a nun, whom Henry had dragged from the monastery at Romney, and had deprived of her veil. Although John does not mention it, Arnulf's accusation was particularly heinous, because the sainted Anselm of Canterbury himself had heard the case of Matilda's mother, had declared her free to marry, and had officiated at the ceremony. After describing Matilda's allegedly dubious birth, John relates that Arnulf disputed Ulger's allegation that Stephen was guilty of perjury for breaking his oath to Henry I to support Matilda.

Ulger snapped back, accusing Arnulf of being a skillful lier, conspicuous even among Normans in this art. He proceeded to demonstrate the archdeacon of Séez knew not whereof he spoke, but Innocent decided shortly that he had heard enough. Without passing judgment, and rejecting the advice of Guy, one of his cardinals, he accepted Stephen's gifts, and confirmed his occupation of England and Normandy. Thereupon Ulger wittily remarked that "The betrothal will take place outdoors, for Peter has left home, and the house is given over to money chargers."

Although John is accused of being biased against Stephen, and of taking impish delight in retailing malicious gossip, his judgments have been found to be fair, and he has only rarely been found to be guilty of factual slips.[28] Since we know that Arnulf had a penchant for poisonous rhetoric, there is no reason to doubt that he did not resort to it on this propitious occasion. As for Innocent, he no doubt already had decided that he preferred the weak Stephen to Matilda with her marriage into the powerful house of Anjou. He did not need to hear the arguments, but in any case he would have been partial to Arnulf, who had just thrown himself mightily into his defense in the schism. Nevertheless, it was appropriate that Stephen should appreciate Innocent's judgment, and reward him commensurately.

---

[27] *John of Salisbury's Mémoires of the Papal Court*, ed. & trans. by Marjorie Chibnall (London, 1956, repr. 1962, 1965), pp. 83-85.

[28] Brooke, *The English Church*, p. 179 & n. 1; Chibnall in the introduction to *John of Salisbury's Mémoires*, p. xxxv; in *The World of Orderic Vitalis*, pp. 200-201, Chibnall suggests that John may have been influenced by later reports.

It may have been Stephen's gift, which Innocent used to pay off the last of Anaclet's supporters in order to hasten the end of the schism.[29] It is probable that Peter the Deacon's assertion to this effect is accurate, since the practice was not foreign to Innocent's party; as we know, for example, Haimeric had used bribes to obtain support for Lambert of Ostia in the papal election of 1124. Innocent and his followers knew that moral opprobrium was attached to such practices, because they had accused Anaclet and his family of disbursing money in similar ways. Yet, in his acquisition and use of funds Innocent differed little from the practices of Calixtus and Honorius. Since there were few institutions for assuring a steady income to the pope and the curia, the temptation to exchange favors for money must have been great. Likewise, the bribing of one's opponents was a time-honored procedure, used most successfully by Anaclet's father in obtaining support for Calixtus in Rome. What is significant about Innocent's conduct is that there are no reports that he lived simply or that his demands were light. On the contrary, the evidence indicates that he lived and dressed in the style of previous popes, and that his requisitions were burdensome. Even granting that a pope would not be expected to live like a monk, one would expect that if Innocent had wanted to set the tone for a church dedicated to internal reform and to stressing pastoral duties, he would have set a proper example. Guigo of Chartreuse and St. Bernard believed that it was incumbent upon the pope to be the model of the good shepherd.

Bernard not only was critical of the display which characterized Innocent's reign, but also of the great acceleration of appeals and *causae maiores* brought before the curia. Innocent encouraged the use of the papal courts as one of his primary means of strengthening and centralizing the papacy.[30] For this task he needed an increasing number of jurists, and of the six who were active during his reign, he appointed four.[31] Bernard, who looked back to the more simple days of St. Peter, however, saw this vastly increased tempo of judicial activity as an abuse. Day and night the curia sounds with the cries of advocates, he complained, and justice becomes ever more remote.[32] Worse, the curia not only heard ecclesiastical cases, but also secular. Justinian's law fills the papal palace, Bernard charged, and while there is constant wrangling, there is little justice.[33] Bernard knew whereof he spoke, because he had had six months in which to observe curial activity after the tribunal held before Roger II in Salerno in the fall of 1137.[34]

---

[29] Petrus Diaconus, *Chronicon*, MGH SS 34:607; Palumbo, *Lo Scisma*, p. 589; Amélineau ("Saint Bernard," p. 101) claims that Peter was not impartial, and that since no other sources reveal Innocent's corruption, Peter's charge should be discounted.

[30] Maleczek, "Das Kardinalskollegium," p. 59.

[31] Zenker, *Die Mitglieder*, p. 212.

[32] *De consideratione, Sancti Bernardi Opera*, ed. cit. 3, pp. 408-410; 435-439.

[33] Ibid., 397-402.

[34] Maleczek, "Das Kardinalskollegium," p. 71.

It is ironical that in his campaign to bring judicial disputes before the curia, the one innovation which Innocent made in his program of reform in the conciliar decrees from Clermont in 1130 to the Lateran in 1139 was that monks and canons regular be prohibited from studying medicine and secular law.[35] The reasoning behind this prohibition was that the study of civil law would interfere with the cure of souls, and that the study of medicine might lead to unchastity. Presumably Innocent was less concerned with the threat either to his own or to his cardinal's pastoral duties. On the very day in which the Council of Pisa reiterated canon 5 of the Council of Clermont forbidding the study of medicine and civil law, Innocent quoted a series of laws out of the *Codex* and the *Digest*.[36] The only constraint on the use of civil law in the curia was that cardinals could draw no argument from secular law which contributed to the practical realization of papal primacy.[37]

The concentration of justice in the papal curia, and the use of secular as well as ecclesiastical law is evidence that Innocent's primary concern was to increase the power of the papacy by centralizing authority therein. If his main objective had been the promotion of the values of the new religious movements, then he would have acted more in keeping with the dictates of Guigo of Chartreuse and St. Bernard.[38] Their support for him, therefore, either was based upon a misconception of his ideology, or upon other factors. Or possibly it was a combination of both.

If Innocent did not himself serve as a model for the new reform movement, he nevertheless did promote it. He would have been resisting current trends if he had not, and there was no reason for him to do so, since these orders supported him even if he did not exemplify their ideals. France was undergoing an economic, political, and spiritual revival, and

---

[35] Canon 5 of the Council of Clermont in 1130; Mansi, *Collectio Sacrorum Conciliorum* 21, pp. 437-440; Maleczek, op. cit., p. 40 & ns. 51-52. The decree was repeated in the councils of Rheims (1131), Pisa (1135) and the Lateran (1139). Mansi's edition of the councils is defective, and must be supplemented by individual studies. See, for example, Robert Somerville's analysis of the decrees of the Council of Pisa. "The Council of Pisa, 1135: A Re-examination of the Evidence of the Canons," *Speculum* 45 (1970), 98-114, esp. 111-114. In this council there was an express prohibition of selling Corsican Christians as slaves, a prohibition probably relating to the competition between Pisa and Genoa for the control of the Corsican church. As far as his reform program was concerned, however, his one innovation was the stricture on studying medicine and secular law.

[36] Maleczek, op. cit., p. 60.

[37] Ibid., 61.

[38] Bernard describes what a pope should be in *De consideratione, Sancti Bernardi Opera*, ed. cit., 3, p. 466: "De cetero oportere te esse considera formam iustitiae, sanctimoniae speculum, pietatis exemplar, assertorem veritatis, fidei defensorem, doctorem gentium, christianorum ducem, amicum sponsi, sponsae paranymphum, cleri ordinatorem, pastorem plebium, magistrum insipientium, refugium oppressorum, pauperum advocatum, miserorum spem, tutorem pupillorum, iudicem viduarum, oculum caecorum, linguam mutorum, baculum senum, ultorem sclerum, malorum metum, bonorum gloriam, virgam potentium, malleum tyrannorum, regum patrem, legum moderatorem, canonum dispensatorem, sal terrae, orbis lumen, sacerdotem Altissimi, vicarium Christi, Christum Domini postremo deum Pharaonis."

the orders reflected this vitality. It was also Haimeric's homeland, and the country which gave Innocent succor in the time of his distress. What is surprising is how little this identification is reflected in Innocent's appointments to the college of cardinals. Of fifty cardinals, only nine were French.[39] Moreover, these appointments were almost his only effort at making the papacy representative of the church at large. He appointed one German—Theodwinus, abbot of Gorze—but his forty other appointments were all Italian.[40]

Even more astonishing was his preference for Benedictines.[41] It was only after his reign that the new orders superseded the older.[42] Innocent appointed seven Benedictines, but only four canons regular and four Cistercians. By contrast, his successors appointed no Benedictines. Celestine II appointed one canon, Lucius II two canons and one Carthusian, and Eugenius III three Cistercians and six canons.[43] Thus, Innocent's promotions to the cardinalate do not reveal that he wished to emphasize the new religious ideology. From the time of Leo IX popes had shown that they wanted to make the papacy more representative of the whole church. Innocent continued that policy, but he did not transcend it.

A brief description of events at Farfa during this period may further help to illuminate what Innocent's attitudes were toward the new and the old monasticism, and also whether Farfa's abbot, Adenulf, supported him because of these attitudes or for other reasons.[44] Farfa was an imperial monastery. Berard III, its abbot at the beginning of the twelfth century, was loyal to Henry V. He participated in Henry's coronation, and in return the emperor presented him with a precious gift. In 1104 Berard was involved in a dispute with Oddo and Octavian, counts of the Sabina, and Anaclet's father and Tebaldus dei Cenci were called in as arbitrators. Petrus Leonis was at first sympathetic to Berard, but swayed by the arguments of the counts, he ultimately voted against him.

Guido succeeded Berard in 1119, and although Calixtus supported him in his struggle with continuing internal problems, he was forced to resign in favor of Adenulf in 1125. Since there was no imperial candidate to support in the papal election of 1130, there was no tradition to guide Adenulf. He decided for Innocent, but for reasons which are not obvious. It could have been that given Farfa's history of antagonism toward Rome,

[39] Zenker, *Die Mitglieder*, pp. 196, 202.

[40] Ibid., 206.

[41] Ibid., 246: "Es wurde schon darauf hingeweisen, dass Innozenze, obwohl er selbst dem Kanonikertum angehört, nicht diese religiöse Gemeinschaft bei seinen Kreationen bevorzugte, sonder in erstaunlich hohem Mass Benediktiner in das Kollegium berief, bei denen es sich auschliesslich um Äbte handelte."

[42] Ibid., 208.

[43] Ibid., 208-210.

[44] Ganzer, *Die Entwicklung des Auswärtigen Kardinalats*, pp. 81-83; I. Schuster, *L'Imperiale Abbazie di Farfa* (Rome, 1921), pp. 247-280; Zenker, *Die Mitglieder*, pp. 160-161.

and its struggle for independence, it was prone to reject anyone favored by the Romans. If in addition it had a grudge against the family of that candidate, there would have been added reason to opt for his opponent.[45] But there were also other strains between Adenulf and Anaclet which are not well documented, but which are alluded to in a letter which Anaclet wrote to a bishop, probably one near Farfa such as Sutri, on May 15, 1130.[46] Anaclet inveighed against Adenulf for breaking his oath and invading the *regalia* of St. Peter after the death of Honorius II. Presumably in retaliation Anaclet's supporters invaded and sacked the lands of Farfa, and Adenulf joined Innocent on his flight to France. Two years later, in gratitude Innocent made Adenulf a cardinal.

As a member of Innocent's entourage Adenulf came into frequent contact with St. Bernard. When Bernard returned to Clairvaux after the end of the schism, he promised a colony of Cistercians to console Adenulf, who had been reimposed as abbot in 1137. True to his word, he dispatched a group of monks under the leadership of Bernard of Pisa, the future Eugenius III. Adenulf received them with great warmth, and housed them in the neighboring monastery of the Holy Savior at Scandriglia.

Innocent also had urged St. Bernard to send the Cistercians to Adenulf, promising them seas and mountains for the reform of the monastery of Scandriglia. He did not keep his promises, however, and in 1140 Bernard of Pisa wrote letters to the pope and to St. Bernard, describing the difficult situation in Scandriglia and complaining that the pope had not kept his word.[47] Innocent's response seems to have been to transfer the group of Cistercians to Acque Salvie, a dreadful place located in the swamps near Rome, where many of the monks contracted malaria.[48] In this whole

---

45 Palumbo suggests these reasons; *Lo Scisma*, pp. 169, 431-432.

46 JL 8390; Palumbo, *Lo Scisma*, "Atti di Anacleto II," XXII, pp. 657-658; PL 179:709: "Hoc idem et de abbate Farfensi noveritis factum, qui post mortem beatae memoriae papae Honorii, contempto juramento quod Romanae Ecclesiae fecerat, beati Petri regalia impudenti temeritate invasit, et nunc Dei Ecclesiam persequi, et in quibus potest juvatus furia infestare non cessat." Note that Anaclet speaks of Honorius "of blessed memory."

47 In the letter to St. Bernard, Bernard of Pisa said: "Caeterum, domine, ut de loco loquar ad quem me misistis, sic cucurri quasi in incertum, sic pugnavi, quasi aerem verberans. Nam dominus papa, cujus litteris evocati sumus, promissionem quam de ejusdem loci confirmatione fecerat, opere non complevit sicut et praesens tempus probat." PL 182:549. To Innocent Bernard of Pisa said: "loquar autem in amaritudine animae meae. Conquerimur, domine, de te, se apud te . . . factum ut imperasti: venimus ad monasterium Sancti Salvatoris sicut mandaveras in litteris tuis servo tuo, patri nostro. Ubi est ergo nunc exspectatio mea, et tua promissio? . . . Crudelissimum quippe videtur, et ab omni humanitatis officio longe remotum, illum [Adenulf] fraudare a desiderio suo, qui nos prium coepit amare quam nosse, qui nos patris affectu in filios adoptavit, adeo ut, si fieri potuisset, oculos suos eruisset, et dedisset nobis . . . " PL 182:547-548.

48 Ernaldus, *Vita Bernardi*, lib. III, PL 185:317: "Abbas Farfensis conventum fratrum a Claravalle vocaverat, monasterium eis aedificaturus; sed Romanus impedivit Antistes, eis et sibi tollens, eos in loco altero ordinavit." This was the monastery at Tre Fontane; see n. 15 above.

affair, Schuster, who has written a history of Farfa during this period, speaks of Innocent as Adenulf's secret antagonist, whose actions damaged the Cistercians.

These events show how complex the interrelationship was at the time of the schism, and the many anomalies indicate that it would be simplistic to reduce them to two sides representing progressive and conservative ideologies.[49] Adenulf's enthusiasm for the Cistercians was mainly ignited when he met St. Bernard in France, after he had already committed himself to Innocent. In all probability he chose Innocent over Anaclet because Anaclet's father had ruled against Farfa, and because Anaclet himself had encouraged a neighboring bishop to retaliate after Adenulf had invaded the *regalia* of St. Peter. Adenulf may have thought that he could take advantage of the upheavals in Rome to enlarge the holdings of Farfa, but Anaclet moved quickly to defend the lands of St. Peter.

Innocent's seemingly close relationship with Adenulf and his own attraction to Cistercian ideals is also called into question by his treatment of the band of Cistercians led by Bernard of Pisa. It is paradoxical that on the one hand he encouraged them to come to Farfa, but that on the other he treated them so inhospitably. At the very least, the fact that he did not attempt to create conditions which would have allowed them to flourish shows that he was less than wholeheartedly committed to their goals.

Innocent's treatment of the Cistercians hints at a side to his nature, which was revealed more dramatically at the Lateran Council of 1139. After Anaclet's death in January 1138, and the short reign of Victor IV, almost all of Anaclet's cardinals came over to Innocent, and worked routinely at curial business. There was apparently a return to normalcy, which Innocent abruptly shattered at the Lateran Council. He delivered a sermon, regaling the throng with the reasons why those who had supported Anaclet must be relieved of their ecclesiastical dignities. Then, singling out individuals by name, he violently grabbed the pastoral staff from their hands, and tore away the *pallia* from their shoulders. In a final humiliating gesture, he removed their pastoral rings *sine respectu misericordiae*.[50] Not forgetting his old enemies, Gerard of Angoulême and Aegidius of Tusculum, he commanded his legate, Geoffrey of Chartres, to go to Gaul and to

---

[49] Schmale (*Studien zum Schisma*, p. 205) conceded that Petrus Leonis' ruling against Farfa may have had some immediate impact on Adenulf's decision to support Innocent, but he thinks that in a broader context ideology was more important. He is confused, however, over whether Petrus or his father was the arbitrator. On p. 205 he correctly identifies him as the father, but on p. 71 he identifies him as the son, and refers to the time as after 1123 rather than 1104. In n. 193 he says that he disagrees with the consequences Palumbo draws from the negative note for Farfa, but of course, he is referring to the wrong person.

[50] The sermon and the incidents thereafter are reported in the *Chronicon Mauriniacense*, Watterich, *Gesta* 2, pp. 250-252; Mansi, *Collectio Sacrorum Conciliorum* 21, p. 535: "His dictis, singulos quos reos cognoverat propriis nominibus exprimens, eisque cum indignatione & jurgio exprobans pastorales baculos de manibus violenter arripuit, & pontificalia pallia, in quibus summa dignitas consistit, de humeris verecundose abstraxit. Ipsos quoque anulos, in quibus ad ipsos pertinens ecclesiae desponsatio exprimitur, sine respectu misericorddiae abstulit."

Aquitaine, and to remove all bishops ordained by them from their offices, and to destroy all altars they had consecrated. Geoffrey carried out his task so thoroughly that not one stone remained upon another.[51]

It was an act of pure vindictiveness, which even St. Bernard, who had rejoiced in Anaclet's death, found to be excessive. He had received Innocent's promise that Peter of Pisa would be received back into the church in good standing, and when Peter was deposed along with the others, Bernard complained that that trust had been betrayed. The complaint fell on deaf ears. The cardinals were not reinstated until the reign of Celestine II. Innocent's disregard for his promise and Bernard's admonitions that he honor it show how little influence the saint had on the pope. Once in office, Innocent was less dependent upon Bernard, and could do more as he pleased. Perhaps the incident provided the impetus for Bernard to examine more carefully the papacy he had fought so intrepidly to install. In *De consideratione* he subjected it to the same sort of criticism that he had previously directed toward Cluny. The practices which he found to be particularly objectionable were those fostered or continued by Innocent.

After the Lateran Council Innocent almost immediately departed on his luckless military campaign against Roger II, and the rest of his reign was frought with squabbles with the Roman commune and Tivoli. Long before, in a dispute in 1137 with Peter the Deacon, an unidentified Greek philosopher summarized how Innocent appeared to some people who viewed the papacy from a distance:

> In the western climate we now see implemented what the Lord says
> through the prophet:
> 'As the people will be, so will be the priest,'
> when pontiffs rush to wars,
> just as your Innocent does;
> They distribute money, they gather together soldiers,
> they are clothed in purple vestments. [52]

---

[51] Mansi, *Collectio Sacrorum Conciliorum* 21, pp. 535-536: " . . . nec reliquens lapidem super lapidem, quem non destrueret, solo funditus adaequavit: & ratione dictante, alia eorum loco restaurare curavit."

[52] *Die Chronik von Montecassino*, MGH SS 34:590-591.

Chapter XIII

THE ANACLETIANS

Standing on spongy legal ground, Innocent's supporters emphasized character, not only as the main criterion for determining which contender should be pope, but also as the rationale for justifying why a minority of cardinals could claim to have elected a pope.[1] St. Bernard and Arnulf of Séez among many others argued that the cardinals who elected Innocent were the *sanior pars*, the more sound part. But an examination of the records of Anaclet's key supporters reveals that Suger did well in describing the cardinals at St. Mark's as the *majores et sapientores*—the greater and the wiser.[2] The French abbot probably accepted without question Peter of Porto's characterization of Anaclet's electors in his letter as the *maiores et priores*.[3]

How, then, did the conception of the Anacletian elector as a southern Italian, who still saw the world as it was before the Concordat of Worms, take form?[4] Let us take Gregory, cardinal priest of the Holy Apostles, as an example of an Anacletian elector, who seems to fit this paradigm almost perfectly.[5] Salient points in Gregory's life which appear to identify him with the allegedly conservative philosophy of the Anacletians are the following:[6] (1) He was born in Ceccano (Southern Italy), and must have received his title in the first decade of Paschal's papacy. (2) In February 1111 he was among the cardinals who participated in the treaty in which Paschal agreed to return the *regalia* to Henry V in return for the imperial renunciation of investitures; still, it is argued, Gregory agreed to the treaty not out of conviction, but only out of necessity. (3) At the Lateran Council of 1112 he was among Paschal's sharpest critics. With Gerard of Angoulême he helped to write the statement condemning the *privilegium*,

---

[1] Suger says that at the Council of Étampes the French clergy advised Louis VI that because the Roman mobs frequently caused so much disorder, it was better to consider the merits of the person rather than the legality of the election. *Vie de Louis VI*, pp. 258-260.

[2] Ibid., 256: " . . . cum ecclesie Romane majores et sapientores ad removendum Ecclesie tumultum consensissent apud Sanctum Marcum et non alibi, et non nisi communiter, romano more celebrem fieri electionem . . ."

[3] Peter of Porto refers to Innocent's electors as *novitii* and Anaclet's as the *maioribus et prioribus*. William of Malmesbury, *The Historia Novella*, ed. cit., p. 8.

[4] Schmale, *Studien zum Schisma*, p. 285, & n. 3.

[5] Hüls, *Kardinäle*, pp. 150, 152-153.

[6] Schmale, op. cit., pp. 60-61.

now dubbed, the *pravilegium* because it had been extracted by force. Significantly Peter of Porto and Guy of Vienne were also opponents of the *pravilegium*. (4) Gregory lost his title, and it may have been because he took an especially extreme stand against Paschal. Again, significantly, it was Calixtus who reinstated him in his title. (5) Gregory was so unshakable in his support for Anaclet's ideals that for a few months after his death, he stood as his successor. It is argued that the picture which one sees distinctly in Gregory is reflected in the other Anacletians.

But if Gregory epitomizes the Anacletian cardinal, according to this view, he also serves as an excellent example of why that image is only an illusion. First, age, as we have already noted with Gregory of St. Angelo, John of Crema, and others, is too insecure a principle to explain the voting pattern among the cardinals. There are many exceptions, and there are also other correlations which have a higher degree of probability. The older cardinals, who voted for Anaclet, could have done so because they rejected Innocent's election as a mockery of legal procedure.[7] Conversely, the more recent appointments to the cardinalate could have voted for Innocent because they owed their advancement to Haimeric, and would therefore have supported his candidate.

Second, being from the South did not necessitate an insulation from the North or an unwillingness to accept ideas coming from there. There was extensive traffic between the curia and the Northerners, and St. Bernard corresponded frequently with the chancellor. Both Petrus Pierleoni and Gregory of St. Angelo as Romans had sympathetic relationships with the leaders of the new reformers as legates to France, and the cardinals unanimously supported a Northerner, Guy of Vienne, as pope. At the request of Calixtus, Gregory of the Holy Apostles himself participated in an attempt to find a solution to a quarrel between the churches of Basel and St. Blasien.[8]

Honorius also used him for at least one assignment in the South. In 1126 he sent him to Montecassino to help to impose Seniorectus as abbot.[9] Although Gregory failed, Honorius' confidence in him suggests that in 1126 there was no cleavage among the cardinals parallel to the split in 1130. The use of Gregory to counter Oderisius with Seniorectus also reveals a defect in the reasoning about the role the older Benedictine monasteries played in the papal schism. According to the theory, as a supporter of Anaclet Gregory should have favored Oderisius against

---

[7] Speaking of the emphasis on legitimacy in the twelfth century, Robert Benson states: "Twelfth-century political thought was preoccupied with the legitimacy of political institutions and of governing authority. Though the problem of legitimacy never strays far from the center of the political theorist's attention, the twelfth century felt this concern with a new intensity, rarely matched during the centuries intervening since the death of Augustine in 430." "Political Renovatio," p. 339.

[8] Zenker, *Die Mitglieder*, pp. 106-107.

[9] Ibid., 107.

Honorius' candidate instead of the reverse. Again, this anomaly points up the complexity of the situation in the church prior to the schism, and emphasizes the difficulty of explaining the allegiances of cardinals by a comprehensive theory based primarily on ideology.

(2) Nothing indicates that Gregory subscribed to the Treaty of February 1111 out of necessity rather than out of conviction. The probable reasoning supporting such a contention is that Anaclet opposed the Concordat of Worms, Gregory voted for Anaclet, and therefore he too must have opposed the Concordat and have been a Gregorian. If he were a Gregorian he could not have favored Paschal's dramatic gesture to return the *regalia* to the emperor in return for a renunciation of investitures. The structure of the argument rests upon the premise that Anaclet opposed the Concordat, and since we have seen that such a premise is unfounded, the rest of the argument collapses. On the basis of what is known it would have to be assumed that Gregory supported the treaty, and that he favored returning the church to a more pastoral orientation.

(3) But, it can be responded, Gregory was one of Paschal's harshest critics at the Lateran Council of 1112. He demonstrated his conservatism by helping Gerard of Angoulême, Anaclet's future loyal supporter, to draft the statement denouncing Paschal's privilege to Henry to invest bishops with ring and staff.[10] This argument, however, is based on a misunderstanding of what was at issue at the Council. The real problem was not the denunciation of the privilege on investitures, which Paschal had already disavowed because it had been extorted under pressure, but whether punitive action should be taken against Henry for having imprisoned Paschal and a number of cardinals, and for having extorted the privilege. Paschal had promised not to excommunicate Henry, and he did not want to break his word. Some, like Guy of Vienne, Jusserand of Lyons, Bruno of Segni, and Kuno of Praeneste insisted that he should, and this insistence caused the impasse at the Council. Gerard of Angoulême came to the rescue, working out a compromise whereby Paschal would publicly retract the privilege and associate himself with the principles of his predecessors without having to break his word to Henry. It was a conciliatory move, which saved Paschal from his critics rather than a harsh attack on the pope.[11] Further evidence that the statement was a gesture toward restoring harmony in the curia is that Gerard was selected as the emissary from the Council to bear the news of its outcome

---

[10] For the Lateran Council of 1112 see Mansi, *Collectio Sacrorum Conciliorum* 21, pp. 73-78.

[11] Gerard's genius as the architect, who resolved the impasse was recognized. See the *Gesta episcoporum et comitum Engolismensium*, MGH SS 26:832: "In qua re nullum remedium a toto concilio inveniri poterat. Girardus episcopus exquisitus tandem tale consilium dedit, quod investiturae revocari poterant salvo sacramento, ita tamen quod imperator dans investituras non excommunicaretur. Quod consilium omne concilium laudans, dixit" 'Non tu locutus es, sed spiritus sanctus in ore tuo.'" Stroll, "Calixtus II," pp. 10-11.

to Henry. The fact that Paschal granted him this commission shows that he had the confidence of both sides. Thus, Gregory's participation in the Lateran Council of 1112 is not a sign of his intransigent Gregorianism, but of his flexibility on problems of *regnum* and *sacerdotium*.

(4) The reasons why Gregory was deprived of his title and was reinstated by Calixtus are too hypothetical to constitute a convincing argument.[12] However, since Calixtus also appointed Haimeric, albeit somewhat later, his reinstatement of Gregory is not ipso facto a sign of Gregory's Gregorianism.

(5) It is only a conjecture that Gregory succeeded Anaclet because he espoused his religious ideology and rejected Innocent's. Gregory may always have felt that Anaclet was the legally elected pope, and that Innocent was a usurper. In that conviction he could have agreed to stand as Anaclet's successor.

The responses stated above suggest that an explanation based upon age and provenance is too simplistic to account for the formation of a cardinal's ideology. Further, they reinforce my previously stated rejection of the view that differences in attitude toward religious reform determined the vote of the cardinals. Oderisius, abbot of Montecassino, is another case in point. His age, southern Italian birth, and membership in an older Benedictine order fit the paradigm of the Anacletian cardinal. Yet, we have seen that there are many other factors going back to his history of animosity with Honorius which could account for his rejection of Innocent. That he did not support Honorius' designated successor, therefore, would have been anticipated apart from any consideration of attitudes toward spirituality and reform.

Peter of Pisa presents so many incongruities with the alleged archetype of the Anacletian cardinal, that no attempt to harmonize them has been successful.[13] Since he had been appointed *scriniarius* by Urban II, he was in the right age bracket, but he was from northern rather than southern Italy. Moreover, he was in no wise provincial, and enjoyed great respect throughout Europe, especially in England. Churchmen admired him not just for his expertise in canon law and theology, but also because of his chaste and religious life.[14]

His delay in criticizing the strong arm tactics used in the election of Honorius, and at first remaining on friendly terms with the pope continues to puzzle and intrigue historians.[15] One suggests that Peter's hesitation

---

[12] Without adducing any evidence Zenker says that it is improbable that Gregory's title was taken away from him because of his sharp criticism of Paschal's policies in 1112. *Die Mitglieder*, p. 106.

[13] Schmale, *Studien zum Schisma*, pp. 62-63; Hüls, *Kardinäle*, pp. 210-211.

[14] Zenker, *Die Mitglieder*, p. 102; concerning his intervention for Archbishop Thurstan of York it is said: "Hic vero Petrus clericus bonus, castus et religiosus, canonum et decretorum et legum scriptarum non mediocriter peritus." *Historia quattuor archiepiscoporum Eboracensium*, Rolls Series 73, 2:174.

[15] *Lib. Pont. Dert.*, p. 205: "Solus Petrus Pisanus, quo non tarde post ab eodem penituit, papae in amicum remansit."

shows that he sympathized with Honorius' religious convictions. This conclusion is substantiated, he believes, by the fact that Peter remained within the pope's inner circle. He also thinks that it is indicative that alone among Anaclet's supporters on the committee of eight, he remained behind with Haimeric and Gregory of St. Angelo at St. Gregory's after Petrus Pierleoni and Jonathan had departed. Peter's late conversion to Innocent under the impetus of St. Bernard implies to him that Peter had not been a blind partisan of Anaclet, but that he had lacked the courage to act upon the understanding which had long been obvious to him. He concludes that Peter's objections to Innocent's election must have been purely legal rather than reservations arising from differences over religious convictions.[16]

Whether they were purely legal is impossible to say. Peter did, after all, hesitate to reject Honorius' patently even less legal election. Legality was not his only consideration, as he demonstrated when he came over to Innocent's side in 1137 just after having presented the legal case for Anaclet. But what Peter's case brings out is that enlightened and dedicated churchmen did object to the way that Innocent was elected. Why should one doubt Peter of Porto's protestations that he rejected Innocent's election for the same reason? Or the archbishop of Milan, or others? Adriaan Bredero rightly points out that in examining the positions taken by Milan and other dioceses of northern Italy, historians have neglected to take the mode of Innocent's election into consideration. He believes that it was a problem which was discussed in good faith, and that the conclusions of the northern Italian bishops led to their long support of Anaclet, in the case of Milan until 1135.[17]

The other factors which are construed to show that Peter did not basically disagree with Honorius' and Innocent's ideology are equally unpersuasive. Peter's inclusion in Honorius' inner circle had nothing to do with his adherence to Honorius' religious convictions, for if membership in that elite body were indicative, Gregory of St. Angelo should have been included, and Peter of Porto relegated to the back benches; in fact the reverse was true. Secondly, it is not a sign of a lack of identification with Petrus that Peter did not leave St. Gregory's with Petrus and Jonathan, since the latter two were sent out on a commission. Peter could not have foreseen that their mission would be thwarted, and that they would not return. When Haimeric engineered the fraudulent election of Innocent, Peter opposed it without hesitation. In an open election he might still have voted for Petrus rather than Gregory of St. Angelo, not because of pro-

---

[16] Zenker (*Die Mitglieder*, p. 104) believes that Peter's objections to Innocent's election were based more on legal considerations than those of a *kirchenpolitischer* sort. She notes, however, that he accepted the election of Honorius, which was just as improper.

[17] Adriaan Bredero, "Une controverse sur Cluny au XIIe siècle," *Revue d'histoire ecclésiastique* 76 (1981), 50.

foundly different visions over what course the church should take, but because Petrus was the more distinguished cardinal.

Saxo, cardinal priest of St. Stephano in Monte Celio, is another important actor in the drama played out in Rome between the elections of 1124 and 1130.[18] As one of the signatories of the Concordat of Worms, seemingly only by straining credulity could he be branded as an uncompromising Gregorian. Nevertheless, it is argued that Saxo could have signed the Concordat while retaining reservations about its provisions. This must have been the case, it is believed, because if Saxo had shared Haimeric's progressive views, the chancellor would have supported his candidacy for the papacy in 1124. Corroborating evidence, it is alleged, is that Pandulphus described Saxo as the candidate of the people—a sure sign of his provincial conception of the papacy, as it also would be later for Anaclet.

But the conclusion does not follow from the premise. Every candidate depended upon the good will of the Roman people to occupy the Roman see, and whether a candidate had this support or not had nothing to do with his conception of the papacy. It was a huge problem for Calixtus coming from Burgundy, and with no previous involvement with the various Roman factions. His acceptance was ensured by Petrus Leonis, who marshalled the allegiance of all of the factions, and had them lined up for the pope's arrival. In 1124 the Frangipani played the decisive role.

The Frangipani probably were cool to Saxo because they feared that with his support in the city, he could dominate them. They had been held in check by Calixtus, and they did not want to continue to live under similar constraints imposed by his successor. To avoid a confrontation between the Frangipani and Saxo, Jonathan nominated the elderly Theobald of St. Anastasia, who was thought to have been too old to be a threat to anyone.[19] The Frangipani, however, remembered Theobald's strenuous efforts to free Gelasius from their captivity, and they were not happy with him either.[20] When Haimeric approached them with the bargain that if they would overthrow Theobald's election as Celestine II, and help to impose Lambert of Ostia as pope in return for a free hand in Rome, they were receptive. The position of the papacy in the church and other ideological considerations did not concern anyone. Not only did neither version of the *Liber Pontificalis* mention any differences, but other factors suggest that there were none. Lambert and Saxo had both been signatories to the Concordat of Worms, and Theobald and Haimeric had both been promoted by Calixtus in 1123.[21] There is no reason to believe that Saxo had reservations about the Concordat, for Calixtus was not

---

[18] Schmale, *Studien zum Schisma*, pp. 63-65; Zenker, *Die Mitglieder*, pp. 132-133; Hüls, *Kardinäle*, pp. 206-207.

[19] Hüls, *Kardinäle* , p. 235.

[20] *Lib. Pont.* 2, p. 313; *Lib. Pont. Dert.*, p. 169; Hüls, *Kardinäle*, p. 268.

[21] Hüls, *Kardinäle*, p. 149.

under any pressure to send a legate with views different from his own. In all probability he would not have used Saxo as a negotiator if the cardinal had not been sympathetic to his wishes.

Of the cardinals appointed before 1123 Jonathan is the only other one about whom much is known.[22] Jonathan was closely associated with Petrus, and indeed followed him in his appointments as cardinal deacon of SS. Cosma and Damiano and as cardinal priest of Santa Maria in Trastevere. Because of this connection his activities are of special interest. Calixtus used him extensively, and as an indication of his good standing with the pope after the Concordat of Worms, Calixtus appointed him as legate to Siena in 1123/24. Even though Jonathan had nominated the pope whom Honorius overthrew, there was no breach between cardinal and pope. Within only a few months after Honorius' accession (May 6, 1125), Jonathan signed a papal bull. Honorius also used him for a most sensitive diplomatic mission—as legate to Farfa along with cardinal priest Conrad of Santa Pudenziana.[23] It was an especially important assignment because it involved the confirmation of the newly-elected abbot, Adenulf, and the accommodation of Farfa with the papacy after its imperial past. Jonathan, then, symbolizes the continuity within the college of cardinals after the reign of Calixtus, and shows that there was no ideological split during the reign of Honorius.

Although little is known about the cardinals appointed after 1123, according to the Klewitz/Schmale thesis their age and provenance identify them with the same tendencies apparent in the older cardinals. The only deviation is Aegidius of Tusculum, who was born near Auxerre.[24] Even though he was French, he is still thought to fit into the framework of the thesis because he had been a monk at Cluny under Pontius. He is admitted to have been a man of great integrity, and he showed his loyalty to Anaclet by withstanding Peter the Venerable's importunities to convert him to Innocent's side. Until Anaclet's death, he remained one of his most steadfast defenders.[25]

Given what now is known about Pontius, however, being a monk under his abbacy no longer carries the negative associations which it once did. Peter the Venerable would not have made such a great effort to bring Aegidius to his side if the abbot had had misgivings about him. In other respects Aegidius also deviates from the model. He was not at all provincial or tied to Roman politics, and he was active during Honorius' reign.

---

[22] Ibid., 225-226; Zenker, *Die Mitglieder*, pp. 54-55.

[23] Zenker (*Die Mitglieder*, p. 54) minimizes the assignment, pointing out that he was the junior person in the legation, and that no initiative was demanded of him. However, she mistakenly refers to Conrad as cardinal bishop of Sabina, and his promotion did not take place until after the legation.

[24] Ibid., 43-44; Hüls, *Kardinäle*, pp. 142-143.

[25] Ep. 40 of Peter the Venerable to Aegidius or Giles of Tusculum, Constable, *The Letters of Peter the Venerable* 1, pp. 134-136; Schmale, *Studien zum Schisma*, p. 78.

Calixtus had used him as a legate to Hungary and Poland, and as late as July 1129 he sailed to Palestine to represent the pope's interests there.

In sum, Aegidius is another exception to the conception of the Anacletian cardinal as an aging Gregorian from Southern Italy, who identified with the older Benedictine houses, involved himself in Roman administration rather than looking to the church at large, and continued the tradition of viewing the Normans as protectors of the church against the German king.[26] The reality was far more complex. Heterogeneity rather than uniformity characterized Anaclet's most active supporters, but one common thread distinguished them; they were men of integrity. In the vicious defamatory campaign unleashed against Anaclet after the election, cardinals such as Peter of Porto, Peter of Pisa, and Aegidius of Tusculum survived unscathed.

---

[26] Schmale, op. cit., pp. 79-82. Schmale repeats these generalizations at the conclusion of his sketches of the Anacletian cardinals.

Chapter XIV

PETRUS PIERLEONI'S RECORD RECONSIDERED

Innocent could hardly have chosen a more daunting opponent, for Petrus had a record which made him eminently *papabile*. Educated in Paris during the time when Abelard and other stellar French masters were active, he also developed a close friendship with Louis VI. Before returning to Rome to become cardinal deacon of SS. Cosma and Damiano, he took monastic vows at Cluny. He played a crucial role in Calixtus II's election, and Calixtus in turn promoted him to cardinal priest of Santa Maria in Trastevere, and twice appointed him as his legate to England and to France. Honorius II seldom used him in special capacities, but he continued to carry on curial business through 1129.

Petrus came from a family which not only was one of the most powerful in Rome, but which had been the strongest bulwark of the reform popes. The propaganda spread at the time of the schism emphasizes its Jewish origins and commercial interests, but that distorts its Christian focus. The Pierleoni were on intimate terms with popes of such disparate character as Gregory VII, Urban II, who died in their house, Paschal II, and Calixtus II. In addition to their financial and military support, the family must have espoused principles and attitudes which inspired the confidence of these popes. Paschal held Petrus Leonis in such high esteem that he asked him to stand surety for his commitment to carry out the agreement of February 12, 1111, stipulating that bishops relinquish their *regalia* in return for imperial renunciation of investitures.[1] Later Petrus Leonis did a masterful job of marshalling all of the factions in Rome to receive Calixtus after the Burgundian pope had spent a somewhat tentative year in France.

The Pierleoni were a very cultivated family, involving themselves in the intellectual and artistic revival of the twelfth century. Sending Petrus to study with the French masters is one indication of this interest. Another is his father's enjoyment in writing poetry. Ordericus Vitalis preserves a

---

[1] *Codex Udalrici, Monumenta Bambergensia*, vol. 5 of *Bibliotheca Rerum Germanicarum*, ed. Philip Jaffé (Berlin, 1869), p. 271: "Si domnus papa hec regi non adimpleverit, ego Petrus Leonis iuro: quod cum tota potentia mea tenebo me ad domnum regem." p. 272: "Ego Petrus Leonis iuro vobis: quia domnus papa proximo die dominico adimplebit regi, quod in carta conventionis scriptum est." For the Pierleoni family see Pietro Fedele, "Le Famiglie di Anacleto II ed Gelasio II," *Archivio della R. Società Romana di Storia Patria* 27 (1904), 400-433; Demetrius B. Zema, "The Houses of Tuscany and of the Pierleoni in the Crisis of Rome in the Eleventh Century," *Traditio* 2 (1944), 155-175.

poem, which Petrus Leonis wrote in 1099 on the death of Urban II. Another, a satire, which he wrote as a memorial to the anti-pope, Guibert of Ravenna, appears to show an acquaintanceship with classical literature. He says of Guibert, "You were an empty name: for that presumption Cerberus keeps a place for you in hell."[2] The family also exhibited its classical proclivities in rebuilding St. Nicola in Carcere, the church so closely associated with them that it was known as the Pierleoni church. The church was constructed out of three Roman temples, and parts of it were painted with classical motifs. At the left of the front entrance was a chapel decorated with frescoes of four Old Testament prophets. For the interior of the church the family donated a paschal candlestick and other religious objects. As a further sign that there was no break between them and Honorius, a plaque commemorating the consecration of St. Nicola is dated 1128 in the pope's name.

But the Pierleoni were a new family, and even if the older noble families were at times deferential to them because of their power, they were also resentful.[3] The Jewish converts had risen from their humble past too quickly, and had usurped the prestige and wealth which the older Roman families also coveted. Why should the Pierleoni have been the confidants of the popes instead of themselves? They saw the family as consumingly ambitious, supporting the pope with their vast fortune in order to gain such favors as a cardinalate for Petrus, and a prefecture for his brother. The psychology of the older aristocracy is understandable, but there was more than adequate reason for Paschal to place his adherents in important positions without suspecting the family of exerting pressure or of using the papacy only to further their own interests. Moreover, there is no reason to assume that Paschal's motives were always political and not religious, or at least ecclesiastical. He may have believed that Petrus Leonis would be the most effective negotiator with the representatives of Henry V, and that Petrus would make a good cardinal.

In fact, at one time it was accepted as obvious that Petrus was the most distinguished of all of the cardinals in 1130, but a newer view holds that his prestige was mainly based upon the power of his family. In addition to his record, the text, "ad illius nutum tota Roma taceat et tota loquatur," provides one of the best clues for deciding which of these positions is correct.[4] The text is usually interpreted to mean that Petrus' prestige was

---

[2] Chibnall, *Ecclesiastic History* 5, pp. 192-195.

[3] Innocent was a member of the Papareschi or de Papa, one of the oldest Roman families. These families tended to see the newer families as interlopers. Giuseppe Marchetti-Longhi, *I Papareschi e i Romani*, vol. 6 of *Le Grandi Famiglie Romane* (Rome, 1947).

[4] The evidence of Petrus' great power in Rome is from a non tendentious source—a conversation between Bishop Guido of Arezzo and a papal legate shortly before Honorius' death. Guido had been in Rome with Honorius. After he returned to Arezzo he described his impressions, including those of the College of Cardinals and of the "überragenden" position of Petrus. The text was discovered by S. Löwenfeld, and published in an article, "Ueber Anaclets Persönlichkeit," pp. 596-597: "episcopus ait nuncio: 'Miror et satis, cum tot sapientes et nobilissimi et summi viri sint in urbe Roma, quod quocies ipsi sua colloquia mira-

so great in Rome just prior to Honorius' death that at a mere nod, men did his bidding. More recently, however, it has been argued that the main import of the text is not as testimony of Petrus' eminence, but of his reliance on Roman support after the younger cardinals had rejected him.[5] This reliance, it is conjectured, accounts for his endeavors to restore the participation of the Roman people in papal elections. He had already associated himself with efforts in that direction in 1124, the argument continues, and in 1130 he appealed to the fact that he had received the support of the Roman people as proof of the legitimacy of his election.

When the text is put in context, its meaning becomes clearer. Löwenfeld says in his introduction that in the comment preceding the text, Bishop Guido of Arezzo was speaking of the College of Cardinals, and accordingly not of the Roman people. The bishop said that even when the wisest and most noble men were speaking, they all deferred to Petrus when he entered their midst. Agreeing with the bishop, Honorius' nuncio elaborated that at Petrus' nod, all Rome spoke or was silent.

The implication of this dialogue is that in the period in which some scholars believe that a de facto schism already existed in the College of Cardinals, and when Petrus was supposed to have been repudiated by the *cardinales novitii*, Guido of Arezzo observes no disharmony. Not only do all of the cardinals show Petrus the greatest respect, but the papal nuncio associates himself with their sentiments. He did not take advantage of his conversation with Guido to make any disclaimers about Petrus' character or religious ideology. Likewise, he did not draw a distinction between the respect which Petrus enjoyed with the Romans, and that accorded him by the cardinals. The text indicates that Petrus was held in the highest honor by both groups, and at least outwardly, by the papacy itself.

But the acclamation of the Roman people did not imply that Petrus was primarily a curial bureaucrat, unmoved by the religious movements of the church at large.[6] Both Petrus and his chancellor, Saxo, who had had the support of the Romans in the election of 1124, were actively involved in international affairs. Moreover, the Romans did not support curial cardinals only. They welcomed the Burgundian, Calixtus II, and Petrus and Saxo likewise worked harmoniously with this pope from the North. When Anaclet and Peter of Porto asserted that the Roman people had approved Anaclet's election, they were saying nothing more than that the statute of Nicholas II had been observed. Their statements did not signify that Anaclet identified with the Romans ideologically or politically, or that he saw the church as centered on Rome rather than as diffused throughout

---

biliter celebrant, et in eis maiestative concionant, mox ut Petrus Leonis accedit, omnes obnubiliantur et liquifiunt.' Nuncius vero episcopo respondit: 'Eius gratiae Petrus Leonis est Romae, ut ad illius nutum tota Roma taceat, et tota loquatur.''' The passage is discussed by Palumbo, *Lo Scisma*, pp. 198-199 & n. 1, 288 & n. 4; see n. 8, ch. X above.

[5] Schmale, *Studien zum Schisma*, p. 72, & n. 196.

[6] Ibid., n. 197.

Christendom. The approbation of the Roman people meant only that like Peter of Porto, Peter of Pisa, and the majority of the College of Cardinals, they accepted Anaclet as the legally elected pope. In all probability Innocent would have welcomed their acclamation, but since he had been elected in secret, he had to forgo this tradition.

If both elections had been held openly, it is difficult to predict which candidate they would have supported. Militating against Petrus is the fact that when Paschal tried to appoint his brother as prefect in 1116, the Romans objected so violently that a virtual civil war broke out. Their objection may not have been specifically to a Pierleoni, however, but to any papal candidate. They were not prone to deep loyalties, and quickly switched to Lothar and Innocent when they were in Rome for Lothar's coronation, and back to Anaclet when they departed.

Moreover, focusing the papacy on Rome rather than thinking in terms of an international church had nothing to do with the Roman people; it concerned attitudes toward ecclesiastical centralization and an openness to developments outside of Rome. Both Anaclet and Innocent were receptive to these new movements, but no one exceeded Innocent in his effort to centralize church governance in Rome. As he said in his sermon at the Lateran Council justifying his deposition of the former supporters of Anaclet, "you know that Rome is the head of the world."[7]

Like Saxo, Petrus is accused of concealing his true feelings for tactical reasons. He feigned support for Paschal's lenient position on investitures in the Lenten Council of 1116 against the opposition of such old line Gregorian opponents as Bruno of Segni and Kuno of Praeneste, it is charged, while in reality harboring views similar to those of these critics. This consonance with Paschal's critics is alleged to be shown in at least two ways: from Petrus' close friendship with Geoffrey of Vendôme, who took a conservative line on investitures, and indeed dedicated one of his tracts to Petrus, and from the vote of the older cardinals representing a conservative point of view.[8]

But the conservative tag on his electors has already been discredited, and to put this same label on Geoffrey of Vendôme does not do justice to the complexity of his thought. His views were, in fact, strikingly similar to those of Ivo of Chartres, in whose diocese his abbey was located. Instead of condemning investitures *per se*, he distinguished between ecclesiastical investitures, which he believed to be a sacrament, and secular investitures. The latter did not threaten ecclesiastical integrity, Geoffrey held, since their purpose was only to provide material sustenance for the bishop and the church. Even more destructive to the conception of Geoffrey as an inflexible Gregorian is the letter he wrote to Gerard of Angoulême defending Paschal's actions in 1111/1112 from his more rigid critics.[9] It is

---

[7] Mansi, *Collectio Sacrorum Conciliorum* 21, 534.

[8] Schmale, op. cit., pp. 21-22, 66.

[9] For Geoffrey of Vendôme's view on investitures see MGH Ldl 2:690-699: "In aec-

not known what position Geoffrey took on the schism, but the congregation of his abbey, la Trinité, quickly recognized Innocent, and Geoffrey was present at the Council of Rheims. Innocent designated him as one of nine commissioners for the regulation of litigation between the monks of Marmoutiers and Saint-Jacoud. Thus, none of the adduced reasons demonstrate that Petrus supported Paschal in the Lenten Council of 1116 not out of conviction, but for strategic reasons.

The English sources are among the most important for evaluating Petrus' character and performance as a legate because they were written outside of the influence of curial politics. Calixtus appointed Petrus legate *a latere* and vicar for England in the summer of 1121. Henry I sent Bernard of St. David's and his nephew and chaplain, John of Bayeux, to conduct him to his court. They had instructions to entertain him directly from the royal demesne without making any procurations from churches and monasteries. Henry received Petrus with great civility, but informed him that it was against the customs of England for anyone other than the archbishop of Canterbury to function as legate. Besides, the king explained, he was too busy with his Welsh expedition to summon a council. Petrus protested that he had no intention of infringing the customs of the Kingdom, and loaded with sumptuous gifts from the king, he began his journey to the coast. On the way he stopped at Canterbury, where the monks received him graciously, and engaged him in pleasant conversation for three days. They asked their guest why Calixtus had intervened on behalf of Thurstan of York to the detriment of Canterbury, and Petrus promised to look into the matter. He read the ancient privileges they showed him, and unaware that they were forgeries, he ruled in their favor. Thereafter he departed for France.[10]

The main sources for this legation are the reports of William of

---

clesiasticis possessionibus, quamvis nec in legibus nec in canonibus inveniatur, tamen propter scandalum et scisma vitandum talis regibus investitura concedatur, ut nec ipsi propter hoc pereant, nec sancta aecclesia detrimentum patiatur. Investituram per virgum et anulum accipere, nisi a suo consecratore, manifestum est esse dampnosum, quia nulli laico illa aecclesiae sacramenta dare, sicut ei non licet episcopum consecrare."

Geoffrey's letter to Gerard of Angoulême is edited in Jacobus Sirmondus, *Opera varia* 3 (Paris, 1696), p. 661: "Non sum ego adeo perturbati cerebri, nec sanctarum inscius scripturarum, quod in eum, qui soli caelo innocentiam debet, sine causa posuissem os meum: in patrem videlicet spiritualem, quem brachiis filialis dilectionis amplecti debeo, et pura veritate venerari; a cujus sancta obedientia non potero vel mortuus separari. Si quis de me aliter sentit, desipit: nec dominum Papam honorare satagit, sed publicare, si quid minus vel nimium egit."

See Wilhelm Schum's long analysis of Geoffrey's views in "Kaiser Heinrich V. und Papst Paschalis II. im Jahre 1112. Ein Beitrag zur Geschichte des Investitur-Streites," *Jahrbücher der königliche Akademie gemeinnütziger Wissenschaften zur Erfurt*, Neue Folge 8 (1877), 281-313; for inconsistencies in Geoffrey's views see Benson, *The Bishop-Elect*, p. 239, n. 42. Geoffrey dedicated Opus II (PL 157:214) to Petrus.

[10] Brett, *The English Church*, p. 41; *Councils and Synods*, pp. 723-725; Helene Tillmann, *Die päpstlichen Legaten in England bis zur Beendigung der Legation Gualas (1218)* (Bonn, 1926), p. 26.

Malmesbury and Eadmer.[11] Taking note that they were composed in cool detachment in England, far from the heated atmosphere of Rome, some scholars conclude that they confirm the Innocentian view of Anaclet. These scholars emphasize William of Malmesbury's report, which they interpret as alleging that like other papal legates to England, Petrus allowed himself to be bribed by the king, and that he did not extend himself to fulfill his assignment. Although other legates were corrupt, they argue, it nevertheless remains a reproach to Petrus that he did not rise above the ordinary.[12]

It is true that Petrus did not succeed in persuading Henry to summon a council, and that he did accept exceptionally fine gifts from the king because of his father's high standing. But do these facts imply that he was corrupt and lax in carrying out his commission? It depends upon what orders Calixtus gave Petrus, and whether the gifts were meant as the sort of inducement Diego of Compostella customarily used to obtain his requests. The council which Henry protested that he was too busy to call was not a general reform council of the sort John of Crema would preside over in 1125, but a council to settle the primacy of England. Calixtus had played a duplicitous game with the English church, and Peter's legation must be seen against that background. After receiving a large payment from Thurstan in 1119, Calixtus had consecrated him archbishop of York. Later the same year Henry met Calixtus at Gisors, and Eadmer says that he received the pope's promise to honor the customs of England, and specifically the archbishop of Canterbury's right to function as legate.[13]

---

[11] William of Malmesbury, *De gestis Pontificum Anglorum*, lib. I, Rolls Series 52:128-129: "Nam et in principio regni Henrici venerat Angliam ad exercendam legationem Guido Viennensis archiepiscopus, qui postea apostolicus fuit; tunc Anselmus, nec multo post quidam Petrus. Omnesque reversi nullo effectu rei, grandi praeda sui, Petrus maxime, quod omnes eum incendere caverent, qui esset filius Petri Leonis, summi Romanorum principis. . . . Nolebat enim ille [Henry] in Angliam praeter consuetudinem antiquam recipere legatum nisi Cantuariensem archiepiscopum, illique libenter refringebant impetum propter violentiam denariorum." Schmale, *Studien zum Schisma*, p. 70, n. 185. In his evaluation of this text he follows Mühlbacher. See also Bernhardi, *Lothar*, pp. 284-285, n. 46.

Eadmer, *Historia Novorum in Anglia*, Rolls Series 81:294-297: "De quorum numero quidam, Petrus nomine, Romanus genere, monachus Cluniacensis professione, venit in Galliam, missus ab ipso pontifice . . . Supercreverat autem fama istius famam omnium ante eum in has partes a Romana sede destinatorum; et abbates ac nonnuli alii, viri videlicet honorati ejus adventum angliae praeconaturi ab eo praemittebantur. Erat enim filius Petri praeclarissimi ac potentissimi principis Romanorum, cujus fides et actio magni consilii et fortitudinis esse solebat iis qui in sede apostolica canonice constituti patres orbis habebantur."

Zöpffel (*Die Doppelwahl*, pp. 304-305) concludes that Anaclet's venality is revealed from the unpartisan testimony of Eadmer, who states that Petrus traveled through the country *mit einem ungeheuren Pompe*, and that he spent three days in Canterbury in *Fröhlichkeit*. Bernhardi (*Lothar*, p. 284, n. 46) rightly disputes Zöpffel's reading of the text, emphasizing that the pomp came from the king, not from Petrus, and that Petrus handled his legation with measure and a feeling for justice.

[12] Schmale, *Studien zum Schisma*, p. 70.

[13] Eadmer, *Historia Novorum*, ed. cit., p. 258; Brett, *The English Church*, pp. 40-47; Stroll, "Calixtus II," p. 30.

But a year later Calixtus offered the legateship to Thurstan, and when the archbishop declined the offer-to accept it would have led to open warfare with Henry and Canterbury—Calixtus offered the dignity to his old confederate, Cardinal Bishop Kuno of Praeneste, well known for his intransigence on issues of *regnum* and *sacerdotium*. Kuno never got to England, perhaps because of Henry's use of what William of Malmesbury refers to as the *violentia denariorum*, and in 1121 Calixtus granted Petrus the legateship.

His assignment most likely was to smooth the ruffled waters. By the summer of 1121 the pope's priorities had changed. He was beginning the process of the negotiations with Henry V to reach a compromise over investitures, and he also desired peace with the other powerful ruler, Henry I. Calling off the inflexible Kuno, he appointed one of his most experienced diplomats, whose distinction was clearly intended to impress the English, and instructed him to be conciliatory. Following these guidelines, Petrus accepted the king's assurances that the customs of England had the papal imprimatur, and he did not insist upon calling a council to settle the question of primacy. The outcome of such a council would have been a foregone conclusion in any case, because Canterbury had a great preponderance of advocates over those of York. After his meeting with the king, in order to reinforce the papal inclination toward Canterbury, Petrus stopped at the cathedral on his way home. Spending three days there in noted amicability, he read the documents presented to him, and pronounced himself convinced of their case against Thurstan. With his mission completed, he departed for the continent.

As for Henry's gifts, there is no reason to believe that they were bribes of the sort which William of Malmesbury mentioned that the king used to safeguard the liberties of the English church and the primacy of Canterbury. Petrus was prepared to recognize these customs when he arrived, so that there was no reason to offer him further inducements. Showing that the same policy was still intact over four years later, John of Crema would again recognize Canterbury's primacy in the winter of 1125/26. Moreover, it was customary for kings to give popes and their emissaries munificent gifts: Henry lavished expensive gifts on Innocent's cardinals when he met Innocent for the first time in Chartres on January 13, 1131, Lothar bestowed magnificent gifts on Innocent when he met him at Liège, and the bishops and monasteries presented John of Crema with "great and splendid gifts" during his English legation.[14] Such gifts did not in themselves constitute bribes. If William saw anything improper in Petrus' conduct in 1121, he must not have considered it to be noteworthy, for when he reported the double election of 1130, he described both Gregory of St. Angelo and Petrus as very celebrated cardinals, who were "outstanding in letters and diligence."[15]

---

[14] *Councils and Synods*, pp. 737, 756.

[15] William of Malmesbury, *Historia Novella*, ed. cit., p. 6: "Eo anno defuncto papa

Eadmer supports this interpretation. William was speaking only in a general way about the practices of legates to England, and he may have known little about Petrus' particular performance outside of the fact that he was especially honored because of his distinguished family. Writing much closer to the actual events, and in greater detail, Eadmer reports that Petrus recognized the English liberties on the basis of papal privileges, not because he had been bribed by the king. He points out that Petrus again adjudicated the dispute between Canterbury and York by the appeal to what he thought were legal documents, and in this case he mentions no gifts. Even granting that Eadmer was a monk from Canterbury, he was not so corrupt himself that he would not have mentioned bribery if he knew of any evidence of it.

The sources together create the impression that Petrus was not venal and corrupt, but a man of probity and dignity. The English bishops were impressed enough to urge Henry to support Anaclet in 1130. Rather than substantiating that the polemics against Anaclet were valid, the English sources show that they were not.

But if the English church at first sided with Anaclet, there was great opposition to him in France. Was this opposition engendered either by an unsavory reputation left in the wake of his legateship, or by his lack of responsiveness to the new reforming orders?[16] Contemporary reports as opposed to polemics written at the time of the schism show that both Gregory and Petrus were well received, and that no discrimination was ever made between them. Moreover, the two of them moved easily between the old and the new orders without distinction.[17]

On October 27, 1123 Petrus and Gregory visited Séez in Normandy on the very day on which Bishop Serlo died. Ordericus Vitalis writes the following account:

> When they were ready to rise from table after the meal, a messenger came with the news that two Roman cardinals, Peter and Gregory, had arrived ... At once the bishop said to his clerks and stewards, 'Go quickly, and wait attentively on the Romans; make generous provision for all their needs, for they are coming as legates of the lord Pope, who is the universal father after God, and no matter who they are, they are our masters.' ... All the others went to meet the cardinals as he had

Honorio [14 February], magna contentione eligendi apostolici Romana fluctuauit ecclesia. Erant tunc in eadem urbe duo famosissimi cardinales, Gregorius diaconus sancti Angeli, et Petrus presbyter cardinalis, filius Leonis Romanorum principis: ambo litteris et industria insignes; nec erat facile discernere populo quisnam eorum iustius eligeretur a clero." William continues to describe the election in an evenhanded way without making any invidious remarks about Petrus. Bernhardi, *Lothar*, pp. 282, n. 40, 284-285, n. 46.

16 Schmale, *Studien zum Schisma*, p. 71, n. 189. Schmale cites Mühlbacher and Zöpffel but no primary sources to show that Petrus left an unsavory reputation in his wake.

17 Theodor Schieffer has catalogued Petrus' and Gregory's legateship in France. Usually they were together, but not always. *Die päpstlichen Legaten in Frankreich vom Vertrage von Meersen (870) bis zum Schisma von 1130* (Berlin, 1935).

ordered, welcomed them ceremoniously in the guest-house, and paid all the respect due to them as the bishop commanded.[18]

In January 1124 Petrus and Gregory visited one of the most spiritual of all of the new religious leaders in France, Stephen, the founder of the order of Grandmont. A. Lecler, working mostly from manuscripts, presents this account of their visit and the Council of Chartres thereafter.[19] Gregory and Petrus learned about Stephen while they were at Limoges, and, accompanied by an abbot of Limoges, they came to see him at Muret, where he was living. They inquired about Stephen's manner of living, and pressed him about whether he was a canon, a monk, or a hermit. Stephen explained that he did not precisely fall within any of those categories, but had learned his way of life from Milon, archbishop of Benevento. He recounted to them many particulars of the court of Rome, and the history of his life. He expressed himself with so much naiveté and wisdom that they wanted to confide in him what was in their hearts, and to get his opinion on the most important affairs. Stephen agreed that each one of them might have a private hour with him. They both were charmed by their conversation, and protested that they had never had an interview so edifying. Assuredly, the Holy Spirit spoke through his mouth, they concluded. "Man of God," they said, "if you persevere as you have begun, without doubt you will receive a recompense equal to that of the holy apostles and of the martyrs, because you follow their route." After Stephen had blessed them, they recommended him in their prayers, and returned to Limoges very satisfied.

Stephen died February 8, 1124, and on March 12th Gregory and Petrus held a synod at Chartres. They spoke to the full council of Stephen's heroic virtues, and prayed for his soul. Then they said, "We have prayed for him, now we pray that he will be our intercessor in the presence of God, because assuredly he reigns with Jesus Christ in heaven."

After the Council of Chartres, they confirmed documents for a number of monasteries including Cluny and its priory, St. Martin-des-Champs. The latter confirmation is of special interest because it was made to Matthew, later bishop of Albano, and Anaclet's implacable foe.[20] Clearly there was no problem in 1124. Stopping at Morigny for a couple of days, they then went on to Châlons where they heard a dispute between the abbot of St. Pierre-au-Mont and the Cluniac monastery of Vitry over rights of burial. Showing their impartiality, they announced their decision from Rheims in favor of the former.

---

[18] Chibnall, *Ecclesiastic History*, pp. 338-339. Since Gregory signed a document dated November 1, 1123 at Montecassino, he may not have been there, or else the two legates may have arrived later. See Schieffer, *Päpstlichen Legaten*, p. 215.

[19] A. Lecler, *Histoire de l'Abbaye de Grandmont* (Limoges, 1911), pp. 24-46.

[20] J. Depoin, *Recueil de Chartes et Documents de Saint-Martin-des-Champs* 1 (Paris, 1912), pp. 274-275, nr. 170: "Petrus Leonis presbiter, et G[regorius], Sancti Angeli diaconus, Sedis Apostolice cardinales et legati, dilecto et venerabili fratri M[atheo], priori Sancti Martini de Campis, salutem et benedictionem."

Still together at Noyen on June 28, 1124, they confirmed the order of the Praemonstratensians, founded by Norbert of Xanten.[21] The charter is of great import, because it not only shows that both Petrus and Gregory approved of the order, but it also reveals that both men greatly admired Norbert's move toward a return to the life of the primitive church. They gave thanks to the omnipotent God that Norbert had renewed the praiseworthy life of the holy fathers, and they lauded his revival of the institutions of the holy doctrine of the early church, which, they lamented, had almost died out. In addition to approving Norbert's order, Petrus is also thought to have been present at his election as archbishop of Magdeburg in 1126, although the "Petrus" mentioned is not further identified.[22] Anaclet expressed astonishment after his own election that given his good will toward Norbert and his order, the archbishop would oppose his election so aggressively.[23]

With Gregory, and at least on two occasions, by himself, Petrus took care of other papal business before returning to Rome by April 2, 1125. One of their stops was at St. Denis, where they were the only two witnesses to a long document issued by Suger.[24] During this stop Suger had the opportunity to observe both men, and his temperate account of the dual elections in 1130 no doubt reflects the opinions he formed at that time.

Since contemporary sources never distinguished between Gregory's and

---

[21] Charles Louis Hugo, *Sacri et canonici ordinis Praemonstratensis annales*, vol. 1 divided into 2 parts. *Probationes primi tomi monasteriologiae* (Nancy, 1734), pp. viij-ix. Charta confirmationis ordinis Praemonstratensis a duobus Legatis in Gallia a gentibus anno 1125: " . . . Omnipotenti Deo cujus misericordia super vitas, gratias agimus, quia vos estis qui sanctorum Patrum vitam probabilem renovatis, et Apostolicae instituta doctrinae, primordiis Ecclesiae sanctae inolita, sed et crescente Ecclesia jam pene deleta, instinctu Sancti Spiritus suscitatis." Giles Constable, "Renewal and Reform in Religious Life," *Renaissance and Renewal in the Twelfth Century*, pp. 37-67 at p. 53.

[22] *Ex Herimanni De Miraculis S. Mariae Laudunensis*, lib. III, ed. Roger Wilmans, MGH SS 12:660: "Cum ergo clerici Magdeburgenses plures quidem eligissent, sed in nullius electione unanimiter consentierent, nuntiatur eis, duos apostolicae sedis legatos, viros religiosos, ab urbe Roma Maguntiacum venisse, quorum unus Petrus, alter vocabatur Gerardus . . ." ed. n. 33: "ni fallor, Leonis filius, post antipapa Anacletus II."

[23] JL 8409. "An, quod veteris amicitiae signa tot dederimus, an quod ordini tuo Praemonstratensi approbationem impertierimus ultro, dum apud Gallos ageremus, idolum fabricas, in Germania erigis?" The letter was written on August 29, 1130, by which time Anaclet probably already knew that Norbert was the most influential advisor in convincing Lothar to recognize Innocent. A possible reason for Norbert's opting for Innocent may have been Anaclet's insistence that Norbert allow his clergy to come to Rome. On May 18, 1130, Anaclet had chided Norbert for deposing his archdeacon, Atticus, who wanted to raise a complaint against his archbishop at Rome. Anaclet commanded him not to interfere with clergy, who wished to come to the pope. JL 8391. Innocent rewarded Norbert for his support by extending the authority of Magdeburg into Poland and Pomerania. JL 7629. See Palumbo, *Lo Scisma*, pp. 320-323. Norbert's biographer reports that Anaclet directly requested Norbert's recognition, but the letters on which he bases his information have not been found, and presumably were destroyed. Bernhardi, *Lothar*, p. 321, n. 91.

[24] A. Lecoy de la Marche, *Oeuvres complètes de Suger* (Paris, 1867), pp. 326-331; Schieffer, *Päpstlichen Legaten*, p. 217.

Petrus' performances as legates, the contention that Gregory made a good impression and Petrus a bad must rely upon voices raised against Petrus during the schism. Even then, no reputable spokesman, such as Suger, criticized him, and partisan sources are suspect. Arnulf of Séez is especially so, since the account of Petrus' and Gregory's visit to Séez reveals that both legates were well received, and that nothing untoward happened. If Petrus had acted as venally as he was later charged, then it would have behooved Gregory to have divorced himself from him, and to have raised a complaint with the pope. Not only did he not do this, but the two men interacted in curial business for the next five years. Both men are also shown to have been strongly attracted to the new spirituality developing in France. Their extensive visit with Stephen of Grandmont, their private, very personal audiences with the saint, and their moving elegy at the Council of Chartres after Stephen's death are all testimony to this attraction. Their praise of Norbert's call to the return to the life of the early church, and the confirmation of his order are further affirmation of this commitment. At the same time both Petrus and Gregory were at ease with Cluniac monasteries, sometimes judging in their favor, and sometimes against them. There simply was no correlation between Innocent with the new orders, and Anaclet with the old.

The general picture of Anaclet which emerges, therefore, is that of a highly respected cardinal, who found favor under all of the popes whom he served. They appointed him to carry out important and long ranging commissions in France and in England, and he performed these tasks fairly. He examined records to adjudicate disputes, and he discussed local problems in a spirit of good will. When he departed from France, he did not leave behind a reputation of venality and corruption, which would be remembered when he tried to curry favor with the French after the papal election. Guigo of Chartreuse and Hugh of Grenoble thought of him as a friend, and Hugh also included Petrus' father in that category.[25] Thus, both Guigo and Hugh had to overlook their feelings when for other reasons they supported Innocent.

Although Petrus' family was constantly accused of being ambitious and of inveigling popes to do its bidding, the accusations are without foundation. More likely they arose out of jealousy or because as a new family the Pierleoni were seen as trying to improve their position to the disadvantage of the established Roman nobility. From this perspective it was to be anticipated that they would manipulate any situation to achieve their personal goals. Likewise, there is no reason to believe that Petrus concealed his true conservatism behind outward support for the progressive reforms of Paschal and Calixtus. His father's intimate involvement in the negotiations with Henry V in February 1111 to resolve the investiture contest, and Petrus' support of Calixtus even after the Concordat of Worms are

---

[25] Le Couteulx, *Annales Ordinis Cartusiensis*, ed. cit. 1, p. 333.

evidence to the contrary. In all probability Peter of Porto's assertion that "the church accepts and reveres this man" encapsulated the attitude of most churchmen toward Anaclet before the post-election invective had time to take its poisonous effect.[26]

---

[26] William of Malmesbury, *The Historia Novella*, ed. cit., p. 9. Very little evidence of Anaclet's attitudes toward ecclesiastic reform remains after his election. However, a charter from the monastery of St. Gregory in Rome dealing with one of its subject churches suggests that those, who wished to rid the church of its opulence, favored Anaclet. Preserved in the Annals of Camaldoli, the charter deals with the church of Sancta Fortunata in Sutri. In 1142 the people of Sutri brought a case before Caccialupus, a judge appointed by Anaclet's brother, Leo, and Leo's son, Peter. Innocent in turn had appointed Leo and Peter as the chief administrators of Sutri after Anaclet's death.

The judge ordered a group called the *Patarenses* to restore the goods, which they held from Sancta Fortunata. The *Patarenses* were in all probability related to the Pataria, a mideleventh century movement in Milan dedicated to reforming the clergy, who regularly were married, and practiced simony. The report associates the *Patarenses* of Sutri with Arnold of Bressia, who, it says, condemned the holding of *temporalia* and other riches by monasteries. Arnold went too far, and was branded a heretic. In like manner, the report says that catholics believed the *Patarenses* to be heretics, schismatics, disturbers of the peace, and lovers of sedition. It also states that they followed Anaclet.

It is impossible to know whether the *Patarenses* were in fact heretics, because after the schism as followers of Anaclet, they would have been seen as such. The text is intriguing, however, because it implies that Anaclet was seen to be sympathetic to the return of the church to its paleochristian state. "Multi e Sutrinis, ut etiam ex Nepesinis finitimis populis, erant Anacletistae; proficiebant ii schismatis tempore & bona ecclesiarum diripiebant, ac sub peccati jugo retinebant. Vigebat pariter hoc tempore Arnaldus Brixiensis haeresiarca, qui inter cetera damnabat monasteriorum temporalia dominia, proventus & divitias, & Romae praesertim turbas plurimas excitaverat." *Annales Camaldulenses*, ed. Johanne-Benedicto Mitterelli & D. Anselmo Costadoni 3 (Venice, 1758), pp. 267-277.

Chapter XV

THE ANATOMY OF THE SCHISM: THE JEWISH ELEMENT

If the schism was not produced by curial parties, distinguished by fundamentally different religious ideologies, and strongly opposed to one another, what, then, was the cause? I suggest that there was no one comprehensive cause, unless it was the quest for power, but if such were the rubric, the quest assumed many forms.

Competition between noble Roman families, especially the Pierleoni and the Frangipani, should not be rejected as a contributing factor. The Frangipani had never espoused any distinct religious principles, but had primarily sought the improvement of their position in Rome and its surrounding territories. They were hostile to Paschal II because he relied upon the Pierleoni to the detriment of their own interests. When Paschal proposed a member of the Pierleoni family for the prefecture of Rome in 1116, they and their colleagues not only thwarted the appointment, but they unleashed hostilities which forced the pope to withdraw from the city. They were furious with the election of Paschal's chancellor, John of Gaeta, as Paschal's successor, and twice attacked him, forcing him to go into exile. They could do nothing about the election of Calixtus because it was held in France, and Calixtus, who had the support of the Pierleoni, was always able to restrain them. Unlike Paschal, however, he kept a better balance between the two families, giving Cencius Frangipani command of a restricted band of troops (the *masnada*), and allowing Leo to participate in important negotiations such as those between Genoa and Pisa for control of the church of Corsica. Their first chance to reassert themselves strongly in papal politics, as well as to regain their former power in the city of Rome, came in the election of 1124.

At this time conditions were propitious for establishing a triumvirate. Haimeric wanted to retain the extensive authority he had wielded during the last years of Calixtus' reign, but a papacy under Saxo would not have allowed him so much freedom. Since Saxo was the most popular candidate, he did not need Haimeric's help, and Haimeric probably did not know him very well. After the signing of the Concordat of Worms little was heard of Saxo, and he seems not to have been active in curial affairs. Lambert of Ostia, who had been active throughout Calixtus' papacy, wanted to become pope, but he clearly was not acceptable to the majority of the cardinals, since they passed him over for the elderly compromise candidate, Theobald. Thus, Lambert, Haimeric, and the Frangipani were all looking for allies to further their own interests. They worked out the strategy carried out in 1124 in which the Frangipani imposed Lambert by force. Then, over Saxo's objections, they bribed key people like Petrus Leonis to ensure Lambert's acceptance by the cardinals and the Roman people.

The election of 1130 was similar to that of 1124 in that there were no ecclesiastical principles at stake. It differed from 1124 in that Gregory of St. Angelo was a less active participant than Lambert had been, and that this time the majority of the cardinals were prepared for any exigencies. In 1124 they had acquiesced in the *coup de main*, reluctant to court the possibility of a schism, and appeased by blandishments which were withdrawn after they had achieved their purpose. Haimeric knew that the same techniques would not work a second time, and had attempted along with Honorius to appoint a sufficient number of sympathetic cardinals to elect their candidate legally. They fell short, however, and again the chancellor had to resort to subterfuge. The difference this time was that his opponents were ready to outmaneuver him, and to use force if necessary.

Haimeric probably selected Gregory as his candidate because he was a Roman, but not from a family powerful enough to give him independent standing within the city. He had a respectable reputation, no important enemies, and what was essential, he was willing to go along with Haimeric's schemes. It says little for his integrity that he was willing to flout legal procedure in tolerating Honorius' mock burial and his own hasty election in order to become pope. There is no sign that Gregory's religious philosophy influenced Haimeric at all. Since his main assignments—as a negotiator for the Concordat of Worms, and as a papal legate to France—were performed with men who opposed him—Saxo and Petrus Pierleoni—they do not signify an ideological position different from that of his opponents. Also, at the time of his election he had no special connection with the new reformers.

In 1130 the majority of the cardinals did not accept Haimeric's *fait accompli*, but elected a pope following legal procedure as closely as they could under the circumstances. As opposed to 1124 the Pierleoni met force with force, making it imperative for Haimeric to convince Bernard of Clairvaux and other reformers of the North that Innocent was the better of the two candidates. It was his only chance of obtaining Innocent's recognition as the true pope. Bernard was not averse to examining the election and the contenders for the papal throne through Haimeric's eyes, even though he had recently fallen out of favor with the chancellor. Perhaps the occasion even provided the opportunity for Bernard to return to his former intimacy with the chancellor and to make his voice heard at the highest levels.[1] Then, too, the abbot must have been

---

[1] Adriaan Bredero, "Une controverse sur Cluny," pp. 50-51: "Innocent reçut l'appui de ce dernier [Bernard of Clairvaux] parce que son élection ouvrait davantage de perspectives à de nouveaux développements, en raison aussi des bonnes relations de l'abbé de Clairvaux

flattered and honored by the requests which Haimeric made of him.

The Jewish origins of Petrus' family made Haimeric's task much easier. Those people who lived in the vicinity of Rome and southern Italy with their mixtures of eastern and western civilizations were relatively tolerant of Jews. There were no uprisings against them, and it was not uncommon for Jews to live side by side with Christians. The inhabitants of the northern continent, however, focused more on Jews as the murderers of Christ. The First Crusade heightened their religiosity, and brought these feelings into the open. The result was not only the well-known pogrom against the Jews in the Rhineland, but also occasional outbreaks of violence in France.[2] The worst was in Rouen, where Guibert of Nogent reports:

> At Rouen on a certain day, the people who had undertaken to go on that expedition [the first crusade] under the badge of the Cross began to complain to one another, "After traversing great distances, we desire to attack the enemies of God in the East, although the Jews, of all races the worst foe of God, are before our eyes. That's doing our work backward." Saying this and seizing their weapons, they herded the Jews into a certain place of worship, rounding them up by either force or guile, and without distinction of sex or age put them to the sword. Those who accepted Christianity, however, escaped the impending slaughter.[3]

Godfrey of Bouillon had sworn that he was going to avenge the blood of Christ by massacring the Jews before he departed on crusade, but he was dissuaded from doing so.[4] However, after Jerusalem had been captured,

---

avec le chancelior pontifical Haimeric, dont le intrigues préparèrent et assurèrent l'élection du pontife." In his letter c. 1130 Bernard complains to Haimeric about the attacks made on him: "Does truth bring hatred even to the poor and indigent, and does not even their misery secure them against envy? Ought I to complain or to exult because I am made an enemy for speaking the truth or for doing right? That is what I leave to be considered by your bretheren, who, against the law speak evil of one who is deaf, and not fearing the malediction of the Prophet, call evil good and good evil. I ask of you, O good men, what in me has displeased your fraternity?" Ep. 48, *Sancti Bernardi Opera*, ed. cit. 7, pp. 137-140.

[2] See Norman Golb, "New Light on the Persecution of French Jews at the Time of the First Crusade," pp. 289-334 of *Medieval Jewish Life*, ed. Robert Chazan (New York, 1976). For good general accounts of the Jews in Western Europe at this time see Salo Wittmayer Baron, *A Social and Religious History of the Jews* 4-5 (New York, 1957); Robert Chazan, *Medieval Jewry in Northern France: A Political and Social History* (Baltimore and London, 1973); Lester K. Little, *Religious Poverty and the Profit Economy in Medieval Europe* (London, 1978), pp. 42-57. For the Jews in Italy see Cecil Roth, *The History of the Jews in Italy* (Philadelphia, 1946). For an impartial assessment of medieval Jews see James Parkes, *The Jew in the Medieval Community* 2nd ed. (New York, 1976), and the many articles by Gavin I. Langmuir.

Much of the current scholarship minimizes the animus against against Jews in Northern Europe prior to the Second Crusade, but I believe that it underestimates the basic hostility which occasionally erupted into violence. Marjorie Chibnall typifies this point of view. Speaking of Ordericus Vitalis she states: "His attitude is a reminder that the more militant approach to non-Christians often associated with the crusading movement only very slowly became general, and only partially replaced older customs of thought and action." *The World of Ordericus Vitalis*, pp. 160-161.

[3] *Self and Society in Medieval France: The Memoirs of Guibert of Nogent*, ed. John Benton (New York, 1970), pp. 134-135; Guibert's memoires are replete with anti-Jewish sentiment. See also Chazan, *Medieval Jewry*, p. 26.

[4] Golb, "New Light on the Persecution of French Jews," pp. 26-27.

the crusaders shut the Jews up in their synagogue, and set the building on fire.

Following the Christian victory the Jews became increasingly isolated. Before the attempt to reconquer Spain from the Muslims in the eleventh century and the First Crusade, Jews had fought side by side with Christians. Now they were excluded for religious reasons. These religious differences festered in the minds of the Christians, who were fired up to fever pitch with the zeal to combat the enemies of God. Moreover, having seen the possibilities of a lucrative trade with the Orient, the crusaders became reluctant to continue to leave this plum to the Jews. Frightened and insecure as a result of the pogroms and the Christian incursions into their old profession, the Jews turned more and more to the less hazardous business of moneylending. Kings and lords protected them so that they could demand ever higher taxes, and the Jews in turn were forced to exact greater and greater rates of interest. By the time of the papal schism Jews were already seen as usurers. In his *Dialogue of a Philosopher with a Jew and a Christian* written in the mid 1130's Abelard has the Jew state:

> Dispersed among all the nations, alone, without an earthly king or prince, are we not burdened with such great demands that almost every day of our miserable lives we pay the debt of an intolerable ransom? In fact, we are judged deserving of such great contempt and hatred by all that anyone who inflicts some injury on us believes it to be the greatest justice and the highest sacrifice offered to God. For they believe that the misfortune of such a great captivity has only befallen us because of God's supreme wrath, and they count as just vengeance whatever cruelty they visit on us. . . . Confined and constricted in this way as if the whole world had conspired against us alone, it is a wonder that we are allowed to live. We are allowed to possess neither fields nor vineyards nor any landed estates because there is no one who can protect them for us from open or occult attack. Consequently, the principal gain that is left for us is that we sustain our miserable lives here by lending money at interest to strangers; but this just makes us most hateful to them who think they are being oppressed by it.[5]

Innocent's supporters used this sentiment toward Jews to good advantage. By exploiting these widely held prejudices, they were able to shift the sympathy, which at first had tilted toward Anaclet to a landslide against him.[6] Soon he came to be seen as the rich Jew, who had gained his wealth

---

[5] Peter Abelard, *Dialogue of a Philosopher with a Jew and a Christian*, ed. & trans. Pierre J. Payer (Toronto, 1979), pp. 32-33. Payer (pp. 6-7) is convinced by the arguments dating the dialogue in 1136. In the preface (pp. XLIX-LXX) to the *Cartulaire de Saint-Vincent de Mâcon* (Mâcon, 1864) Camile Ragut notes that there were several colonies of Jews in the environs of Mâcon. Until the end of the eleventh century they preserved the liberty of their persons and the free disposition of their property, but the First Crusade occasioned hate to be raised against them as the murderers of Christ. As a result their personal and social position changed. Nobles profited from this change, not only to impose a very heavy yearly tax on them, but also to confiscate their goods and property.

[6] Mühlbacher, *Die streitige Papstwahl*, pp. 124-132. Mühlbacher shows that before this campaign became effective, there was much support and good will for Anaclet. Peter the Venerable was criticized by many of the Cluniacs for adhering to Innocent, and for cam-

through usury, and who had bought his way up to the papacy. It was not
that people saw Innocent as a crusader for a more spiritual church, in the
way that Gregory VII must have appeared as the liberator of the church
from secular control, but that they saw Anaclet as a descendant of the
people who had killed Christ. Viewed from this perspective, any evil inti-
mation against him would be believed—e.g., that he had initiated violence
before rather than after the election, that he attained his position in the
college of cardinals only because of his family's ill-gotten money, that he
was motivated by ambition rather than by religious convictions, and that
he had sired a child by his sister.[7] The protests of men like Peter of Porto
and Peter of Pisa were of no avail against this inexorably moving wave of
malicious rumors.

The campaign of vilification against Anaclet was well coordinated.[8] The
scurrilous accusations made by Bishop Manfred of Mantua correspond
closely with the monstrous charges leveled later from the North by Arnulf
of Séez in the *Invectiva in Girardum Engolismensem Episcopum.*[9] Manfred's
first charges are fairly moderate, comparing Anaclet unfavorably with
Innocent, and deploring the Jewish perfidy and Leonine madness of the
heretic, Petrus, which rages in the church. Later he becomes more expansive, claiming that Anaclet engaged in sexual relations with nuns, with
married women, and even with his own sister, copulating at random as
though he were a dog.[10] Arnulf, archdeacon of Séez, and later bishop of

---

paigning so vigorously against a former Cluniac monk, he points out. He notes that according to Arnulf of Séez, Gerard of Angoulême tried to keep Spain in Anaclet's camp, and that
until at least 1134 Diego of Compostella attempted to remain on good terms with both sides.
And he observes that King Henry of England, on the urging of Gerard, and most of the the
English bishops were inclined toward Anaclet. The bishops tried to keep Henry from recognizing Innocent, but the king finally gave in, according to Ernaldus, when St. Bernard agreed
to take Henry's sins upon himself, but more probably after the Council of Étampes when
Louis VI opted for Innocent.

[7] Ibid., 120.

[8] Bloch, "The Schism of Anacletus II," p. 167, n. 29.

[9] Ibid., 166-167. Bloch says of the *Invectiva*, "As to vileness of language and monstrosity
of charges, this pamphlet easily tops the whole rich literature of the *Libelli de lite*." Quoting
other authors Bloch notes that Haller (*Das Papsttum* 2, pt. 2, p. 544) says, "Das ungeheuer-
liche Pamphlet Arnulfs von Lisieux verdient Beachtung nur als Zeugnis für dem schmutzige
Character seines Verfassers." Bloch also says that Zöpffel (*Die Papstwahlen*, pp. 299-301,
371) admitted that the tract was unreliable. However, I note that Zöpffel at times did rely
upon it, and he seemed to be more or less in agreement with its contents. Palumbo (*Lo Scisma*, pp. 21-22) grants Manfred and Arnulf the dubious honor of writing the most violent
pages of all of the Innocentian propaganda. On pp. 95-100 Palumbo discusses Anaclet's Jewish extraction. The *Invectiva* is edited in MGH Ldl 3:85-108; MGH SS 12:707-720; Watterich,
Gesta 2, pp. 258-275.

[10] Watterich, *Gesta* 2, n. 1, pp. 275-276: "Nunc igitur quanto magis iudaica perfidia et
Leonina rabies et Petri haeresis in ecclesiam furiunt et virum innocentem, iustum, castum,
bene morigeratum, catholice electum et consecratum, Innocentium nomine, cum suis per-
dere et omnia bona moliuntur subvertere, . . . et ille iniquus Petrus, perditionis filius, cum
suis aut per vos poeniteat aut per vos pereat. . . . Qui licet monacus, presbyter, cardinalis
esset, scorta, coniugatas, monachas, sororem propriam, etiam consangineas ad instar canis,
quoquomodo habere potuit, non defecit. Et quod intrusus sit et execratus, symoniacus eius
introitus adprobat. A tempore enim Calixti beatae memoriae, ut sedem Apostolicam at-

Lisieux, was not to be outdone in his use of invective. He speaks of Anaclet's family in the usual terms, and contends that the anti-pope's Jewishness was visible in his face. He then repeats the story of Anaclet's libidinous relationship with his sister, and notes in the most explicit terms how the law of nature was confused by the progeny resulting from their union.[11] Later, again returning to Anaclet's family, Arnulf expressed what was widely believed—that Anaclet's family had still not been purified from the yeast of Jewish corruption.[12]

The anti-Jewish propaganda began immediately after the election, and was quickly picked up by the annalists. Archbishop Walter of Ravenna was in the neighborhood of Rome at the time of Honorius' death, and in a letter to Norbert, he informed him of Anaclet's origins, and admonished him to alert the king and the German bishops to this fact so that the heresy of Jewish treachery might be extirpated.[13] The cardinal bishops

---

tingeret, nisus est cardinales episcopos muneribus pollicitis, blanditiis circuiendo (quod per memetipsum cognosco: rogatus enim ab illo et a fratribus eius saepenumero fui) et cives Romanos donationibus et sacramentis subvertendo . . ." See also Bernhardi, *Lothar* p. 313 and n. 80.

[11] Watterich, *Gesta* 2, pp. 259-260: "Libet igitur praeterire antiquam nativitatis originem et ignobilem similem prosapiam nec iudaicum nomen arbitror opponendum de quibus ipse non solum materiam carnis, sed etiam quasdam primitias ingeniti contraxit erroris. Ipse enim sufficiens est et copiosa materia neque quidquam domui eius ipso turpis vel esse vel fuisse coniecto. Cuius avus cum inestimabilem pecuniam multiplici corrogasset usura, susceptam circumcisionem baptismatis unda damnavit. Pudebat eum impotentiae suae potius, quam erroris, nec genus eius, infidelitatis opprobrio confusum, perpetua damnaret obscuritas: susceptis itaque fidei sacramentis, ubi novus civis insitus, est factus dignitate Romanus. . . . Ex hac itaque diversorum generum mixtura, Girarde, Petrus iste tuus exortus est, qui et iudaicam facie repraesentet imaginem et perfidiam voto referat et affectu."

p. 262: "Profusa vero convivia tanta libidinum spurcitia sequebatur, ut ab ipso passim, quidquid occurreret, adiretur. Sororem Tropeam (sed nec dici fas est) bestiali polluisse narratur incestu et ex ea abominabili prodigio eosdem sustulisse filios quos nepotes! Nepotum pater, filiorum factus avunculus—sic naturae iura confudit, ut eosdem sibi invicem fratres faceret et cognatos. Iam nec Iudaeus quidem, sed Iudaeo etiam deterior. Nulla sexuum, nulla loci vel temporis, nulla professionum ratio."

[12] Ibid., 274: "Infidelis universitas illa, quam sequeris, familia Petri Leonis est, nondum fermento iudaicae corruptionis penitus expiata." This is the same Arnulf, it is to be remembered, who defamed Matilda at the hearing over the kingship of England during the Lateran Council of 1139. During the Second Crusade Arnulf squabbled with his colleague, Bishop Godfrey of Langres: "both were smoothe-tongued, both extravagant, both (it is said) mischief-makers, devoid of the fear of God; but of the two the bishop of Langres was more prudent and high-minded. Few if any have brought more harm on the Christian army and whole community. Each had his own following who believed in him, and both received large sums of money from the sick and dying whom they attended and absolved in the name of the pope, claiming to be his representatives. Indeed they are believed to have accumulated more wealth during the expedition than they paid out of their own pockets." *John of Salisbury's Memoirs*, ed. cit., pp. 54-55.

[13] *Monumenta Bambergensia*, ed. Jaffé, *Bibliotheca Rerum Germanicorum* 5, pp. 423-425. Gualterius archiepiscopus Ravennae Norberto archiepiscopo Magdeburgensi (March-April 1130): "Innocentius . . . per electionem venerabilium fratrum et dominorum nostrorum unanimiter in unum convenientium. . . . Postmodum vero Petrus Leonis, qui papatum a longis retro temporibus affectaverat, parentum violentia, sanguinis effusione, decrustatione sanctarum imaginum, facta etiam conspiratione, inverecunde facie rubeam sibi cappam assumens, universalem matrem nostram sanctam Romanam ecclesiam turpiter usurpare et symonicae occupare contendit. . . . Praedictum vero Petrum, vere leonis rugientis filium

who voted for Innocent noted that Anaclet had been elected in the very hour in which Judaea crucified Christ,[14] and in describing the schism the *Chronicle of Maurigny* emphasized the conversion of Anaclet's forefathers.[15] Matthew of Albano was one of the four cardinal bishops who correlated the time of Anaclet's election with the crucifixion of Christ. Both he and Peter the Venerable, with whom he was very close, were outspoken in their antagonism toward Jews. Since they were so influential in rallying Western Christendom to Innocent, their attitudes must be given special consideration.[16]

Peter mentions approvingly that as prior of St. Martin-des-Champs Matthew had prohibited his monks from borrowing money from Jews.[17] Peter himself, as I have already noted, wrote a long tract against Jews, and its tone was of more than customary violence.[18] Peter asks, for example, if there is any race of men who does not think that the Jews are the most vile slaves, and he asserts that whereas in religion the Jews had once been the head of all peoples, that now they have become the tail.[19] And later,

---

querentem quem devoret, tamquam non electum sed contra Deum et sanctam ecclesiam erectum, non assumptum sed intrusum, non apostolicum sed apostaticum, non catholicum sed hereticum, non consecratum sed execratum, divina ei in omnibus et per omnia contradicente auctoritate, condempnantes abdicamus. . . . quatenus tam per domum regem quam et per vos pax ecclesiae reformetur, et Iudaicae perfidiae heresis, quae nuper in eadem ecclesia exorta est, praestante Domino funditus exstirpetur."

In a letter of May 11, 1130 to Lothar Innocent commends Walter of Ravenna as his legate and contrasts his own lack of ambition for the papacy with Petrus' striving (nr. 247, ibid., 427-429): "Postmodum vero P[etrus] Leonis, qui papatum a longis retro temporibus affectaverat parentum violentia, sanguinis effusione, decrustatione sanctarum imaginum beati Petri cathedram occupavit." In Anaclet's letter to the bishops, abbots, and other clergy of Germany of February 24, 1130 he does not malign Innocent (ibid., 421-422, nr. 243). Anaclet describes his own election and then says: "Si quid autem sinistri rumoris acceperitis, non multum miremini. Solius enim Dei est, unire vota et omnium voluntates. Falsum tamen, quicquid praeter id, quod diximus, delatum fuerit, habeatis; . . ."

[14] Watterich, *Gesta* 2, p. 182: "Petrus Leonis hora sexta, qua Judaea Christum crucifixit et tenebrarum caligo mundum involvit . . . pontificatus insignia arripuit." Mühlbacher, *Die streitige Papstwahl*, pp. 23-25; Bernhardi, *Lothar*, p. 314, n. 80.

[15] *Chronicon Mauriniacensis*, Watterich, *Gesta* 2, pp. 183-184: "Fuit hic Petrus, Petri filius, filii Leonis. Leo vero a Judaismo Pascha faciens ad Christum a Leone baptisari et eius nomine meruit insigniri. Hic vir, quia scientissimus erat, in curia Romana magnificentissimus effectus, genuit filium nomine Petrum, magnae famae magnaeque potentiae post futurum."

[16] Mühlbacher, *Die streitige Papstwahl*, p. 127. Mühlbacher emphasizes that Peter the Venerable exerted a profound effect on the French church by receiving the fleeing pope so ceremoniously, and that Peter in turn credited Matthew with being especially influential in rallying support for Innocent. *De Miraculis* II, c. 16, PL 189:928: "studio praecipue Matthaei papa jam dictus univit."

[17] *De Miraculis* II, c. 15, PL 189:927. Speaking of Matthew, Peter says: "Requirens ille creditores, quosdam ex ipsis Judaeos esse cognovit. Statimque ad fratres ista sibi referentes conversus: 'Et inde,' inquit,'hoc vobis quod Christiani et monachi a Judaeis et impiis mutas accipere pecunias voluistis?' "

[18] Bloch, "The Schism of Anacletus II," p. 167, n. 30.

[19] *Tractatus Contra Judaeos*, PL 189:507-650 at p. 560: "Quae enim gentes Judaeis non imperant? Quibus populis Judaei non serviunt? Quod genus hominum non eos ut vilissima mancipia conculant? Vere sicut olim eis in Deuteronomio interminatus est Deus, cum quantum ad religionem, cunctorum populorum caput exstiterint, nunc in caudam omnium gentium conversi sunt. (Deut. 28)"

where in the context of the schism Peter might have substituted "pope" for "king," he asks whether one could accept a Jew, that is an exile or a slave, as king?[20]

No doubt some of Peter's hostility arose from Cluny's economic difficulties, and the consequent pressure on him to borrow from Jews.[21] But it is clear from a letter which he wrote to Louis VII at the time of the second crusade that his hate also originated from traditional religious causes. In the letter he states that the Jews are even worse than the Saracens. At least the Saracens have the virtue of being at a great distance, he observes, while the Jews are here in our midst. He accuses them of blaspheming Christ and the Christian sacraments, and of treating them with contempt. The Saracens ought to be detested for their views, he believes, but at least they believe in the virgin birth and other Christian doctrines. The Jews, however, deny God, and even worse, the son of God, whose death and resurrection made possible man's salvation. How much more, therefore, he asks, ought the Jews to be cursed and hated? The severity of God in damning the Jews from the time of the passion of Christ until the end of the world, is absolutely just, he concludes.[22]

Since Peter was closely associated with those who specifically tied Anaclet to his Jewish heritage, it is probable that he too saw Anaclet as one who had not yet rid himself of the taint of his past.[23] Nevertheless there is no evidence that he explicitly exploited Anaclet's lineage as Innocent did. In a letter to Archbishop Hugh of Rouen on October 6, 1131, Innocent took note of the fact that Hugh had been an intrepid supporter of the church in its time of trial. He said that he was aware that Hugh detested the ambition of the invader, Petrus Leonis, and that he had ground down the madness of Jewish perfidy by his frequent exhortations. Innocent was

---

20 Ibid., 560: "Dabis ergo mihi, Judaee, de talium numero regem? Dabis pro rege exsulem? Produces pro rege servum? Propones pro duce mancipium?"

21 Bredero, "Une controverse sur Cluny," p. 68.

22 Constable, *The Letters of Peter the Venerable* 1, ep. 130, pp. 327-330: "Sed quid proderit inimicos Christianae spei in exteris aut remotis finibus inseque ac persequi, si nequam blasphemi, longeque Sarracenis deteriores Iudaei, non longe a nobis, sed in medio nostri, tam libere, tam audacter, Christum, cunctaque Christiana sacramenta, impune blasphemauerint, conculcauerint, deturpauerint? Quomodo zelus dei comedet filios dei, si sic prorsus intacti euaserint, summi Christi ac Christianorum inimici Iudaei . . . Si detestandi sunt Sarraceni, quia quamuis Christum de uirgine ut nos natum fateantur, multaque de ipso nobiscum sentiant, tamen deum deique filium quod maius est negant, mortemque ipsius ac resurrectionem, in quibus tota summa salutis nostrae est, diffitentur, quantum execrandi et odio habendi sunt Iudaei, qui nichil prorsus de Christo uel fide Christiana sentientes, ipsum uirgineum partum, cunctaque redemptionis humanae sacramenta abiiciunt, blasphemant, subsannant? . . . Sic de dampnatis dampnandisque Iudaeis ab ipso passionis mortisque Christi tempore iustissima dei seueritas facit, et usque ad ipsius mundi terminum factura est."

23 A statement from *Contra Judaeos* makes this probability all the more likely. Peter indicates that the spirit of God has not yet been placed within a Jew, and without that spirit, no Jew can ever be converted to Christ. This would presumably hold true for Anaclet's family. "Nescio, inquam, utrum homo sit, de cujus carne nondum cor lapideum ablatum est, cui non datum est cor carneum, in cujus medio nondum positus est divinus Spiritus, sine quo ad Christum nunquam converti potest Judaeus." PL 189:551.

pleased that Hugh's efforts had met with success—that the hearts of princes and others had been made steadfast in the catholic faith, and in their obedience to himself.[24]

Rouen was not just any city, and Hugh was not just any archbishop. It is to be recalled that one of the worst pogroms against the Jews had occurred at Rouen at the time of the First Crusade, and that Hugh was a powerful churchman close to both Rome and Henry I. A kinsman of Matthew of Albano, he had been abbot of the royal abbey of Reading in England. Honorius summoned him to Rome in 1129, and sent him back to England, not exactly as a legate, but as a special cleric of St. Peter and the Roman church with the particular duty of collecting Peter's Pence. Innocent immediately confirmed his promotion to the archbishopric of Rouen on March 28, 1130, and Hugh probably functioned as his chief advocate when Henry sailed to Normandy in the autumn of 1130 to decide which papal contender to recognize. The negotiations reached a climax at Rouen in May. There, Innocent's chief supporters had gathered to overcome any hesitations Henry might still have had. Among them were Geoffrey of Chartres, Suger, Peter the Venerable, and St. Bernard; in Henry's entourage were the bishop of Lisieux, Arnulf of Séez, and Hugh of Rouen. It was from Rouen that Innocent issued the summons to the great council to be held at Rheims on October 18th. Hugh acted as Henry's chief representative there after the king returned to England.[25]

Hugh, then, operated at the highest level—with the king, with the papacy—Haimeric as well as Innocent—and with the most influential churchmen of Northern Europe. Even though we do not know that all of these people echoed his outrage over Anaclet's Jewish perfidy, we know that Innocent and Arnulf of Séez did, and it is a reasonable assumption that their sentiments were not isolated.

Bernard at least shared them, and no matter what other factors he might have taken into consideration, it is improbable that he ever could have recognized a pope, who still had not been cleansed of his Jewish heritage. In his practical position on Jews Bernard was more temperate than Peter the Venerable and Matthew of Albano, to say nothing of Arnulf of Séez.[26] For example, he never went so far as Peter in proposing that Jewish funds be confiscated for use by the crusaders.[27] He also forcefully opposed killing Jews, and heeded an urgent appeal to stop Radulph, a Cistercian monk, who was encouraging mobs to massacre Jews during the second

---

[24] PL 179:103: ". . . et ambitionem invasoris Petri Leonis detestans, ac Judaicae perfidiae furorem conterens . . ."

[25] JL 7472-6; PL 179:93-97; William of Malmesbury, *The Historia Novella*, ed. cit., p. 10; *Synods and Councils*, pp. 755-757, and n. 1, for further sources.

[26] For a detailed description of Bernard's attitude toward Jews see David Berger, "The Attitude of St. Bernard of Clairvaux toward the Jews," *Proceedings of the American Academy for Jewish Research* 40 (1972), 89-108.

[27] *The Letters of Peter the Venerable*, ed. cit., 1, nr. 130, pp. 327-330.

crusade. But as strong an opponent as he was of the destruction of Jews, he was at the same time a perpetuator of anti-Jewish stereotypes.[28] In a letter to Haimeric he reveals his general position on Jews. Quoting from Acts 7:51, the chapter which describes Stephen's stoning by the Jews, he says, "or certainly harken with the Jews, 'you always are resistant to the holy spirit.' "[29]

Like Peter the Venerable, Bernard was imbued with the idea of Jewish servitude. In *De consideratione* he said, "There is no more disgraceful slavery, none worse than that of the Jews: whithersoever they go they drag the chain, and everywhere displease their masters."[30] Servitude was considered to be the punishment for the greatest of all crimes, the crucifixion. In his sixtieth sermon on the *Cantica Canticorum* Bernard speaks of Jews as viperous venom for laying their impious hands upon the Lord of Glory.[31] Joseph had to hide Mary while she was pregnant, Bernard says, lest "that stiff-necked people . . ., those cruel and incredulous Jews, would have mocked at him and stoned her . . . What would they have done to him whilst yet unborn, on whom afterwards, when glorified by miracles, they did not hesitate to lay sacrilegious hand?"[32]

Bernard believed that the Jews were intransigent because of their stupid and bovine intellect, but at least he placed them above the animals in intelligence, the reverse, as he pointed out, of Isaiah's order.[33] In economic matters, Bernard saw the Jews as almost everyone else did, namely as devoted to the pursuit of gain.[34] It was he who first used the term, *judaizare*, to mean to lend at interest. In the letter to the clergy and people of Eastern France urging them to undertake the crusade, but not to persecute Jews, he says that where there are no Jews, Christian moneylenders extort even worse usury (*pejus Judaizare*). He then speculates that such people might better be called baptized Jews than Christians.[35] The latter statement indicates that he believed that it was possible to exhibit Jewish characteristics even though baptized; this seems to have been his view of Anaclet.

---

[28] Berger, "The Attitude of St. Bernard," pp. 106-107.

[29] Ep. 311, *Sancti Bernardi Opera*, ed. cit. 8, p. 239: "Immo vero aut acquiescat Apostolo dicenti: SPIRITUM NOLITE EXTINGUERE, aut certe audia cum Iudaeis: VOS SEMPER SPIRITUI SANCTO RESTITISTIS . . ." See also Amélineau, "St. Bernard," pp. 105-106.

[30] Lib. I, c. 3, *Sancti Bernardi Opera*, ed. cit. 3, p. 398.

[31] "Sancti Bernardi Sermones super Cantica," *Sancti Bernardi Opera*, ed. cit. 2, p. 144.

[32] "Second Sermon on the Virgin Mother," *St. Bernard's Sermons for the Seasons and the Principal Festivals of the Year*, tr. a priest of Mt. Melleray (Westminster, Maryland, 1950), 1, pp. 86-87; Berger, "The Attitude of St. Bernard," p. 100.

[33] "Sermones super Cantica," ed. cit. 2 p. 144; Berger, "The Attitude of St. Bernard," p. 103.

[34] Ibid., 143: "Nam actus in bellis, affectus in lucris totus erat, intellectus in crassitudine litterae, cultus in sanguine pecundum et armentorum."

[35] Ep. 363, *Sancti Bernardi Opera*, ed. cit. 8, p. 316: "Taceo quod sicubi desunt, peius iudaizare dolemus christianos feneratores, si tamen christianos, et non magis baptizatos Iudaeos convenit appellari." Berger, "The Attitude of St. Bernard," p. 104.

Bernard made frequent innuendos which suggested Anaclet's Jewish identity. Speaking of him in a letter to Peter the Venerable, Bernard exulted that the fruitless growth, the rotten branch, had been lopped off. That impious one, who had made Israel to sin, has been swallowed up in death and has gone down into the pit, he said with obvious satisfaction.[36] Bernard had no doubt that Peter would understand the metaphors, for in other contexts he associated the images of a flower without fruit, of withered grass, and of a fruitless tree with the Jews.[37] In his long letter to the bishops of Aquitaine Bernard refers to Anaclet as a beast, a term often used by Peter the Venerable for Jews.[38] But the statement which most directly reveals that Bernard believed that even a descendant of a Jew should not be pope appears in a letter to Lothar written in 1134. Indicating that the sins of the father were visited upon the son, Bernard said of Anaclet, "For just as it is clear that it is an insult to Christ that the offspring of a Jew has occupied the chair of Peter, so without a doubt, anyone who makes himself king in Sicily, acts in opposition to Caesar."[39]

Although more discreet than Arnulf of Séez, both Bernard and Peter the Venerable implied that they agreed with him when they indicated that

---

[36] Ep. 147, *Sancti Bernardi Opera*, ed. cit. 7, pp. 350-351.

[37] *De Laude Novae Militia*, c. 7, *Sancti Bernardi Opera*, ed. cit. 3, p. 225; *De Laudibus Virginis Matris Sermo* I, ibid. 4, p. 17; *Sermones Super Cantica*, ibid. 2, pp. 143-144: "The fig tree puts forth her green figs; and as I think, by that is meant the nation of the Jews. . . . And again, it is a fig tree upon which he [the Savior] pronounces a curse, because he has found upon it no fruit. . . . Whence hast thou these figs crude and course? And in truth, what is there in that people which is not crude and course, whether we consider their actions, their inclinations, their understanding, or even the rites with which they worship God? . . . If you ask me at what moment this [the production of green figs] took place with the [Jewish] people, I reply, when it killed Christ. For it was then that its malice was consumated. . . . O what a consumation of its continued production of crude and coarse fruits did that fig tree, so accursed and condemned to perpetual sterility, reach at length!" Berger, "The Attitude of St. Bernard," p. 105.

St. Augustine was most probably the source for these metaphors. In his own *Contra Judaeos* he stated that because of their unbelief Jews had been cut off from the root of the olive tree to which the Patriarchs belong. Because of their humble faith Gentiles have been grafted on. PL 42:51. Later he says it is not for us to boast over them as branches broken off; ibid., 64; see A. Lukyn Williams, *Adversus Judaeos: A Bird's Eye View of Christian Apologiae until the Renaissance* (Cambridge, 1935), pp. 313, 317. Peter the Venerable claimed to be following St. Augustine who wrote against Julian the heretic, Faustus the heathen Manichaean, and also against the Jews. PL 189:652. For the views of St. Augustine on Jews see Bernhard Blumenkranz, *Die Juden predigt Augustins*, vol. 25 of Basler Beiträge aus Geschichtswissenschaft, ed. E. Bonjour, W. Kaegi, F. Stähelin (Basel, 1946).

[38] Ep. 126, *Sancti Bernardi Opera*, ed. cit. 7, pp. 309-319. Berger, "The Attitude of St. Bernard," p. 106, n. 76. Speaking of Jews in ch. v of *Contra Judaeos* Peter says: "Take an ox or an ass, the stupidest animal there is. What difference is there from thee? An ass will hear but not understand, and so it is with a Jew. I lead out then a monstrous animal from its den, and show it as a laughing stock in the amphitheater of the whole world, in the sight of all peoples. I bring forward thou Jew, thou brute beast, in the sight of all men, . . ." PL 189:602.

[39] Ep. 139 to Lothar in 1134, ibid., 335-336: "Ut enim constat Judaicam sobolem sedem Petri in Christi occupasse injuriam; sic procul dubio omnis qui in Sicilia regem se facit, contradicit Caesar." See Bloch, "The Schism of Anacletus II," pp. 166-167.

they valued his services at the time of the schism. Peter called him an "amicum schismatis tempore," and extolled his "in iuuenili aetate morum maturitatem."[40] Bernard referred to him as "the uterine son of the Roman church," and with Peter the Venerable, he came to his aid in 1141 when he was elected bishop of Lisieux. He did so again in 1146.[41]

When St. Bernard insinuated that Jewish character could remain unaffected by conversion, he no doubt was reflecting the common opinion. The same view had been expressed earlier about Anaclet's forefather, Leo, whose habit of usury, it was claimed, was not removed by baptism.[42] In general, Bernhardi explains how most people felt about Jews, and why anti-Jewish propaganda could be so effective.[43] He emphasizes how despised Jews were, and says that a clever Jew who had raised his status through the acquisition of money particularly irritated people. Even those who did not openly express their antisemitism nevertheless believed all of the calumnies uttered against Jews. Thus, the mere mention that Anaclet was a Jew implied that he possessed all of their negative characteristics. Christians thought that it was good that Jews be converted to their religion, Bernhardi states, but not that they become popes.

No anti-Jewish slurs were made against Anaclet while he was a papal legate in France because he was not then an object of controversy. However, it was known that his family had converted to Christianity, and in the Council of Rheims in 1119, his brother was made an object of derision. The brother, Gratianus, had been a hostage, and was released to the care of Calixtus II during the Council. The French and others attending the pope noted his dark, but pallid coloring, and said that he looked more like a Jew or a Saracen than a Christian. They observed that he was dressed beautifully, but that his body was deformed, and they expressed their dislike for his father, who, they claimed, had accumulated his riches through usury.[44] Considering the large number of French prelates and

---

[40] Ep. 101, Constable, *The Letters of Peter the Venerable* 1, pp. 261-262.

[41] Bloch, op. cit., p. 167 & ns. 30, 31.

[42] *Benonis Aliorumque Cardinalium Schismaticorum contra Gregorium VII. et Urbanum II.*, ed. Kuno Francke, MGH Ldl 2:379: "Brunoni [Leo IX] igitur in itinere multa loquendo se subposuit. Et, ut Romam venit, optinuit ab eo, ut fieret unus de custodibus altaris beati Petri. Et in brevi loculos implevit, et cui pecuniam illam committeret, filium cuisdam Iudei noviter quidam baptizatum, sed mores nummulariorum adhuc retinentem, familiarem sibi fecit." Palumbo, *Lo Scisma*, p. 98.

[43] Bernhardi, *Lothar*, p. 314. William of Malmesbury denounced the Jews as being an "accursed" and "infidel" people, especially because of their denial of the doctrine of incarnation. *El libro 'De laudibus et miraculis Sanctae Mariae' de Guillermo de Malmesbury*, ed. José M. Canal (Rome, 1968), pp. 73-76; Chibnall, *The World of Orderic Vitalis*, p. 160.

[44] Chibnall, *Ecclesiastic History* 6, pp. 266-268: "Filium quoque Petri Leonis, quem obsidem habebat [Archbishop of Cologne] ob amoris specimen gratis reddidit. Haec dicens, quasi ob insigne tripudium laetiamque mirabilem, digito monstravit nigrum et pallidum adolescentem, magis Judaeo vel Agareno quam christiano similem, uestibus quidem optimis indutum, sed corpore deformen. Quem Franci, aliique plures papae adsistentem intuentes, deriserunt, eique dedecus perniciemque citam imprecati sunt, propter odium patris ipsius, quem nequissimum foeneratorem nouerunt." Palumbo, *Lo Scisma*, p. 130 & n. 1; Schmale, *Studien zum Schisma*, p. 71, n. 190.

laymen at the Council, it seems that the prejudices against the Pierleoni family were widespread long before the election of 1130. For the supporters of Haimeric and Innocent to tap this reservoir required little effort.

Thus, even though Innocent's most prominent supporters had their individual reasons for preferring him to Anaclet, they had, in Anaclet's Jewish background, a devastating weapon in their arsenal. They were not just using it because it would be effective, however, for it is clear from their writings that they also believed their own rhetoric.

A. Grabois ("Le schisme de 1130 et la France," pp. 610-611) interprets this account as an expression of anti-semitism. Following Schmale, Marjorie Chibnall suggests that opposition to the Pierleoni was already forming in curial circles in 1119, and was seeking justification in charges of usury against Peter Leonis. She also wonders whether in writing 16 years after the incident, Ordericus might have been reading back the hostility against the Pierleoni, which prevailed at the time of the schism. Both of these suggestions appear to me to be improbable. The incident itself was too specific to have been interpreted in hindsight, and as I have attempted to show, Schmale's analysis of this period is not convincing.

Chibnall also may be anxious to exculpate Ordericus from harboring any anti-Jewish sentiment. She previously noted that when Ordericus spoke of the Jews as persecutors of Christ or St. Stephen in his account of the First Crusade, that he was simply copying Baudry of Bourgueil. In the case of the Council of Rheims she emphasizes that Ordericus linked the reference to Jews to the infidel Saracens, but that linkage does not attenuate the charge. As I have already pointed out, Peter the Venerable asserted that the Jews were even worse than the Saracens. Ordericus no doubt reflects the prevailing view when he associates negative physical characteristics with Jews, but he does not include himself among those, who laughed scornfully and called down imprecations on the head of the hostage because of his origin and appearance. I see no reason to doubt that he correctly reported the actions and sentiments of the French delegates.

Chapter XVI

THE PROPAGANDISTS

Anaclet was no match for his rival in the contest to win the allegiance of Christendom after their elections. Some obvious reasons account for Innocent's success: that he appeared to embody legitimacy by retaining his predecessor's chancellor; that his legates were already known to the men of the North, while on the whole Anaclet's were not; that Honorius, Haimeric or both had performed many services for the most influential ecclesiastical leaders; and that Anaclet's chancery was less experienced. Beyond these pragmatic reasons, it is generally believed that Innocent's strongest supporters weighed the worth of each man and found Innocent to be the superior of the two in character. They also judged him to be the the more legitimately elected. Ecclesiastical and secular leaders alike accepted the opinions of these religious leaders, and opted for Innocent.

But for the most part churchmen received their impressions of Innocent and Anaclet through lenses ground by Haimeric and his allies. If the images were distorted, then the decisions based upon them do not reflect the merits of each case. It is true that there was some opportunity for forming independent judgments by assessing the diplomatic activities of the two candidates, and their participation in Gelasius' and Calixtus' entourage. Gerhoh of Reichersberg states that the regular canons knew even before the election that Innocent was a friend of chastity and religion, and that Anaclet was an enemy of the church.[1] In this instance, however, Gerhoh is unreliable. He had his own agenda, and he desperately needed Innocent's support for his heterodox position. He believed that sacraments performed by simoniacal or unchaste priests were invalid, and he argued vigorously for his view. His opponents regarded his position as heretical, and sought support for their case against him with the French theologians. Gerhoh resoundingly rejected the authority of these theologians, but when Archbishop Walter of Ravenna came to Regensberg in the fall of 1130 as Innocent's legate, his opponents took advantage of the legate's arrival to decide the issue of simoniacal priests.

Walter was a German from the same circle as Gerhoh, and was

---

[1] Gerhoh of Reichersberg, *Epistola ad Innocentium papam (Dialogus inter clericum saecularem et regularem)*, ed. E. Sackur, Ldl 3:203-239, at p. 227: "quem [Innocentium] et ante papatum novimus castitatis et religionis fuisse amicum, sicut illum alterum Dei et aecclesiae novimus fuisse inimicum."

sympathetic to him as a person. For this reason he was reluctant to condemn the zealous canon, but he recommended moderation, and along with Archbishop Conrad of Salzburg, commanded silence. Gerhoh complied as long as he could, but by the fall of 1131, he could stand it no longer. He appealed to Innocent in a letter, which was also a dialogue between secular and regular canons. In this tract/letter Gerhoh equated his own fight against the validity of sacraments performed by simonist priests with Innocent's fight against Anaclet.[2] He identified his side of the dispute with the regular canons, and the simonist side with the secular canons. Just as no supporter of Anaclet—the mercenaries, simonists and Nicolaites—could raise the host, he argued, so also no secular canon could do so.

Gerhoh requested, and was granted an audience with Innocent to present his case in person. The pope called him to Rome, where he received the support of Walter of Ravenna, Haimeric, and ultimately of Innocent himself. In opposition to St. Bernard and other Frenchmen, Innocent gave his imprimature to Gerhoh's *Dialogue*. No doubt realizing what a powerful weapon Gerhoh's views would be in the struggle against Anaclet, the pope and his advisors embraced them on tactical rather than theological grounds.

Bernard, the less pragmatic theologian, no doubt had read his St. Augustine, and saw the analogy between the views of the Donatists and those of Gerhoh. Just as the bishop of Hippo rejected the view that sacraments performed by an apostate priest were invalid, so also Bernard rejected Gerhoh's view that simoniacal, or—relating the issue to the schism—schismatic priests could not perform sacraments. Bernard's rejection of Gerhoh's view did not endear him to the purist canon. Gerhoh reveals his displeasure in a change he made in describing his summons to the pope in 1131 to present his case. In the first version he says, *consulente venerabili viro Bernhardo*, but later, omitting any reference to the abbot, he adds in the margin, *pulsatus a quibusdam schismaticis*. However, the abbot's concurrence in his view on simoniacal priests was too important to forfeit out of mere pique, and for this reason Gerhoh tried again, dedicating his *Libellus de quod princeps huius mundi iam iudicatus sit (Liber de Simoniacis)* to him in 1135. Again, he emphasized the schism, not because it was the main focus of his concern, but in order to win the powerful abbot over to his cause.[3]

Bernard refused to be swayed by such flattery, and his steadfast adherence to his position and Gerhoh's to his, shows what profound ideological

---

[2] Ibid. 235.

[3] *Libellus de eo quod princeps huius mundi iam iudicatus sit*, ed. E. Sackur, MGH Ldl 3:240-272; see p. 243 where Gerhoh ties his argument to the schism: "quomodo cogitatis a Petro Leone populum sibi adhaerentem separare, quamdiu ipse ab ecclesia precisus creditur idem sacrificium quod nos offerimus, offere . . ." See also Peter Classen, *Gerhoch von Reichersberg: Eine Biographie* (Wiesbaden, 1960), pp. 81-82.

differences existed among the northern reformers. Rather than being the source of any ideological dispute itself, the papal schism became a pawn to rally Anaclet's opponents to Gerhoh's unorthodox positions. By extending the category of invalid sacraments from those performed by simoniacal and unchaste priests to those performed by schismatics and heretics, Gerhoh hoped to rally all of Innocent's followers to his side. Similarly, by the nature of his argument, all of those whom he accused of simony fell under the suspicion of sympathizing with Anaclet. He did not support Innocent on ideological grounds, and reject Anaclet on those same grounds; rather he coopted the schism as part of his strategy to win the adherence of churchmen to a position, which had nothing to do with the schism.

Just as Gerhoh's characterization of Anaclet is unreliable, so also are those of the other northern religious leaders. It is improbable that they had accurate information, and because Anaclet's Jewish heritage may have weighed more heavily in their considerations, their recognition of Innocent does not imply a shared ideology. Further, their support is not ipso facto proof that Innocent represented the highest ideals of the reform, and that Anaclet did not.

Like the churchmen and secular leaders of the twelfth century, many scholars seem to have accepted the opinions of the northern reformers with little questioning. Because of their admiration for these figures—particularly for St. Bernard—and because of their inclination to see the candidate recognized by the church as the one deserving of that recognition, they tend to examine the evidence from this perspective. They may also be influenced by the fact that the great preponderance of extant sources favors Innocent.

Zöpffel and Amélineau are scholars within this tradition, whereas Mühlbacher's approach represents a more judicious assessment of the sources.[4] Both he and Palumbo are openly sceptical of the charges leveled at Anaclet, because they came from his enemies. By contrast, while

---

[4] Amélineau, "Saint Bernard," pp. 48-112. One of the first things he mentions about Anaclet is that he was from a family of converted Jews. He believes the Innocentian charges that Petrus was very ambitious, and appears to assume that his ambition resulted from the huge fortune made so quickly by his family. He also accepts all of the negative propaganda spread about Gerard of Angoulême, believing without hesitation St. Bernard's contention (the only source) that Gerard turned to Anaclet only after Innocent had rejected his request to become that pope's legate. Ep. 126, *Sancti Bernardi Opera*, ed. cit. 7, pp. 309-319. Toward the end of his study Amélineau transmits Bernard's oration presented before Roger II in which he convinces Peter of Pisa to convert to Innocent. In this speech Bernard implies that Anaclet was even worse than the pagans and the Jews of old because he dared to rend the tunic of Christ. Would it make sense, he asks, that the entire world should perish in order that the kingdom of heaven be given to Petrus Leonis "whose life is openly what it has shown itself to be?" Ernaldus, *Vita Bernardi*, PL 185:294-295. Since Amélineau is viewing the schism from the perspective of Bernard rather than from that of Innocent, however, he then points out that after Bernard's inestimable help, Innocent turned against him once he occupied the Holy See. Bernard's value presumably was in gaining his office rather than in influencing his policies thereafter.

admitting that Arnulf of Séez was not a wholly reliable source, Schmale
still lends some credence to his invective. Many other scholars are more
critical of Arnulf, but they find it difficult not to be moved by St.
Bernard's thundering denunciations. Bernard, after all, was a holy man of
such towering stature that his judgments must be given the most serious
consideration. At the same time, however, he was wont to throw himself
into causes of questionable merit.

According to legend his mother, Aleth, believed that God had designated her son to communicate His will. Whether because of her influence
or from other causes, Bernard seldom flinched from his assurance that his
perceptions and opinions were correct. Further, he was a genius at convincing others of the rectitude of his views. A gifted psychologist, and a
magnetic rhetorician, he would soften an adversary by first castigating him
for his erring behavior. Frequently he would claim that it had inflicted
grievous distress upon him personally, and he conjured up dreadful
images of punishment if the miscreant continued in his wrongful ways.
When the subject had been rendered abject by these repeated verbal
blows, Bernard would then become the gentle helpmate, offering his assis-
tance in leading him along the right path. Count William IX of Aquitaine,
who had supported Anaclet until 1135, fell on the steps of the church in a
kind of fit after Bernard had carried the host outside, and had held it up
dramatically while appealing to William to relent. William did so, as did
most of the others who underwent similar emotional persuasion. Those
who did not succumb were usually the more learned and sophisticated,
men like Gerard of Angoulême and Roger II, for example.

Many of Bernard's judgments tended to be rash, and his temperament
was given to extremes. On the one hand he could be sweet and gentle,
moving men to adore him, and on the other he could be self-righteous
and abrasive. In evaluating situations where his own interests were
involved he often lacked perspective, viewing confrontations in terms of
black and white rather than observing shades of grey. The schism of 1130
was only one of many conflicts seen in these terms.

The contested episcopal election at Langres in 1138 was another.[5] The
dispute was caused primarily by a split within the cathedral chapter, but it
had ramifications far beyond the diocese. Clairvaux lay within its boundaries, so that it was a matter of great interest to St. Bernard who the
bishop was. Peter the Venerable was involved because the bishop-elect,
William of Sabran, was a Cluniac monk. The case is complicated, but it is
generally agreed that there was no clear cut case of malevolence on the
part of Bernard's opponents.[6] Yet, in a flurry of letters, Bernard unleashed

---

[5] For an analysis of the election see Giles Constable, "The Disputed Election of Langres
in 1138," *Traditio* 13 (1957), 119-152. For a brief discussion of the dispute as an example of
Bernard's intemperance see Anselme Dimier, "Outrances et Roueries de Saint Bernard,"
Pierre Abélard, Pierre le Vénérable, pp. 655-670 at pp. 656-658.

[6] Constable, "The Disputed Election," p. 139: "The consecrators were hardly the type of
bishops to lend themselves to a flagrant breach of canon law. Only Bishop Josserand of

a volley of invective against them. He compared the bishop-elect to Baal, and accused him of being consecrated with the complicity of the archbishop of Lyons and the bishops of Mâcon and Autun, all friends of Cluny.[7] In another letter to Innocent he said that shame forbade him to repeat all of the rumors which were being spread about the bishop-elect.[8] But he saved his strongest words for Archbishop Peter of Lyons and Peter the Venerable. In a letter to the cardinals and bishops at Rome he referred to the archbishop and the abbot as powerful gods of the earth, who had risen not only against himself, but also against the men to whom he was writing, against themselves, against God, and against all equity and honesty.[9]

By contrast, Peter the Venerable responded calmly, recounting the history of the case from the vantage point of his involvement. He explained that the accusations made against the bishop-elect came from hardened enemies of Cluny, and that they should not have been taken before bishops and judges until their truth had been ascertained. On the basis of a personal interview Peter was satisfied that the charges were without foundation, and he asked Bernard not to lend credence to them. In the spirit of accommodation Peter said that Cluniacs and Cistercians should not fear, but love and trust one another, and he assured Bernard that the bishop-elect would do exactly that if he became bishop.[10]

Bernard did not heed Peter, however, but continued his campaign to a successful conclusion. William of Sabran was removed and replaced by the prior of Clairvaux after Bernard himself had humbly declined the nomination.

Mâcon is a somewhat obscure figure, and even he had been bishop for more than ten years at the time of the consecration. The bishop of Autun in 1138 was Stephen of Baugé, of whose virtue and wisdom Peter the Venerable wrote in the highest terms in his letter 5.6 and who was a theologian of some note and author of a treatise *De sacramento altaris*. He had been bishop since 1112 and was a man well advanced in years by 1138. Archbishop Peter of Lyons was also, as has been seen, an elderly and highly respectable prelate. Whatever his part in the so-called sacrilegious consecration, and in spite of Bernard's scathing attacks, he remained sufficiently in the good graces of Innocent II to be sent in the following year as a legate to the Holy Land."

[7] Ep. 166, *Sancti Bernardi Opera*, ed. cit. 7, pp. 377-378.

[8] Ep. 167, ibid., 378-379.

[9] Ep. 168, ibid., 380-381; Constable, "The Disputed Election," pp. 139-140. Speaking of these and other letters of the same kind Constable says, "In these letters the abbot of Clairvaux made use of every weapon in his well-stocked armory of words. He was in turn pathetic, cajoling, pleading, threatening, and abusive. He skillfully played upon the fears of the pope and the curia that the great regional prelates might assert their independence."

[10] Ep. 29, Constable, *The Letters of Peter the Venerable* 1, pp. 101-104. Urging Bernard not to be so credulous of the evil rumors being spread about the elect, Peter says: "Eapropter tantis tamque manifestis inimicis credere, tantis tamque manifestis hostibus fidem dare, nec uestrum nec aliquorum bonorum est. Credite magis domesticis quam extraneis, notis quam ignotis, amicis ueridicis quam inimicis maledicis. Credite michi, qui et domestici et noti et amici apud uos nomine glorior, qui etsi a communi mendacio quo *omnis homo mendax* est immunis esse non possum, absit tamen ut tibi non caueam mandacium, ubi cauere possum."

Bernard's violent verbal assaults on Peter the Venerable and Archbishop Peter of Lyons reveal his compulsion to denigrate those with whom he disagreed, no matter what sort of men they were.[11] Archbishop William Fitzherbert of York, canonized by Honorius III, Gerard of Angoulême, Abelard, and Anaclet all received similar treatment. Frequently he used animal imagery, which had the effect of dehumanizing his opponents. His attack on Abelard gave him the opportunity to use his considerable learning, and his Shakespeare-like skill in making plays on words. In a letter to Innocent he compares Abelard with Anaclet, pointing out to the pope that he had escaped the roaring of Petrus Leonis (the lion), and that now he must face Peter the dragon (Abelard), who attacks the faith of Peter. Like a ravishing lion Anaclet persecuted the church of God, he charges, and Abelard waits in ambush like a dragon to kill the innocent (Innocent).[12] In other letters Abelard is also a serpent,[13] and a new Goliath.[14]

These examples reveal that Bernard was more than usually drawn to disputes. Once involved, instead of evaluating the evidence as impartially as possible, he frequently believed what he wanted to hear or what supported an opinion he already held. He could argue his case eloquently, but the argument almost always involved blackening the character of his opponents. At times he simply lashed out in what seemed to be a blind fury. His attacks on Anaclet should be compared with those on Peter the Venerable and Archbishop Peter of Lyons as an indication or measure of their credibility. As in the case of William of Sabran, his attitude toward Anaclet may have been formed by listening to malicious rumors spread by Anaclet's enemies. Believing them, he then acted against the pope in Rome with his customary extravagance.

A letter from Louis VI to Haimeric, the cardinal bishops, and other cardinals, who had voted for Innocent, shows how Innocent's communication's network functioned.[15] In May 1130 Louis was already

---

[11] Although Elphège Vacandard, Bernard's foremost biographer, believes that Bernard's causes were good, he admits that his violence of expression dishonored them. *Vie de Saint Bernard* 2 (Paris, 1895), p. 158.

[12] Ep. 330, *Sancti Bernardi Opera*, ed. cit. 8, pp. 266-268. The play on words is based upon Psalm 90.13: "Super aspidem et basiliscum ambulabis, et conculabis leonem et draconem." Dimier, "Outrances," pp. 659 & n. 13.

[13] Ep. 331, ibid., 269-270.

[14] Ep. 189, ibid., 12-16.

[15] Ms. Olmütz, Domkapitelbibliothek (now Opava Státni Archiv) 205, fol. 212ra; Wilhelm Wattenbach, "Reise nach Österreich in den Jahren 1847, 1848, 1849," *Neues Archiv für ältere deutsche Geschichtskunde* 10 (1851), 682; repr. Reuter, "Zur Anerkennung," pp. 415-416; for a discussion of the churchmen responsible for Innocent's quick recognition, ibid., 395-414: "(P)alatinis episcopis Hostiensi, Albanensi, Prenestino, Abinensi, Tiburtino, cancellario ceterisque cardinalibus qui vobiscum sunt, L. Dei gratia Francorum rex in Domino salutem. Litteris vestris susceptis per filium vestrum et karissimum fratrem nostrum Ymarum de electione domni GG. Sancti Archangeli cardinalis in summum pontificem, Deo et vobis—quos ecclesiam tenemus—gratias retulimus et consilio domni Remensis et quorundam de palatio nostro Romane ecclesie fidelibus rescribere non distulimus. Iustam itaque peticionem vestram benigne amplectentes domnum papam Innoc(entium), virum honestum tante dignitati personam congruentem, in patrem et universis ecclesie pastorem indubitanter suscep-

writing a response to a letter he had received from these cardinals, which means that they had to have sent their letter to him immediately after the election. Louis gives no indication that the letter he received said anything at all about a second election. After seeking the advice of Archbishop Rainald II of Rheims and his clerical advisors, whom we know to be Suger and Algrin, he formally recognized Innocent, a man of good character. In closing he states that what he had decided in consultation with his advisors would be affirmed in a general council, which he was calling for May 25th. Accordingly, by the time the Council of Étampes convened, Louis had already made his decision.

The missing element in the letter is any reference to the schism, which he surely knew about from many sources by May. Were it not for his explicit mention that he had consulted his advisors, and would be calling a general council, his letter would appear to be a routine approval of a papal election. These measures are the giveaway that Louis was dealing with the dilemma raised by the dual elections. His first information of what had taken place in Rome came from Ymarus, the messenger who delivered the letter from the cardinals. According to a late fifteenth century Cluniac source Ymarus had been a monk at the priory of Saint Martin-des-Champs when Matthew was prior. Matthew was one of the cardinal bishops, who had sent the original letter to Louis, and Ymarus would have received his information from him and Haimeric. It was their version of the events in Rome, which Louis heard first.

But the king was not so naive as to accept this view unquestioningly. The problem for him was not so much whether Ymarus was presenting an accurate picture of what had happened in Rome, but what the significance of the crisis would be for the French monarchy. To gain that assessment he consulted his local advisors, even though they were hardly dispassionate. Archbishop Rainald had made at least one trip to Rome during Honorius' reign, and showed his disposition to recognize that pope's chosen successor by recognizing Innocent when he first arrived in France, and the schism was raging.[16] Louis no doubt knew the archbishop's bias when he consulted him, but he may have been somewhat more inclined to accept his advice in return for the aid Rainald had granted him in an uprising in Flanders in 1127. Suger was a sage counselor, with broad experience, and could be counted on to give Louis wise advice. Although he was a friend of St. Bernard and Peter the Venerable, his primary loyalty was to the French crown. From his past associations with Petrus, he most

imus, omnemque reverenciam et debitam obedienciam ei plenarie offerentes, sibi suisque legatis totum regnum nostrum exponimus. Super hoc et in octavis pentecostes conventum sollempnem convocabimus, ut quod fidelium nostrorum actum est consilio, hoc in generali affirmetur concilio. Valete.''

[16] *Chronicon monasteri S. Andreae castri Cameracesii* III 37, MGH SS 7:549: [Innocent] in Gallias devenit, et a Remensi metropolitano maximeque abbate Claraevallis ut papa susceptus, in has provincias pervenit.''

probably respected him, and he knew that his candidacy would have support in France. But he was also aware of St. Bernard's preternatural persuasive talents, and the extraordinary power of the Cluniac conglomerate once mobilized. This system would be supplemented by the coterie of northern French bishops to which he himself belonged—Geoffrey of Chartres, Goslen of Soissons, Stephen of Paris, and Bartholomeus of Laon. These bishops were already in frequent contact, thanks especially to a series of six councils, which Matthew of Albano had summoned in Northern France between June 1128 and March 1129.[17] Suger informed Louis that the combination of these powerful prelates and the systems they commanded would win over the French church for Innocent. Louis would have been foolhardy to have rejected his recommendation, and to have examined the elections evenhandedly. His choice was obvious.

It took longer for Innocent's French champions interlocking with their counterparts in Germany, England, and Normandy to convince Henry I and Lothar, both of whom had more complicated relations with the papacy. But once Louis had made his decision, Henry's and Lothar's were easier. Innocent's smoothly running chancery helped, and after Saxo's death, the discrepancy between the effectiveness of the two chanceries widened all the further. The destruction of any literature not favorable to Innocent's cause increased the difficulty of gaining access to information on the basis of which to make a reasoned judgment. Even so, while it lasted, the contest was bitter.

There were, however, a few men, even in France, who were not caught up in the hysteria, and who tried to stem it. An obscure satire ridiculed the struggle in Aquitaine, but the most important source for revealing the tactics of the propaganda warfare is a letter of Reimbald, canon of St. Lambert of Liège.[18] The letter was written in the last month of 1130, and inserted into a funeral *rotulus* to assure as broad a dissemination as possible. Its even-handedness and objectivity inspire trust.[19]

Reimbald cautions the clergy against making a precipitous decision over which candidate should be the rightful pope, because such haste could redound to the detriment of the church. He singles out the Cluniacs as the

---

[17] Hüls, *Kardinäle*, pp. 97-98.

[18] Wilhelm Wattenbach, "Mitteilungen aus Handschriften," 2 *Neues Archiv für ältere deutsche Geschichtskunde* 8 (1883), 191-193. The author seems to have been a partisan of Anaclet and William. Palumbo, *Lo Scisma*, p. 41.

[19] *Epistola de schismate, Reimbaldi Leodiensis Opera Omnia*, Corpus Christianorum Continuatio Mediaevalis 4 (Turnhout, 1966), pp. 117-121: "Sic docet in euangelio Dominus: *Nolite iudicare*. Et Apostolus: *Nolite ante tempus iudicare* . . . Ceterum interim de inuidia taceamus. Ignorantia hic in causa est; quae quidem quodammodo tolerabilis esset, nisi, temeritati commixta, ante tempus ad iudicium proueret. Haec est, quae Cluniacenses ipsos, tam sacrum aliquando, tam sollempnem, tam undique oculatum conuentum non preteriit, sed et per ipsos non modo Occidentalem Ecclesiam infecit, uerum etiam Orientalem iamiamque inficit; . . . Hac heu confusione, hoc errore iam paene tota Aecclesia, quasi frenesi quadam circumfertur ac uertigine . . .''

most active agents in whipping up people's emotions, and in demanding that they make immediate decisions before they had gained access to as much information as they could obtain. He praises Cluny's ancient customs of prudence, severity, and openness, but regrets that now through a combination of ignorance and temerity, its monks keep both the eastern and the western churches from learning the truth. He cannot understand why they excised Gerard of Angoulême's letter from the funeral *rotulus* in which the bishop had inserted it to inform as many people as possible what had happened in Rome. Gerard was known as a man of sanctity, Reimbald says, and his letter should have been allowed to be read. If there were mistakes they should have been corrected in the spirit of fraternal friendship. What gives the Cluniacs the right to decide for others, he asks. In this poisonous atmosphere he discerns that envy and personal motives hide behind alleged general causes as the real reasons for condemning one side or the other. The result of such pernicious behavior, he laments, is that the seamless tunic of Christ was being rent, and that the whole church was reeling under the concussion caused by the errors and confusion.

The importance of Reimbald's letter for understanding the anatomy of the schism cannot be overemphasized. It reveals that there was no debate over religious ideology, but only a campaign of personal defamation. The destruction of information and the insistence that people respond emotionally rather than reflectively indicates that for the supporters of Innocent, philosophical differences and questions over the procedure of the elections were not the points of contention. If they had been, there would have been no reason not to air them publicly. The outcome of the schism was not determined by a mass response to what happened in Rome in 1130, and by an assessment of the two candidates and the principles for which they stood, but by a reaction to carefully manipulated information diffused by a few influential men.

Reimbald indicates that Anaclet's supporters were not passive, but that they also contributed to the creation of the charged atmosphere following the schism. However, it would be inaccurate to conclude that their contribution equaled that of Innocent's supporters. Even though they responded in kind to the personal attacks, basic differences remained. They did not attempt to thwart the communication of information, and they did not vilify Innocent. They also tried to bring the issue of the election before the public through the letters of Pandulphus (or Peter or Pisa, if he was the author), Peter of Porto and Gerard of Angoulême. St. Bernard's distorted and sketchy versions cannot be considered to be their counterparts.

By concentrating on other data, recent studies of the schism have glossed over the hysteria described by Reimbald, and his attempts along with those of others like Archbishop Hildebert of Tours to extend a cooling hand. There were also other efforts to shift the issue from one of mutual accusations to a consideration of criteria relevant for deciding who should be pope. Anaclet's attempts to submit the dispute to a tribunal is one, and the examination of the election from a legal perspective by the author of the chronicle of St. Andrew of Château-Cambrésis is another.[20] Although the monastery of St. Andrew was a strict reforming order, it escaped the influence of St. Bernard, and rejected Innocent on the ground that his election was illegal.

But the attempt to insert an element of sanity into the decision making process had no chance against the welter of feeling whipped up against Anaclet. Rather than becoming informed about his character and his record, people were guided by a series of legends which grew up about him. One, originating from Ernaldus, attributed the success of the Pierleoni to the continued support of the Jews, even after their conversion.[21] The money they were able to accumulate allowed them to buy power within the city, it was alleged, and ultimately, the papacy. Another legend held that the family resorted to violence, and that it pillaged churches and pilgrims. A third charged that as legate Petrus had demanded huge payments, and that he continued this practice as a member of the curia. A fourth contended that as was to be expected from a descendant of converts and bankers, he loved pomp and lavish living.[22]

In the end, the outcome of the schism was determined not by the legitimacy of either election, not by the qualifications of the two men, and not by their characters. It was determined by a skillful propaganda campaign which neutralized law as a factor, and perpetuated such a pernicious image of Anaclet that it was even speculated that he was the beast of the apocalypse.[23]

---

[20] After speaking of Honorius' quick burial by Haimeric and his followers the author says: "Quod ubi cardinales ceteri parsque civium comperunt, raptim convenientes, sepulti corpus effodiunt ac debita funeris officia complentes apostolico more denuo sepeliunt, ac deinde unum ex suis scilicet Petrus Leonis . . . papam constituunt." *Chronicon monasteri S. Andreae*, MGH SS 7:549. The annalist was one of the few men outside of Rome, who concentrated on the legality of the election. Palumbo thinks that he may have been influenced by Peter of Porto's letter. *Lo Scisma*, p. 204, n. 1. Mühlbacher, *Die streitige Papstwahl*, p. 133.

[21] Ernaldus, *Vita Bernardi*, PL 185:202.

[22] Palumbo, *Lo Scisma*, p. 606; see also pp. 284-286, 364.

[23] Gerhoh of Reichersberg, *Epistola ad Innocentium*, Ldl 3:238: "quod Petrus cum suis consentaneis pertineret ad corpus filii perditionis, si tamen ipse non est ipsa illa bestia, cuius in apocalipsi plaga mortis dicitur curata."

SUMMARY

Ideological differences did not give rise to the dual elections of 1130, and the positions attributed to Innocent and Anaclet both then, and for the most part now, do not reflect their true thinking. Before 1130 Anaclet had been active in the church primarily outside of Rome, and had shown profound sympathy for the new religious mentality. Innocent supported the religious foundations which grew out of a desire of their founders to return to the *vita canonica*, but he oriented the papacy toward an *imitatio imperii*. In this respect he disappointed the religious leaders of the North. Guigo of Chartreuse forthrightly criticized his practices, and St. Bernard revealed his disillusionment in *De consideratione*. There, he decried the tendencies which Innocent had greatly accelerated, and advised Eugenius III to look to Peter and Gregory the Great as his models rather than to his recent predecessors.[1]

As opposed to those who see Innocent's reign as a watershed defining a new direction for the church, I see no sharp break. Rather, I see a continuous progression. New orders of canons and monks were founded, but older ones such as Cluny and Farfa were reformed. There was an easing of the competition between the emperor and the pope for control of the church and Christian society, but problems between *regnum* and *sacerdotium* persisted. Before their elections Anaclet and Innocent faced these changing situations in basically the same way.

The schism occurred essentially for political reasons, and evolved in the following way. Haimeric allied himself with the Frangipani, who had a record of seeking their own personal advantage even at the expense of such reform popes as Paschal II and Gelasius II. Haimeric may not have been as unprincipled as they, but his actions were just as unscrupulous. He used the Frangipani to impose Honorius by force, and to intimidate the opposition to assure Innocent's irregular election.

Innocent had been a negotiator of the Concordat of Worms and a papal legate to France before becoming pope. He was considered to be a decent, but not an outstanding, cardinal. His papacy deviated from that of other reform popes not in that it more closely conformed to the ideals of St. Bernard, but in that it emphasized papal authority. Not a pastoral Pope, he made the papacy into a juridical center, which coopted the judicial functions formerly exercised by the lower echelons of the ecclesiastical hierarchy.

---

[1] *De consideratione, Sancti Bernardi Opera* ed. cit. 3, pp. 407-408.

His relationship with the emperor was good in general, but problems continued. Some points of contention were investitures, which Lothar wanted returned to their status prior to the Concordat of Worms, authority over the imperial abbey of Montecassino, and jurisdiction in Southern Italy. Innocent granted privileges to religious establishments including the new orders, but he also relied on the older Benedictine houses such as Cluny, Farfa, and St. Denis. He perpetuated the policy of Calixtus and Honorius of expanding papal authority, especially by intervening aggressively in the affairs of Montecassino. He did not distinguish himself by a simple or an abstemious style of living. He had strong support from the leaders of the new religious orders such as St. Bernard, Norbert of Xanten and Guigo of Chartreuse, but he also had dedicated followers among the old orders such as Peter the Venerable, Matthew of St. Martin-des-Champs, and Adenulf of Farfa.

The Pierleoni were the bankers of the reform papacy, and undeviatingly supported it. There is no evidence that they did so principally for personal gain, or that they made demands upon the popes whom they helped to sustain. As a cardinal, Petrus professionally carried out the tasks requested by the popes whom he served. There is every reason to believe that he accepted the Concordat of Worms and the *modus vivendi* with the emperor entailed by it. Likewise, he favored the new forms of Benedictinism and the orders of canons regular. His character was impugned only after the elections, and then not by neutral sources, but by Innocent's supporters. He was reviled for his Jewish ancestry, especially in France. There the status of the Jews was declining, due in part to an increase in mass piety stimulated by the reform movement, and to an awareness heightened by the Crusades of the alien character of the Jew both nationally and religiously. Furthermore, leaders of religious institutions blamed Jews for many of their economic problems. Peter the Venerable felt particularly aggrieved.[2] Anaclet was defended as staunchly as he was attacked, especially by Peter of Porto and Peter of Pisa, who saw him as a man of integrity and the legally elected pope.

Not enough is known about most of the cardinals who voted for Innocent to determine whether they shared a common ideology, much less that it was that of the northern reformers. Among those about whom we have more extensive information, the picture is too mixed to establish that they voted for Innocent because of any ecclesiastical world view which he espoused. From what we do know about the cardinals, however, their vote can far more readily be accounted for on the basis of their relationship with Haimeric and the members of his circle. Haimeric was very much involved in the appointment of the younger cardinals, and they would have identified with him. If he had lost his influence, they would have lost

---

[2] David Berger, *The Jewish-Christian Debate in the High Middle Ages: A Critical Edition of the NIZZAHON VETUS* (Philadelphia, 1979), pp. 17-18.

theirs. It was thus the better part of wisdom to support his candidate for the papacy. The fact that more of them came from the North also makes sense, since this was the area in which he was born, and in which he had functioned until he became chancellor in 1123.[3]

The cleavage between the new and older Benedictine houses is now known to be less sharp than it was once thought to be. Likewise the differences between Cluny under Pontius and Cluny under Peter the Venerable are no longer held to be as great as they once were. The tenuous identification of Anaclet with Pontius, and the direct association between Innocent and Peter the Venerable, therefore, no longer carry the significance of decadence versus reform. In all probability Peter the Venerable worked so indefatigably for Innocent for other reasons: Innocent's patrons—Honorius and Haimeric—had taken Peter's side in his dispute with Pontius, Anaclet was still tainted with Jewish blood, and St. Bernard zealously championed Innocent.

St. Bernard's motives for supporting Innocent were no doubt complex, but among them probably was his wish to maintain his access to the curia through Haimeric. For this reason he would have been receptive to Haimeric's negative portrayal of Anaclet. In Bernard's eyes, Anaclet's Jewish ancestry would have solidified this image. Even though the learned abbot argued that Innocent was the more legally elected pope, his arguments hint of sophistry, and it is improbable that he actually believed that he was. But whether Innocent was legally elected or not was of no great moment to the saint, because he was insensitive to the importance of procedure for achieving the goals of the reform. Secure in his conviction that Innocent was the better man, Bernard believed that he must do everything in his power to ensure that he could occupy his see. His talent for playing on people's emotions, and his skill as an orator assured his success. Together with his friends in the other religious orders of the North, he overwhelmed the opposition.

In essence, profound ideological differences neither produced the disputed elections, nor secured Innocent's triumph. The causes of the schism were mainly local, and concerned the ambitions of Haimeric, powerful cardinals, and Roman aristocratic families. Once the two camps had joined arms, religious leaders from the church at large became participants. With an organization honed by years of involvement with secular leaders and ecclesiastical prelates from throughout Western Europe, Innocent waged a decisively more effective campaign. Anaclet's vulnerability as a scion of a family of wealthy Jewish converts tipped the scale. Voices of reason like those of Reimbald of Liége and Peter of Porto, who encouraged people to make a reflective assessment of the two candidates and their elections, were lost in the din.

---

[3] He had been a canon at Santa Maria in Bologna, and may later have been one at St. John's of the Lateran. Hüls, *Kardinäle*, p. 236.

SELECT BIBLIOGRAPHY

Manuscripts

Vatican City, Biblioteca Apostolica Vaticana
    Barb. Lat. 2733.
    Iacobus Grimaldi. Instrumenta autentica Translationum Sanctorum corporum et Sacrarum Reliquarum E Veteri in novum Templum Sancti Petri cum multis memoriis, Epitaphiis, Inscriptionibus, Delineatione patris Basilicae demolitae, et Iconicis Historiis Sacrae Confessionis Ab eodem Summo Pontifice magnificentissime exornata (1619).

Rome, Biblioteca Vallicelliana
    G 99
    Regesta Anacleti II

Montecassino, Biblioteca Abbaziale
    MS 159
    Regesta Anacleti II

Sources

ABELARD, PETER. *Dialogue of a Philosopher with a Jew and a Christian*, ed. & trans. Pierre J. Payer. Toronto, 1979.

ANACLET II (Petrus Pierleoni). *Anacleti antipapae epistolae et privilegia*. PL 179:690-732.

ANGOULÊME. *Cartulaire de l'église d'Angoulême*, ed. J. Nanglard. Angoulême, 1890.

———. *Gesta episcoporum et comitum Engolismensium*, MGH SS 26:822-823.

Annales Monastici. Ed. H.R. Luard, 4 vols., Rolls Series 36. London, 1879.

CARDINALIS ARAGONIA. *Vitae nonullorum pontificum Romanorum 1050-1241*. Ed. Ludovicus Antonius Muratori, *Rerum Italicarum Scriptores* 3, pp. 273-587. Milan, 1723.

ARNULF OF SÉEZ. *Arnulfi Sagiensis archidiaconi postea episcopi Lexoviensis invectiva in Girardum Engolismensem episcopum*, ed. L. Dieterich, MGH Ldl 3:81-108.

AUGUSTINUS EPISCOPUS (Sanctus). *Sermo contra Judaeos, Paganos et Arianos*. PL 42:1117-1130.

Benonis Aliorumque Cardinalium Schismaticorum contra Gregorium VII. et Urbanum II., scripta. Ed. Kuno Francke, MGH Ldl 2:366-422.

BERLIÈRE, URSMER. *Documents inédits pour servir à l'histoire écclésiastique de la Belgique* 1. Maredsous, Abbaye de Saint-Benoit, 1894.

BERNARD OF CLAIRVAUX. *Sancti Bernardi Opera*, ed. Jean Leclercq & H. Rochais, 8 vols. Rome, 1956-1977.
    Apologia ad Guillelmum Abbatem. 3:80-109.
    Corpus Epistolarum 1-180. 7.
    Corpus Epistolarum 181-547. 8.
    De Consideratione ad Eugenium Papam. 3:393-493.
    De Laude Novae Militiae. 3:214-239.
    De Laudibus Virginis Matris Sermo I. 4:12-21.

Sermones super Cantica. 2.

——. *Five Books on Consideration: Advice to a Pope.* Ed. & trans. John D. Anderson & Elizabeth T. Kennan, vol. 13 of Cistercian Fathers series. Kalamazoo, Michigan, 1976.

——. *The Letters of Saint Bernard of Clairvaux.* Ed. Bruno Scott James. London, 1953.

——. *St. Bernard's Sermons for the Seasons and the Principal Festivals of the Year.* Tr. by a priest of Mt. Melleray. Westminster, Maryland, 1950.

Bertholdi Zwifaltensis Chronicon, ed. H.F.O. Abel. MGH SS 10:93-124.

Biblia Sacra cum Glossa interlineari, Ordinaria, Nicolae Lyrani expositionibus, Burgensis Additionibus & Thoringi Replicis 4. Venice, 1588.

Calixtus II Pontifex Romanus epistolae et privilegia. PL 163:1093-1358.

CAMALDOLI. *Annales Camaldulenses,* ed. Johanne-Benedicto Mittarelli & D. Anselmo Costadoni 3. Venice, 1758.

CECCANO. *Annales Ceccanenses,* ed. G.H. Pertz. MGH SS 19:275-301.

CHARTREUSE. *Annales Ordinis Cartusiensis ab anno 1084 ad annum 1429,* ed. D. Carolo Le Couteulx, vol. 1 *1084-1141.* Monstrolii Typis Cartusiae. S. Marie de Pratis, 1888.

——. *Lettres des premiers Chartreux,* ed. Un Chartreux, vol. 1 *S. Bruno, Guiges, S. Anthelme.* Sources Chrétiennes 88. Paris, 1962.

CHATEAU-CAMBRESIS. *Chronicon S. Andreae castri Cameracesii a. 1001-1133,* ed. L.C. Bethmann. MGH SS 7:526-550.

CLAIRVAUX. *Recueil des chartes de l'abbaye de Clairvaux 1,* ed. J. Waquet. Troyes, 1950.

CLUNY. *Bibliotheca Cluniacensis,* ed. Martin Marrier. Paris, 1614.

——. *Ex Chronico Cluniacensi,* ed. M. Bouquet, *Recueil des historiens des Gaules et de la France* 12, pp. 313-316. Paris, 1781, repr. 1968.

——. *Recueil des chartes de l'abbaye de Cluny 5,* ed. A. Bernard & A. Bruel. Paris, 1894.

Codex Udalrici. Monumenta Bambergensia, vol. 5 of *Bibliotheca Rerum Germanicarum,* ed. Philip Jaffé. Berlin, 1869.

Conciliorum Oecumenicorum Decreta. Ed. Josephus Albergo, Perikle-P. Joannou, Claudio Leonardi, Paolo Prudi, consultente Herbert Jedin. Centro di documentazione istituto per le scienze religiose Bologna. Basle, Barcelona, Fridbourg, Rome, Bologna, 1962.

Corpus Iuris Canonici. Ed. Aemilius Friedberg. Leipzig, 1879-81, repr. Graz, 1959.

Cronisti e Scrittori sincroni Napoletani editi e inediti, ed. Giuseppe Del Re, vol. 1 *Storia della Monarchia Normanni.* Naples, 1845.

Decretum de electione papae. MGH Const. et Acta 1:537-541.

Deliciae eruditorum seu ueterum Anekdoton opusculorum collectanea, ed. J. Lamius 3. Florence, 1737.

EADMER. *Historia Novorum in Anglia,* ed. M. Rule. Rolls Series 81:1-302. London, 1884.

ERNALDUS. *Vita Bernardi.* PL 185:267-302.

FALCO. *Chronicon Falconis Beneventani,* ed. Ludovicus Antonius Muratori, *Rerum Italicarum Scriptores* 5, pp. 82-133. Milan, 1724.

Gaufredi de Bruil prioris Vosiensis ex Chronico, ed. M. Bouquet, *Recueil des historiens des Gaules et de la France* 12, pp. 421-451. Paris, 1781, repr. 1968.

GERHOHUS REICHERSBERGENSIS. *De Investigatione Antichristi*, ed. E. Sackur. MGH Ldl 3:304-395.

———. *Epistola ad Innocentium Papam missa quid distet inter clericos seculares et regulares*, ed. E. Sackur. MGH Ldl 3:203-239.

———. *Libellus de eo quod princeps huius mundi iam iudicatus sit*, ed. E. Sackur. MGH Ldl 3:240-272.

———. *Libellus de ordine donorum sancti spiritus*, ed. E. Sackur. MGH Ldl 3:273-304.

GERVASE OF CANTERBURY. *Gesta Regum et Actus Pontificum*, ed. William Stubbs. Rolls Series 73. London, 1880.

GRANDMONT. *Scriptores ordinis grandimontensis*, ed. I. Becquet. Corpus Christianorum, continuatio Mediaevalis 8. Turnhout, 1958.

GREGORY DI CATINO. *Chronicon Farfense*, ed. Ugo Balzani, 2 vols. Rome, 1903.

GRENOBLE. *Cartulaires de l'église cathédrale de Grenoble, dits Cartulaires de Saint-Hughes*, ed. Jules Marion. Paris, 1869.

HARIULF. *Chronicon Aldenburgense Majus, Appendix da Hariulfum*. PL 174:1544-1554.

Henrici Archidiaconi Huntendunensis Historia Anglorum, ed. T. Arnold, Rolls Series 74. London, 1879.

Ex Herimanni de Miraculis S. Mariae Laudunensis, ed. Roger Wilmans. MGH SS 12:653-660.

Hessonis scholastici de concilio Remensi relatio, ed. W. Wattenbach. MGH SS 12:422-428.

HILDEBERT, ARCHBISHOP OF TOURS. *Curiae Romanae Discriptio*, ed. Ortuin Gratius, *Fasciculus rerum expetendarum et fugiendarum*. Cologne, 1535, new ed. *Opera et Studi Edwardi Brown*. London, 1690.

HINSCHIUS, PAUL, ed. *Decretales Pseudo-Isidorianae et Capitula Angilramni*. Leipzig, 1863.

Historia Compostelana. Ed. Henrique Florez, vol. 20 of España Sagrada. Madrid, 1765.

INNOCENT II. *Innocentium II Pontifex Romanus epistolae et privilegia*. PL 179:21-686.

IVO CARNOTENSIS EPISCOPUS. *Decretum*. PL 161:9-1036.

———. *Panormia*. PL 161:1038-1344.

John of Salisbury's Memoires of the Papal Court (Ioannis Sareberiensis Historia Pontificalis), ed. & trans. Marjorie Chibnall. London, 1956, repr. 1962, 1965.

Liber Censuum de l'église Romaine. Ed. Paul Fabre & Louis Duchesne. Bibliothèque des Écoles Française d'Athènes et de Rome. 2e serie, 2 vols. Paris, 1905.

Liber Pontificalis. Ed. Louis Duchesne. 2 vols. Paris, 1886-1892.

Liber Pontificalis prout exstat in codice manuscripto Dertusensi. Textum genuinum complectens hactenus ex parte ineditum Pandulphi, scriptorii pontificii. Ed. Josè María March. Barcelona, 1925.

LOTHAR III. *In Anacletum papam sententia*. MGH Leges 2:81; MGH Const. et Acta 1:167.

LUCCA. *Memorie e documenti per servire all'istoria del ducato di Lucca*. Pub. R. Accademia Lucchese di Scienze, lettere et arti 5:1. Lucca, 1844.

LUDOLFI DE SANCTO PAULO. *Historia Mediolanensis a 1097-1137*, ed. Ludwig Bethmann & Philipe Jaffé. MGH SS 20:17-49.

MÂCON. *Cartulaire de Saint-Vincent de Mâcon*, ed. Camile Ragut. Mâcon, 1864.

MANSI, JOANNES. *Sacrorum Conciliorum Nova et Amplissima Collectio* 21. Venice, 1776.

Mirabilia urbis Romae. Ed. Roberto Valentini & Giuseppe Zucchetti, *Codice Topografico della Città di Roma* 3, vol. 90 of *Fonti per la Storia d'Italia*, pp. 17-65. Rome, 1946. Percy Ernst Schramm, *Kaiser, Könige und Päpste* 3, pp. 322-328. Stuttgart, 1968.

MONTECASSINO. *Die Chronik von Montecassino (Chronica monasterii Casinensis)*, ed. Hartmut Hoffmann, MGH SS 34:1-773. Hanover, 1980.

Narratio de electione Lotharii. MGH SS 12:510-512.

Necrologium ecclesiae S. Mariae trans Tiberim. Ed. Pietro Egidi, *Necrologi e libri affini della provincia di Roma* 1, *Necrologi della città di Roma*. Rome, 1908.

ORDERICUS VITALIS. *The Ecclesiastic History of Orderic Vitalis*, ed. Marjorie Chibnall. 6 vols. Oxford, New York, 1969-1978.

OTTO OF FREISING. *Chronicon ab Ottone Frisingensi episcopo*, ed. Roger Wilmans. MGH SS 20:83-301.

PETER THE VENERABLE. *The Letters of Peter the Venerable*, ed. Giles Constable. Harvard Historical Studies 78, 2 vols. Cambridge, Massachusetts, 1967.

———. *De Miraculis.* PL 189:851-954.

———. *Tractutus adversus Iudaeorum inveteram duritiem.* PL 189:507-650.

PETRUS PICTAVENSIS MONACI. *Panegyricus Petro venerabili dictus in primo adventu ejus ad Aquitaniam secundam.* PL 189:47-58.

PONTIUS. *Pontii Cluniacensis Abbatis Gesta Quaedam*, ed. M. Bouquet, *Recueil des historiens des Gaules et de la France* 14, pp. 196-197. Paris, 1806, repr. 1968.

PRÉMONTRÉ. *Sacri et canonici ordinis Praemonstratensis annales* 1, ed. Charles Louis Hugo. Nancy, 1734.

Reimbaldi Leodiensis Opera Omnia. Cura et studio Caroli de Clercq. Corpus Christianorum Continuatio Mediaevalis 4. *Epistola de schismate*, pp. 117-121. Turnholt, 1966.

Roberti de Monte Chronica. Ed. D.L.C. Bethmann, MGH SS 6:480-535.

SAINT ANDRÉ-LE-BAS. *Cartulaire de l'abbaye de Saint André-le-Bas de Vienne*, ed. Ulysse Chevalier. Lyons, 1869.

SAINT BERTIN. *Les Chartes de Saint Bertin* 1, *648-1240*, ed. Daniel Haigneré. Saint Omer, 1886.

SAINT MARTIN-DES-CHAMPS. *Recueil de Chartes et Documents de Saint-Martin-des-Champs* 1, ed. J. Depoin. Paris, 1912.

Sigiberti Gemblacensis chronica, cont. Anselmi a. 1112-1135. Ed. D.L.C. Bethmann, MGH SS 6:375-385.

SIRMONDUS, JACOBUS. *Opera varia* 3. Paris, 1696.

SUGER, ABBÉ DE ST. DENIS. *Oeuvres complètes de Suger*, ed. A. Lecoy de la Marche. Paris, 1867.

———. *Vie de Louis VI le Gros*, ed. & tr. Henri Waquet. Paris, 1929.

TIBURTINA. *Chronica Pontificum et Imperatorum Tibertina*, ed. O. Holder-Egger. MGH SS 31:226-265.

Vita Innocentii Papae II ex MS. Bernardi Guidonis. Ed. Ludovicus Antonius Muratori, *Rerum Italicarum Scriptores* 3, pp. 433-434. Milan, 1723.

Vita Norberti Archiepiscopi Magdeburgensis. Ed. Roger Wilmans, MGH SS 12:663-703; PL 170:1254-1358.

WATTERICH, JOHANN MATTHIAS. *Pontificum Romanorum qui fuerunt inde ab exeunte saeculo IX usque ad finem saeculi XIII vitae ab aequalibus conscriptae, quas ex Archivi pontifici, bibliothecae Vaticanae aliarumque codicibus adiectis suis cuique et annalibus et documentis gravioribus.* Vol. 2 *Paschalis II.-Coelestinus III. (1099-1198).* Leipzig, 1862, repr. Scientia Verlag Aalen, 1966.

WILLIAM OF MALMESBURY. *De gestis Pontificum Anglorum,* ed. N.E.S.A. Hamilton. Rolls Series 52. London, 1870.

____. *The Historia Novella,* tr., intro. & notes K.R. Potter. London, Edinburgh, Paris, Melbourne, Toronto, New York, 1955.

____. *El libro 'De laudibus et miraculis Sanctae Mariae' de Guillermo de Malmesbury,* ed. José M. Canal. Rome, 1968.

Secondary Works

AMÉLINEAU, E. "Saint Bernard et le schisme d'Anaclet II (1130-1138)," *Revue des questions historiques* 30 (1881), 47-112.

BALZANI, UGO. *Italia Papato e Impero nel Secolo XII.* vol. 11 of *Biblioteca Storica Principati* a cura di Pietro Fedele. Messina, 1930.

BAUMGARTEN, PAUL MARIA. "Ein Brief des Gegenpapstes Anaclet (II)," *Neues Archiv der Gesellschaft für ältere deutsche Geschichtskunde* 22 (1897), 576-578.

BARON, SALO WITTMAYER. *A Social and Religious History of the Jews,* vols. 4-5. New York, 1957.

BENSON, ROBERT. *The Bishop-Elect: A Study in Medieval Ecclesiastical Office.* Princeton, N.J., 1968.

____. "Political *Renovatio*: Two Models from Roman Antiquity," pp. 339-386 of *Renaissance and Renewal in the Twelfth Century,* ed. Robert L. Benson & Giles Constable with Carol D. Lanham. Cambridge, Massachusetts, 1982.

BENTON, JOHN, ed. *Self and Society in Medieval France: The Memoirs of Abbot Guibert of Nogent.* New York, 1970.

BERGER, DAVID. "The attitude of St. Bernard of Clairvaux toward the Jews," *Proceedings of the American Academy for Jewish Research* 40 (1972), 89-108.

____. *The Jewish-Christian Debate in the High Middle Ages: A critical edition of the NIZZAHON VETUS.* Philadelphia, 1979.

BERNHARDI, WILHELM. *Lothar von Supplinburg.* Berlin, 1879, new ed. 1975.

BEUMANN, HELMUT. "Das päpstliche Schisma von 1130, Lothar III. und die Metropolitanrechte von Magdeburg und Hamburg-Bremen in Polen und Dänemark," pp. 479-500 of *Wissenschaft vom Mittelalter: Ausgewählte Aufsätze.* Cologne, Vienna, 1972.

BIGGS, ANSELM GORDON. *Diego Gelmirez, First Archbishop of Compostela.* Washington, D.C., 1949.

BISCHKO, CHARLES JULIAN. "The Spanish Journey of Abbot Ponce of Cluny," *Ricerche di storia religiosa* 1 (1957), 311-319.

BLOCH, HERBERT. *Montecassino in the Middle Ages.* 2 vols. Rome, Cambridge, Massachusetts, 1987.

———. "The Schism of Anacletus II and the Glanfeuil Forgeries of Peter the Deacon of Monte Cassino," *Traditio* 8 (1952), 159-264.

BLUMENKRANZ, BERNARD. *Die Judenpredigt Augustins*. Vol. 25 of Basler Beiträge zur Geschichtswissenschaft, ed. E. Bonjour, W. Kaegi, F. Stähelin. Basel, 1946.

———. *Juifs et chrétiens dans le monde occidental 430-1096*. Paris. 1960

BOSL, KARL. *Regularkanoniker (Augustinerchorherren) und Seelsorge in Kirche und Gesellschaft des europäischen 12. Jahrhunderts*. Bayerische Akademie der Wissenschaften, Philosophische-Historische Klasse Abhandlungen; neue Folge, vol. 86. Munich 1979.

———. "Das Verhältnis von Augustinerchorren (Regular-kanoniker) Seelsorge und Gesellschaftsbewegung in Europa im 12. Jahrhunderts," pp. 419-549 of *Istituzioni monastiche e istituzioni canonicali in Occidente (1123-1215)*. Atti della settima settimana internazionale di studio Mendola, 28 agosto—3 settembre 1977, Milano, *Vita e Pensiero*. Pubblicazioni dell'Università Cattolica del Sacro Cuore, Miscellanea del Centro di Studi medioevali 9, 1980.

BOUTON, JEAN DE LA CROIX. "Bernard et les Chanoines Réguliers," pp. 263-288 of *Bernard de Clairvaux*, ed. Thomas Merton. Paris, 1953.

———. "Bernard et l'Ordre de Cluny," pp. 193-217 of *Bernard de Clairvaux*, ed. Thomas Merton. Paris, 1953.

BREDERO, ADRIAAN H. "A propos de l'autorité abbatiale de Pons de Melgueil et de Pierre le Vénérable dans l'ordre de Cluny," *Mélanges E.-R. Labande: Etudes de Civilisation Médiévale*, ed. under the direction of the University of Poitiers by C.É.S.C.M., pp. 63-75. Poitiers, 1974.

———. "Cluny et Cîteaux au XIIe siècle: Les origine de la controverse," *Studi Medievali* 12, nr. 1 (1971), 135-175.

———. "Pierre le Vénérable: les commencements de son abbatiat à Cluny (1122-1132)," pp. 99-118 of *Pierre Abélard: Pierre le Vénérable: Les courants philosophiques, littéraires et artistiques en occident au milieu du XIIe siècle*. Colloques internationaux du centre national de la recherche scientifique no. 546. Abbaye de Cluny, 2 au 9 juillet, 1972. Paris, 1975.

———. "S. Bernardo di Chiaravalle: Correlazione tra fenomeno cultico e storico," *Studi su S. Bernardo di Chiaravalle nell'ottavo centenario della canonizzazione*; convegno internazionale Certosa di Firenze (6-9 Novembre 1974), pp. 23-48. Rome, 1975.

———. "Une controverse sur Cluny au XIIe siècle," *Revue d'histoire écclésiastique* 76 (1981), 48-72.

BRETT, MARTIN. *The English Church under Henry I*. Oxford, 1975.

BYNUM, CAROLINE. "Did the Twelfth Century Discover the Individual?" *Journal of Ecclesiastical History* 31 (1980), 1-17.

———. *Jesus as Mother: Studies in the Spirituality of the High Middle Ages*. Berkeley, Los Angeles, London, 1982.

CASPAR, ERICH. *Roger II. (1101-1154) und die Gründung der normannisch-sizilischen Monarchie*. Leipzig, 1907.

CHALANDON, FERDINAND. *Histoire de la Domination Normande en Italie et en Sicile* 2. New York, 1907, repr. 1960.

CHAZAN, ROBERT. *Medieval Jewry in Northern France: A Political and Social History*. Baltimore and London, 1973.

CHIBNALL, MARJORIE. *The World or Orderic Vitalis*. Oxford, 1984.

CHODOROW, STANLEY. *Christian Political Theory and Church Politics in the Mid-Twelfth Century: The Ecclesiology of Gratian's Decretum*. Berkeley, Los Angeles, London, 1972.

――. "Ecclesiastical Politics and the Ending of the Investiture Contest: The Papal Election of 1119 and the Negotiations of Mouzon," *Speculum* 46 (1971), 613-640.

CHROUST, ANTON. "Das Wahldekret Anaclets II.," *Mitteilungen des Instituts für österreichisches Geschichtsforschung* 28 (1907), 348-355.

CLASSEN, PETER. *Gerhoch von Reichersberg: Eine Biographie*. Wiesbaden, 1960.

――. "Zur Geschichte Papst Anastasius IV," *Quellen und Forschungen aus italienischen Archiven und Bibliotheken* 48 (1968), 36-63.

CLAUDE, HUBERT. "Autour du schisme d'Anaclet: Saint Bernard et Girard d'Angoulême," *Mélanges Saint Bernard*, pp. 80-94. Dijon, 1954.

CONSTABLE GILES. "Cluny, Cîteaux, La Chartreuse: San Bernardo e la diversità delle forme di vita religiosa nel XII secolo," pp. 93-114 of *Studi su S. Bernardo di Chiaravalle nell'ottavo centenario della Canonizzazione*: Convegno internationale Certosa di Firenze (6-9 Novembre 1974). Rome, 1975.

――. "The Disputed Election at Langres in 1138," *Traditio* 13 (1957), 119-152.

――. "The monastic policy of Peter the Venerable," pp. 119-142 of *Pierre Abélard: Pierre le Vénérable: Les courants philosophiques, littéraires et artistiques en occident au milieu du XIIe siècle*. Colloques internationaux du centre national de la recherche scientifique no. 546. Abbaye de Cluny, 2 au 9 juillet, 1972. Paris, 1975.

――. "Renewal and Reform in Religious Life," *Renaissance and Renewal in the Twelfth Century*, ed. Robert L. Benson & Giles Constable with Carol D. Lanham. pp. 37- 67. Cambridge, Massachusetts, 1982.

CONSTABLE, GILES & KRITZECK J., ed. "The Reforming decrees of Peter the Venerable," *Petrus Venerabilis, 1156-1956: Studies and texts commemorating the eighth centenary of his death* (Studia Anselmiana 40). Rome, 1956.

Councils and Synods, with other documents relating to the English Church. Ed. Dorothy Whitelock, Martin Brett, & Christopher N.L. Brooke, pt. II, *1066-1204*. Oxford, 1981.

COWDREY, H.E.J. *The Age of Abbot Desiderius: Montecassino, the Papacy, and the Normans in the Eleventh and Early Twelfth Centuries*. Oxford, 1983.

――. "Two Studies in Cluniac History 1049-1126. II. Abbot Pontius of Cluny (1109-22/26)," *Studi Gregoriani* 11 (Rome, 1978), 178-298.

DEÉR, JOSEF. *The Dynastic Porphyry tombs of the Norman Period in Sicily*, tr. G.A. Gillhoff. Dumbarton Oaks Studies V. Cambridge, Massachusetts, 1959.

――. *Papsttum und Normannen: Untersuchungen zu ihren lehnsrechtlichen und kirchenpolitischen Beziehungen*. Cologne, Vienna, 1972.

DIMIER, ANSELME. "Outrances et roueries de Saint Bernard," pp. 655-670 of *Pierre Abélard; Pierre le Vénérable: Les courants philosophiques, littéraires et artistiques en occident au milieu du XIIe siècle*. Colloques internationaux du centre national de la recherche scientifique no. 546. Abbaye de Cluny, 2 au 9 juillet, 1972. Paris, 1975.

DUBOIS, J. "Les ordres religieux au XIIe siècle selon la Curie romaine," *Revue Bénédictine* 78 (1968), 283-309.

DUBY, GEORGES. "Économie domaniale et économie monétaire: le budget de Cluny entre 1080 et 1155," pp. 155-171 of *Annales Économies, Sociétés,*

Civilisations 7. Paris, 1952, repr. 1977.

——. *La Société aux XIe et XIIe siècle dans la région mâconnaise.* Paris, 1955, repr. 1971.

DUCHESNE, LOUIS. "Le Nom d'Anaclet II au palais de Latéran," *Mémoires de la Société des Antiquaires de France*, 5th ser., 9 (1888), 197-206.

EICHMANN, EDUARD. "Das Officium Stratoris et Strepae," *Historische Zeitschrift* 142 (1930), 16-40.

ELZE, REINHARD. "Die päpstliche Kapelle im 12. und 13. Jahrhundert," *Zeitschrift der Savigny-Stiftung für Rechtsgeschichte* KA 36 (1950), 145-204.

FALCO, GIORGIO. "I communi della Campagna e della Marittima," *Archivio della R. Società Romana di Storia Patria* 42 (1919), 537-605.

FEDELE, PIETRO. "L'Êra del Senato," *Archivio della R. Società Romana di Storia Patria* 35 (1912), 583-610.

——. "Le Famiglie di Anacleto II e di Gelasio II," *Archivio della R. Società Romana di Storia Patria* 27 (1904), 399-433.

——. "Sull'origine dei Frangipani," *Archivio della R. Società Romana di Storia Patria* 33 (1910), 493-506.

——. "Una Chiesa del Palatino: S. Maria 'in Pallara'," *Archivio della R. Società Romana di Storia Patria* 26 (1903), 343-380.

FLETCHER, RICHARD A. *The Episcopate of the Kingdom of Leon in the Twelfth Century.* Oxford, 1978.

——. *St. James Catapult: The Life and Times of Diego Gelmirez of Santiago de Compostela.* Oxford, 1984.

GANZER, KLAUS. *Die Entwicklung des Auswärtigen Kardinalats im Hohen Mittelalter: Ein Beitrag zur Geschichte des Kardinalkollegiums vom 11. bis 13. Jahrhundert.* Munich, 1965.

GIESEBRECHT, WILHELM. *Geschichte der deutsche Kaiserzeit* 4. Braunschweig, 1877.

GIRAUD, PAUL. *Essai historique sur l'abbaye de St. Barnard et sur la ville de Romans.* vol. 2 *Cartulaire de Romans et autres pièces justicatives inédites servant du preuves à la Première Partie.* Lyons, 1856.

GOLB, NORMAN. "New Light on the persecution of French Jews at the time of the first Crusade," pp. 289-334 of *Medieval Jewish Life*, ed. Robert Chazan. New York, 1976.

GOLZIO, VINCENZO AND ZANDER, GIUSEPPE. *Le Chiese di Roma dall'XI al XVI secolo.* vol. 4 of *Roma Christiana*, ed. Carlo Galassi Paluzzi. Bologna, 1963.

GRABOIS, ARYEH. "Le Schisme de 1130 et la France," *Revue d'histoire écclésiastique* 76 (1981), 593-612.

GRAY, J.W. "The Problem of Papal Power in the Ecclesiology of St. Bernard," *Transactions of the Royal Historical Society*, 5th series, vol. 24, pp. 1-17. London, 1974.

GREGOROVIUS, FERDINANDO. *Storia della Città di Roma nel Medio Evo* 2, 3rd. ed. Rome, 1912.

GROTZ, HANS. "Kriterien auf dem Prüfstand: Bernhard von Clairvaux angesichts zweier kanonisch strittiger Wahlen," pp. 237-263 of *Aus Kirche und Reich: Studien zu Theologie, Politik und Recht im Mittelalter.* Festschrift für Friedrich Kempf, ed. Hubert Mordek. Sigmaringen, 1983.

GUNDLACH, WILHELM. "Der Streit der Bisthümer Arles und Vienne um den

Primatus Galliarum," 2 "Die Epistolae Viennenses," *Neues Archiv der Gesellschaft für ältere deutsche Geschichtskunde* 15 (1890), 9-102.

HAEGERMANN, D. "Untersuchungen zum Papstwahldekret von 1059," *Zeitschrift der Savigny-Stiftung für Rechtsgeschichte* KA 56 (1970), 157-193.

HAHN, HANNO. *Die frühe Kirchenbaukunst der Zisterzienser*. Berlin, 1957.

HALLER, JOHANNES. *Das Papsttum: Idee und Wirklichkeit* 2:2. Munich, 1950-53, repr. 1965.

HEFELE, CHARLES-JOSEPH VON. *Conciliengeschichte*. Nach den Quellen bearbeitet; trans. & notes, H. Leclercq, *Histoire des Conciles d'après les documents originaux* 5:1. Paris, 1912.

HEHL, ERNST-DIETER. *Kirche und Kreig in 12. Jahrhundert: Studien zu kanonischen Recht und politischer Wirklichkeit*. Vol. 19 of Monographien zur Geschichte des Mittelalters. Stuttgart, 1980.

HERKLOTZ, INGO. "Der Campus Lateranensis im Mittelalter," *Römisches Jahrbuch für Kunstgeschichte* 22 (1985), 1-43.

HESSEL, A. "Cluny und Mâcon. Ein Beitrag zur Geschichte der päpstlichen Exemptions und Privilegien," *Zeitschrift für Kirchengeschichte* 22 (1901), 516-524.

HOFFMANN, HARTMUT. "Petrus Diaconus, die Herren von Tusculum und der Sturz Oderisius' II. von Montecassino," *Deutsches Archiv für Erforschung des Mittelalters* 27 (1971), 1-109.

HOLTZMANN, R.. *Der Kaiser als Marschall des Papstes: Eine Untersuchung zur Geschichte der Beziehungen zwischen Kaiser und Papst im Mittelalter*. Heidelberg, 1928.

――――. "Zum Papstwahldekret von 1059," *Zeitschrift der Savigny-Stiftung für Rechtsgeschichte* KA 27 (1938), 135-153.

――――. Zum Strator- und Marschalldienst," *Historische Zeitschrift* 145 (1932), 301-350.

HORST, UWE. *Die Kanonessammlung Polycarpus des Gregor von S. Grisogono: Quellen und Tendenzen*. Munich, 1980.

HÜLS, RUDOLF. *Kardinäle, Klerus und Kirchen Roms 1049-1130*. Vol. 48 of Bibliothek des deutschen historischen Instituts in Rom. Tübingen, 1977.

HUGO, CHARLES LOUIS. *La Vie de S. Norbert, archevêque de Magdebourg et fondateur de l'Ordre des Chanoines Prémontrez*. Luxembourg, 1704.

Le istituzioni ecclesiastiche della 'Societas Christiana' dei secoli X-XII, (1) Papato, cardinalato ed episcopato, (2) *Diocesi, pievi e parocchie*. Pubblicazioni dell'Università Cattolica del Sacro Cuore; Miscellanea del Centro di Studi Medioevali 7, 8. Milan, 1974, 1977.

Istituzioni monastiche e istituzioni canonicali in Occidente (1123-1215). Atti della settima settimana internazionale di Studio Mendola, 28 agosto - 3 settembre 1977, *Vita e Pensiero*. Pubblicazioni dell'Università Cattolica del Sacro Cuore, Miscellanea del Centro di Studi medioevali 9. Milan, 1980.

JACQUELINE, BERNARD. "Bernard et le schisme d'Anaclet II," pp. 349-354 of *Papauté et épiscopat selon saint Bernard de Clairvaux*. Saint-Lo, 1963.

――――. Épiscopat et Papauté chez saint Bernard de Clairvaux. Saint-Lo, 1975.

JANSSEN, WILHELM. *Die päpstlichen Legaten in Frankreich vom Schisma Anaklets II bis zum Tode Cölestins III (1130-1138)*. Kölner historische Abhandlungen 6. Cologne, Graz, 1961.

JORDAN, KARL. "Die Entstehung der römische Kurie," *Zeitschrift der Savigny-*

Stiftung für Rechtsgeschichte KA 59 (1939), 96-152.

———. "Zur päpstlichen Finanzgeschichte im 11. und 12. Jahrhundert," *Quellen und Forschungen aus italienischen Archiven und Bibliotheken* 25 (1933/1934), 61-104.

KAMP, NORBERT. "Der unteritalienische Episkopat im Spannungsfeld zwischen monarchischer Kontrolle und römische 'libertas' von der Reichsgründung Rogers II. bis zum Konkordat von Benevento," *Società, Potere e Popolo nell'età di Ruggero II*, pp. 99-132. Università degli studi di Bari. Centro di studi normanno-svevi. Bari, 1979.

KEHR, PAUL. "Die Belehnungen der süditalienische Normannenfürsten durch die Päpste (1059-1192)," *Abhandlungen der preussischen Akademie der Wissenschaften*, phil.-hist. Kl. n. 1. Berlin, 1934.

———. "Diploma purpureo di Re Ruggero II per la Casa Pierleoni," *Archivio della R. Società Romana di Storia Patria* 24 (1901), 253-259.

KENNAN, ELIZABETH. "The 'De Consideratione' of Bernard of Clairvaux and the Papacy in the Mid-Twelfth Century: A Review of Scholarship," *Traditio* 23 (1967), 73-115.

KINNEY, DALE. *S. Maria in Trastevere from its founding to 1215*. Diss. New York University, 1975.

KITZINGER, ERNST. "The Arts as Aspects of a Renaissance: Rome and Italy," pp. 637-670 of *Renaissance and Renewal in the Twelfth Century*, ed. Robert L. Benson & Giles Constable with Carol D. Lanham. Cambridge, Massachusetts, 1982.

KLEWITZ, HANS-WALTER. "Das Ende des Reformpapsttums," *Deutsches Archiv für Geschichte des Mittelalters* 3 (1939), 371-412. Repr. *Reformpapsttum und Kardinalkolleg*, pp. 207-253 with "Die Entstehung des Kardinalkollegiums" and "Studien über die Wiederherstellung der römischen Kirche in Süditalien durch das Reformpapsttum." Darmstadt, 1957.

KNONAU, GEROLD MEYER VON. *Jahrbücher des Deutschen Reiches unter Heinrich IV. und Heinrich V.* Berlin, 1907, repr. 1965.

KNOWLES, DAVID. "Cistercians and Cluniacs: The Controversy between St. Bernard and Peter the Venerable," (1955) in *The Historian and Character and Other Essays*. Cambridge, England, 1963.

KRAUSE, HANS-GEORG. *Das Papstwahldekret von 1059 und seine Rolle im Investiturstreit*. Studi Gregoriani 7. Rome, 1960.

KRAUTHEIMER, RICHARD. *Rome: Profile of a City, 312-1308*. Princeton, 1980.

LADNER, GERHARD B. "I mosaici e gli affreschi ecclesiastico-politici nell'antico palazzo Lateranense," *Rivista di archeologia Christiana* 12 (1935), 265-292.

———. *Die Papstbildnisse des Altertums und des Mittelalters*. 2 vols. Vatican City, 1941-1970.

———. *I Ritratti dei Papi nell'Antichità e nel Medioevo*. 2 vols. Vatican City, 1941-1970.

LAMMA, PAOLO. *Momenti di storiografia Cluniacense*. Rome, 1961.

———. "Su alcuni temi di storiografia Cluniacense," pp. 258-273 of *Spiritualità Cluniacense*. Todi, 1960.

LAUER, PHILIPPE. *Le Palais de Latran*. Paris, 1911.

LECLER, A. *Histoire de l'abbaye de Grandmont*. Limoges, 1911.

LECLERCQ, JEAN; BREDERO, ADRIAAN; ZERBI, PIETRO. "Encore sur Pons de Cluny et Pierre le Vénérable," *Aevum* 48 (1974), 134-149.

LITTLE, LESTER K. *Religious Poverty and the Profit Economy in Medieval Europe*. London, 1978.

LÖWENFELD, S. "Kleinere Beiträge. 2. Ueber Anaclets Persönlichkeit," *Neues Archiv der Gesellschaft für ältere deutsche Geschichtskunde* 11 (1885-86), 595-597.

MACCARONE, MICHELE. "I Papi del Secolo XII e la Vita Comune e Regolare del Clero," pp. 349-398 of *La Vita comune del Clero nei Secoli XI e XII*. vol. 1 *Relazioni e Questionario*. Miscellanea del Centro di Studi Medioevali III. Atti della Settimana di Studio Mendola Settembre 1959. Milan, 1962.

———. "Primato romano e monasteri dal principio del secolo XII ad Innocenzo III," pp. 49-132 of *Istituzioni monastiche e istituzioni canonicali in Occidente (1123-1215)*. Atti della settima settimana internazionale di Studio Mendola, 28 agosto - 3 settembre 1977, *Vita e Pensiero*. Pubblicazioni dell'Università cattolica del Sacro Cuore, Miscellanea del Centro di Studi medioevali 9. Milan, 1980.

MALECZEK, WERNER. "Das Kardinalskollegium unter Innocenz II. und Anaklet II.," *Archivum Historiae Pontificiae* 19 (1981), 27-78.

MARATU, M. L'ABBÉ. *Girard, Évêque d'Angoulême Légat du Saint-Siège (vers 1060-1136)*. Angoulême, 1866.

MARCHETTI-LONGHI, GIUSEPPE. *I Papareschi e i Romani*. Le Grandi famiglie romane 6. Rome, 1947.

MARIO DA BERGAMO. See Luigi Pellegrini.

MORRIS, COLIN. *The Discovery of the Individual 1050-1200*. London, 1972.

MÜHLBACHER, EMIL. *Die streitige Papstwahl des Jahres 1130*. Innsbruck, 1876, repr. Aalen: Scientia Verlag, 1966.

MÜLLER, ERNST. "Der Bericht des Abtes Hariulf von Oudenburg über seine Prozessverhandlungen an der römischen Kurie im Jahre 1141," *Neues Archiv der Gesellschaft für ältere deutsche Geschichtskunde* 48 (1930), 97-115.

NILGEN, URSULA. "Maria Regina - Ein politischer Kultbildtypus," *Römisches Jahrbuch für Kunstgeschichte* 19 (1981), 1-33.

NOONAN, JOHN T. *Bribes*. New York, London, 1984.

PALUMBO, PIER FAUSTO. "La cancelleria di Anacleto II," *Scritti di paleografia diplomatica in onore di Vincenzo Federici*, 81-131. Florence, 1944, repr. *Studi Salentini* 17 (1964), 3-53.

———. "Nuovi Studi (1942-1962) sullo scisma di Anacleto II," *Bollettino dell'istituto storico italiano per il medio evo e Archivio Muratoriano* 75 (1963), 71-103.

———. *Lo Scisma del MCXXX: I precedenti, la vicenda Romana e le ripercussioni europee della lotta tra Anacleto ed Innocenzo II col registro degli atti di Anacleto II*. Miscellanea della R. Deputazione di Storia Patria. Rome, 1942.

PANVINIO, ONORPHRIO. *De praecipuis urbis Romae sanctioribusque basilicis quas septem ecclesias vulgo vocant*. Rome, 1570.

PARKES, JAMES. *The Jew in the Medieval Community*. 2nd ed. New York, 1976.

PARTNER, PETER. *The Lands of St Peter: The Papal State in the Middle Ages and Early Renaissance*. Berkeley, Los Angeles, 1972.

PELLEGRINI, LUIGI (Mario da Bergamo). "Cardinali e Curia sotto Callisto II (1119-1124)," pp. 507-556 of *Raccolta di studi in memoria de S. Mochi Onory*. Milan, 1972.

———. "La duplice elezione papale del 1130: I precedenti immediati e i protagonisti," pp. 265-302 of vol. 2 of *Contributi dell'Istituto di Storia Medioevale*,

Raccolta di studi in memoria di Giovanni Soranzo. Milan, 1968.

——. "Osservazioni per la duplice elezione papale del 1130," *Aevum* (1965), 45-65.

PETKE, WOLFGANG. *Kanzlei, Kapelle, und Königliche Kurie unter Lothar III. (1125-1137).* Cologne, Vienna, 1985.

ROBERT, ULYSSE. *Bullaire du Pape Calixte II.* Paris, 1891.

RODOCANACHI, EMMANUEL. *Le Saint-Siège et les Juifs: Le ghetto à Rome.* Paris, 1891.

ROTH, CECIL. *The History of the Jews of Italy.* Philadelphia, 1946.

RÜTHING, H. "Ein Brief des Kardinals Matthäus von Albano an die Grande Chartreuse," *Revue Bénédictine* 78 (1968), 145-151.

RUSSO, A. "La doppia elezione papale del 1130 e l'opera di S. Bernardo di Chiaravalle," *Rivista di letteratura e di storia ecclesiastica* 7 (1975), 41-52.

SCHIEFFER, THEODOR. *Die päpstlichen Legaten in Frankreich vom Vertrage von Meersen (870) bis zum Schisma von 1130.* Berlin, 1935.

SCHMALE, FRANZ-JOSEF. "Die Bemühungen Innocenz II um seine Anerkennung in Deutschland," *Zeitschrift für Kirchengeschichte* 65 (1954), 240-296.

——. *Studien zum Schisma des Jahres 1130.* Forschungen zur kirchlichen Rechtsgeschichte und zum Kirchenrecht 3. Cologne, 1961.

SCHRAMM, PERCY ERNST. *Kaiser, Könige und Päpste* 4:1. Stuttgart, 1970.

SCHREIBER, GEORG. *Kurie und Kloster in 12. Jahrhundert* 2 vols. Stuttgart, 1910, repr. Amsterdam, 1965.

SCHUM, WILHELM. "Kaiser Heinrich V. und Papst Paschalis II. im Jahre 1112. Ein Beitrag zur Geschichte des Investitur-Streites," *Jahrbücher der königliche Akademie gemeinnütziger Wissenschaften zu Erfurt*, Neue Folge 8 (1877).

SCHUSTER, I. *L'imperiale abbazia di Farfa: Contributo allo studio del ducato romano nel M. Evo.* Rome, 1921.

SEGL, P. *Königtum und Klosterreform in Spanien. Untersuchungen über die Cluniacenser Klöster in Kastilien-Léon vom Beginn des 11. bis zur Mitte des 12. Jahrhunderts.* Kallmünz, Opf., 1974.

SERVATIUS, CARLO. *Paschalis II. (1109-1118): Studien zu seiner Person und seiner Politik.* Vol. 14 of *Päpste und Papsttum*, pub. Georg Denzler. Stuttgart, 1979.

SOLMI, ARRIGO. *Il Senato Romano nell'alto Medio Evo (757-1143).* Rome, 1944.

SOMERVILLE, ROBERT. "The Council of Pisa, 1135: A Re-examination of the Evidence of the Canons," *Speculum* 45 (1970), 98-114.

SPÄTLING, L. "Kardinallegat Petrus im Pontifikat Honorius II." *Antonianum* 38 (1963), 162-192.

STROLL, MARY. "Calixtus II: A Reinterpretation of his Election and the end of the Investiture Contest," *Studies in Medieval and Renaissance History* 3 (1980), 3-53.

——. "The Struggle Between Guy of Vienne and Henry V," *Archivum Historiae Pontificiae* 18 (1980), 97-115.

STUERNER, W. "Der Königswahlparagraph im Papstwahldekret von 1059," *Studi Gregoriani* 9 (1972), 37-52.

SYDOW, JÜRGEN VON. "Cluny und die Anfänge der apostolischen Kammer: Studien zur Geschichte der päpstlichen Finanzverwaltung im 11. und 12. Jahrhundert," *Studien und Mittheilungen zur Geschichte des Benediktinerordens* 63

(1951), 45-61.

———. "Il 'Concistorium' dopo lo Scisma del 1130," *Rivista di storia della chiesa in Italia* 9 (1955), 165-176.

SYNAN, EDWARD A. *The Popes and the Jews in the Middle Ages.* London, 1965.

TELLENBACH, GERD. "Der Sturz des Abtes Pontius von Cluny und seine geschichtliche Bedeutung," *Quellen und Forschungen aus italienischen Archiven und Bibliotheken* 42/43 (1963), 13-55.

TIERNEY, BRIAN. *Origins of Papal Infallibillity 1150-1350.* Leiden, 1972.

TILLMANN, HELENE. *Die päpstlichen Legaten in England bis zur Beendigung der Legation Gualas (1218).* Bonn, 1926.

———. "Ricerche sull'origine dei Membri del Collegio Cardinalizio nel XII Secolo: I. La Questione dell'Accertamento delle Origini dei Cardinali," *Rivista di Storia della chiesa in Italia* 24 (1970), 441-464.

———. "Ricerche sull'origine dei Membri del Collegio Cardinalizio nel XII Secolo: II/I. Identificazione dei Cardinali del Secolo XII di Provenienza Romana," *Rivista di Storia della Chiesa in Italia* 26 (1972), 313-353.

TOUBERT, HÉLÈNE. "Le renouveau paléochrétien à rome au debut du XIIe siècle," *Cahiers Archéologique fin de l'Antiquité et Moyen Age* 20 (1970), 99-154.

ULLMANN, WALTER. "Foundations of Medieval Monarchy," a lecture pub. in *Sewanee Mediaeval Colloquium occasional papers.* Sewanee, 1982.

———. *The Growth of Papal government in the Middle Ages: A Study in the ideological relation of clerical to lay power.* London, 1955, 2nd ed. 1962, repr. 1965.

———. *Medieval Papalism: The Political Theories of the Medieval Canonists.* London, 1949.

VACANDARD, ELPHÈGE. "Saint Bernard et le schisme d'Anaclet II en France," *Revue des questions historiques* 43 (1888), 61-123.

———. *Vie de saint Bernard.* Paris, 1895.

VAN DAMME, J.B. "Bernard de Clairvaux et Pons de Cluny: Controverse au subject d'une controverse," *Cîteaux* 25 (1974), 271-286.

VAN DEN EYNDE, DAMIEN. "Les premiers écrits de saint Bernard," *Recueil d'études sur saint Bernard et ses écrits* 3, ed. Jean Leclercq. Rome, 1969.

VAN ENGEN, JOHN. "The 'Crisis of Cenobitism' Reconsidered: Benedictine Monasticism in the years 1050-1150," *Speculum* (1986), 269-304.

VERDIER, PHILIPPE. *Le Couronnement de la Vierge: Les origines et les premiers développements d'un thème iconographique.* Montreal, Paris, 1980.

VONES, LUDWIG. *Die 'Historia Compostellana' und die kirchen Politik des Nordwestspanischen Raumes 1070-1130: Ein Beitrag zur Geschichte des Beziehungen zwischen Spanien und dem Papsttum zu Beginn des 12. Jahrhunderts.* Cologne, Vienna, 1980.

WALTER, CHRISTOPHER. "Papal Political Imagery in the Medieval Lateran Palace," *Cahiers archéologiques fin de l'Antiquité et Moyen Age* 20 (1970), 155-176; 21 (1971), 109-136.

WHITE, HAYDEN V. "The Gregorian Ideal and St. Bernard of Clairvaux," *Journal of the History of Ideas* 21 (1960), 321-348.

———. "Pontius of Cluny, the Curia Romana and the End of Gregorianism in Rome," *Church History* 27 (1958), 195-219.

WIECZOREK, GEORG. *Das Verhältnis des Papstes Innocenz II. (1130-1143) zu den*

Klöstern. Diss. Greifswald, 1914.

WIERUSZOWSKI, HELEN. "Roger II of Sicily, Rex-Tyrannus, in Twelfth Century Political Thought," *Speculum* 38 (1963), 46-78.

WILLIAMS, A. LUKYN. *Adversus Judaeos: A Bird's-Eye View of Christian Apologiae until the Renaissance.* Cambridge, 1935.

WILLIAMS, WATKIN. *Studies on Saint Bernard of Clairvaux.* Manchester, 1935.

WILMART, A. "Deux pièces relatives à l'abdication de Pons, abbé de Cluny en 1122," *Revue Bénédictine* 44 (1932), 351-353.

YDARDENI, MYRIAM, ed. *Les Juifs dans l'histoire de France.* Premier Colloque International de Haifa. Institut d'histoire et de Civilisation Françaises de l'Université de Haifa. Leiden, 1980.

ZEMA, DEMETRIUS B. "The Houses of Tuscany and of the Pierleoni in the Crisis of Rome in the eleventh Century," *Traditio* 2 (1944), 155-175.

ZENKER, BARBARA. *Die Mitglieder des Kardinalkollegiums von 1130 bis 1159.* Diss., Würzburg, 1964.

ZERBI, PIERO. "Cluny e Cîteaux. Riflessioni e ipotesi sui rapporti fra i due 'ordines' durante lo scisma di Ponzio (1122-26)," *I Cistercensi e il Lazio.* Atti delle giornate di studio dell'Istituto di storia dell'Arte dell'Università di Roma. Rome, 1978.

———. "Intorno allo schisma de Ponzio Abate di Cluny (1122-26)," pp. 835-891 of *Studi Storici in honore di Ottorino Bertolini* 2, ed. Pacini. Pisa, 1972.

ZÖPFFEL, RICHARD. *Die Papstwahlen und die mit ihnen im nächsten Zusammenhange stehenden Ceremonien in ihrer Entwicklung vom 11. bis 14. Jahrhundert.* Nebst eine Beilage: *Die Doppelwahl des Jahres 1130.* Göttingen, 1872.

INDEX